A loving exploration into subtle energies of the Heart, and their role in our personal evolutionary path. A comprehensive overview that contributes to a "wholehearted" expression of Self, along with practical guidance for today's energy worker.

—Peggy Phoenix Dubro, author of *Elegant Empowerment: Evolution of Consciousness* and developer of the EMF Balancing Technique®

Mark Greenia has performed a great service in clearly translating the obscure energetic concepts of chakra and energy centers into life as we live it. The benefit,—a better understanding of how to achieve health of personality and heart, and rise to loftier spiritual levels. A very good service,—and we need more of this.

—Maurie D. Pressman, M.D.
co-author of *Twin Souls* and author of *Enter the Supermind.*

The time is now to open our hearts and heal. This is the powerful message found in *Living from the Heart.* In these pages you will find both practical and intuitive information on our most precious energy center, the Heart.

—Marilyn Schaal, Reiki Master

Living from the Heart is essential reading for energy workers, and anyone else who seeks to understand our "interconnectedness" with the Universe. This book explains elegantly how we can make a positive impact interacting from the Heart Center via our energy signature with compassion and love.

—Chris Lowe, Energy Worker, EMF Balancing Practitioner

Living from the Heart:

Exploring Subtle Energy in the New Millennium

Blending Quantum Physics and the Energy of Compassion

by Mark Greenia

Unlimited Publishing
Bloomington, Indiana

Luminarch

Dedication

*To the thousands of people who lost their lives
on September 11, 2001,*

and to their families

and to those who fought to save, rescue

and rebuild...

Acknowledgements

It is hard to express the tremendous support I received throughout the production of this book. At times I felt guided by spirit, and at times driven by spirit. I am very grateful to have had the opportunity to compile this work and through this process, to meet so many wonderful people. Many loving souls have participated in this co-creative project by providing their thoughts, words, inspiration and guidance. Many gave from the heart, and it has made all the difference. Although it is not possible to name everyone, the following are those I want to specifically mention.

Thanks go to my dear friends, fellow energy workers, and bringers of high vibrational energies, Peggy Phoenix Dubro, Steve Dubro (of the EMF Balancing Technique/Energy Extension), Lee Carroll (who brings forth the Kryon energies), Debbie Callbeck, Sharon Wegrzyn and Diane Cohen of "Into the Light"; to Melinda De-Boer, Patty Rosser, Linda Nichole Carrington, Michelle Brennan, and to Patricia Tenant a beautiful energy worker who made her transition to the next level of her journey. Thanks to Ronney Aden of InnerWords Magazine for her continued support.

Special (high vibrational) thanks to Dr.Todd Ovakaitys, M.D. for the information on his breakthroughs in laser energized nutritional supplements (Gematria).

Thanks go to Dr. Maurie D. Pressman for permission to include his article on bridging personality and spirit, to Dr. Clancy McKenzie, for his article on Love Energy, and to Cheryl Rose for the beautiful cover illustration of Gaia. Thanks go to my talented brother Matt for his artwork drawings used in this text and for his support through this project, and to my sister Chris for sharing her personal poem on goals.

Thanks go to John and Anna Chitty for the use of information extracted from their article *"The Language of Yin and Yang;"* thanks to Kay Cook for permission to include her "Healer's Creed;" thanks to Doven Starr for her article on "What is Reiki?;" and thanks to Karen Ball for the guidelines on working with people with immune deficiency. Thanks to Angela for the use of the Anahata symbol. Thanks also to Dan Snow, Dave Shearer and the Unlimited Publishing staff for their help and creativity.

Very special thanks to Kathy and Jason who have given me infinite patience and loving support through my many hours of writing and for understanding the sometimes far away look in my eyes as much of this material was being formed. Thanks to my daughter Bridgette for her loving support and gentle spirit.

Very special thanks go to Marilyn Schaal for sharing her experiences in working with heart energies, for her review of various manuscript sections and for her gift of support and encouragement throughout the development of this material.

I sincerely hope you find this book helpful in your personal journey. May you discover your own inner passion and embrace it, and may you continue *living from the heart*.

Contents

Chapter Four
Personal Experiences with Healing, Spiritual Growth and the Energy of the Heart

Chapter Five
The Physical Heart

Tables

Figures

Prologue

This book is about an exploration into the heart energies of love and compassion. Love in its many forms, is the most powerful energy we know. It can transform lives, enable us to overcome insurmountable obstacles, and even be the impetus to create new life.

As I worked on the material that was to become this book, the world was shocked by a catastrophe on September 11, 2001. In response, a war was declared against terrorism, an unseen enemy. An enemy with no fixed location in time or space, a war against that enemy's ideals and methods. I think someone said more than 50 years ago that future wars would be wars of ideas and ideals, more so than disputes over boundaries or possessions. As the world evolves to higher levels of consciousness, pockets of hatred will be exposed to the light. As they become exposed, they will vanish. It will not be an easy or quick process, but it will happen.

We are deep into this archetypal struggle against an unseen enemy that has chosen fear and hatred as its battle cry. However, we must not forget that in the larger picture, we are each responsible, every day, every moment, for the future that we co-create with our actions and intentions. How we treat our family, friends, neighbors and acquaintances in our daily life is just as important as how we treat strangers elsewhere on the planet. There is an infiltration of love energy occurring on our planet at this time. Many people are resisting this energy because they feel if they "give in" to this energy they will cease to exist! This is a misconception based on fear.

We must learn to hold in our minds and in our hearts a vision of a future that is based on unity and compassion. This does not mean that we fail to act when responsible action is called for. Love is not a passive state. Love is a conscious activity, motivated by spirit. If your children were being harmed, you would not sit idle taking no action. You would take responsible action rapidly to protect their lives and their future. This is an act of love. You would act to stop those attacking your children. You would apply your energies to the formation of a better future. Action is appropriate if it is done without hatred and vengeance. Hatred and vengeance only provide dark forces with more of what they wish to create, which is fear. As humans on the planet become closer to one another, love grows. This is a natural occurrence. As love grows, the remaining pockets of fear are exposed to the light in full force.

Let us strive to feel the energies of love and compassion in our hearts and learn how to transmute fear and hatred into more constructive energies. Let us experience and transmit the energies of love to wherever they are needed around the globe. What we do on an individual basis, within our personal spheres of influence affects the global consciousness. You are a being of light and you do make a difference in the world. Your thoughts, emotions and interactions with others change the consciousness of your environment in ways you do not even perceive. You are a positive force for change in the world in every moment that you exist.

Introduction I

My Personal Journey

My interests in physics, the nature of energy and the subject of philosophy go back to my childhood. I was an avid reader of science texts on electromagnetics in early grade school and entered an accelerated learning science program in junior high which continued into high school and beyond. Concurrent with this I read much of the ancient philosophical writings on the nature of man and spirit. I remember when I was 14 years old, my excitement (and my parents' disbelief) when I came home with a 30 volume encyclopedia on the "Philosophies of the World," which I bought at the local Goodwill store for $15.00. While my classmates played baseball, I read Marcus Aurelius and Isaac Azimov. I constructed a science lab in the basement complete with blue lightning from high voltage generators. Soon, I found that my questions regarding the energy of electromagnetics and the biological energies of living organisms, and the nature of the spirit were leading me down a common path. But I did not know where that path was leading. It seemed for years I had nothing but questions.

My formal training in subtle energy work began some years later. At the university, my intended major was biochemistry. However, I found an even greater attraction to the world of subtle energies. I was introduced to the practice of Tai Chi, from a Chi master named Damien, learned Aikido from a Japanese master, and at the same time began training in the art of massage therapy.

I found that the subtle energies we deal with in Tai Chi pervade the entire body and surround the body. I found that I could sense the energies very strongly, even visually at times. My classmates in the Tai Chi class thought I was odd when I said I could strongly sense and feel the Chi energy. The Tai Chi master said, "well, of course you can." I said, "well, the other student's don't." He said, "they have not yet learned how to feel and sense with their whole being."

As I studied under Professor Uno of Japan, it became obvious that the "Ki" in Aikido and the "Chi" in Tai Chi were the same energies. In fact these and all other martial arts involve the directing of unseen energies, and of integrating the mental, emotional and physical selves with the higher energies of spirit.

I found that when doing massage therapy I was interacting with the body's muscle and tissue systems, but also with the body's energy system. I could sense where tight muscles were by sensing energy blockages in the body's energy field.

Over the years this lead me into studying various methodologies and techniques for understanding the body's energy system, including yoga, reflexology, the chakra system (energy vortexes), Ayurveda, Reiki (subtle energy balancing techniques), and most recently the EMF Balancing Technique of Peggy Phoenix Dubro.

I wrote my previous book *Energy Dynamics* because I wanted to share what I have learned about the human energy anatomy. I feel that it is very important for us at this time to understand and appreciate how we are essentially Energy Beings. Our physiology, our emotional interactions with others, our sense of stability and power in our personal lives is all a direct reflection of how we handle our selves energetically.

I also had a major life-changing event when experiencing the Kundalini Rising process, and also wanted to share what I learned through this process. The Kundalini Rising process vastly increased my ability to sense subtle energies, while opening the chakras and blowing apart old energy blockages. It can also cause many other changes which turn one's world upside down. Western doctors rarely even acknowledge this event, so there is little help within the field of traditional medicine for those who are seeking more information as to what is happening. I dove back into the world of subtle energies and there I have found the answers to what was taking place then, and even now. I found the energies of the heart to be the most profound, and that is what spawned this new book.

Kundalini sparks an evolutionary process. Surviving it and integrating its effects into your life requires a balancing of subtle yet powerful energies. Energy balancing is a combination of unblocking stuck energy flows in the body's energy field, and allowing the energy to flow, as well as facilitating the interaction and calibration of the body's own energy field with the surrounding energy framework of the earth and the universe.

Since childhood, my love of science, especially physics and biology, has led me in recent years through an examination of quantum physics as it relates to human energy anatomy. Much more information is available today on quantum theories than there was just a few years ago. Still, many people find the concepts too esoteric to rely on as an explanation of what is occurring today in our world of complex energetic forces. It is becoming clearer, however, that quantum physicists have been making discoveries that strongly support the world of energetic medicine and subtle energy healing.

Throughout this book, I have tried to bring forth and attempt to answer several questions: What is energy?, How we are connected with our environment? Why are emotions important?, What are the benefits of energy balancing?, What are some of the fundamental principles of the energy universe in which we live? and, How can we use this information to better our lives and the lives of those around us?

In many parts of this book I include what are called "Axioms," which are explained in the next section. Basically an Axiom describes in concise terms a fundamental principle of existence. They are useful in aligning our thoughts and in interpreting other information. The Axioms are a product of intuitive channels, provided here as a gift from the heart.

It would be irresponsible to talk about the energies of the heart without acknowledging that, on a physical level, heart and circulatory system related diseases take the lives of more people each year than any other disease. This situation is so widespread that you as a reader of this book probably know someone who has been affected by heart related problems, or perhaps you have experienced this yourself. Perhaps you have lost a loved one. This is not meant to be a medical or nutritional guidebook of any kind. There are already excellent sources available for that kind of information. The goal of this book is to bring about an increased awareness of the power of the subtle energies of the heart center and how they relates to not only our physiology, but our mental, emotional and spiritual state as well.

There is a correlation between the blockages in the energies of the heart and the problems we see on a physical level. I believe that solutions that address only the physical side of the problem will not reach enough people in time. A greater understanding of the four-fold approach to healing is needed. This means Spiritual, Mental, Emotional and Physical.

To understand the physical side of what is happening, I have included a chapter on the Physical Heart. It is not fun to write about the diseases of the heart, and not fun to read about them either. It does help put things in perspective on a global scale.

There is no doubt whatsoever that human physical anatomy is an extension of our energy anatomy. Most physical problems have energetic causes at their root. The ancient Tibetans knew this. The ancient Vedic teachings of India were based on this. We are re-awakening this knowledge within us now. If you look inside yourself you will feel this is true. For each of us, understanding the nature of the mind, emotions and the body as extensions of the spirit is a consciousness raising activity. The most joyous part of this journey of re-discovery is that we get to share it with each other.

At the deepest level, our physical body is a painting etched on a canvas of energetic particles. Each cell in the body is composed of molecules, which are composed of atoms and sub atomic particles. Separated mostly by empty space, subatomic particles are essentially vibrational energy packets. They are not solid. They are vibrational energy in a constant state of flux. So in fact our entire cellular structure is composed of mostly empty space and vibrational energy packets. Sounds like science fiction, but it is true. Cells are alive and know how to perform their functions since they have access to the energetic information stored in the DNA. DNA is a molecule composed of atoms and subatomic particles, which are again, energy vibrations. What is unique in all this is the concept that all of this is "conscious" activity— that is, an activity of Consciousness. Some Doctors know that the real role of medicine is to facilitate the body's own healing mechanisms, so that the body's inherent wisdom, its inner consciousness, brings about a proper energetic alignment that allows a restoration of the body's inner health.

What is important for us at this time is to interact with our fellow human beings directly. Energy balancing is a consciousness raising activity at an energetic level. I have found that the benefits to come from energy work include: an increased sense of balance, increasingly stable energy levels, improved mental and emotional outlook, increased creativity, increased vitality (aging reversal) and more.

I have learned that our emotions play a key role in subtle energy work and in our general health. Emotion is Energy in motion. Emotions are energy. The level of vibration determines the level of the emotion.

Love is a very high vibrational energy. Fear is an erratic, low vibrational energy. Low vibrations cause energy blockages just like squeezing off a garden hose.

Confusion, depression, anxiety, ulcers, circulatory problems, emotional problems, drug and alcohol addiction, prescription medication abuse, all have an energetic counterpart. Viewing the person as a whole, and addressing the energetic causes will take us farther towards a longer lasting solution.

Our state of awareness and our *intent* influence our energy anatomy on a minute-by-minute basis. Conscious intent can direct energy flows. Focused intent is extremely powerful creative energy. Embracing a higher spiritual intent for our growth process allows us to come into harmony with the higher intents of others. Co-creation is an activity of focused intent for higher growth.

I sincerely hope that the information in this book brings you added insight into your personal relationship with yourself, and with those around you.

I continue to meet fantastic people with loving, open hearts while continuing on my personal journey and I wish you the same joyous experience.

Mark Greenia

Introduction II

Our Shifting Global Consciousness

We live in a beautiful world that is filled with endless wonders. We are also living in a time of a major shift in global consciousness. Events are taking place and spiritual energies are being released into our timeline that have never been experienced before.

You have already felt this shift on an energetic level and you have been drawn to this book because of it. This book will not yet become mainstream since its concepts are beyond the belief systems of most people in our western society. This book is about shifting consciousness. It is about spiritual energy and spiritual growth. If you are reading this book you are undoubtedly on the leading edge of this wave of evolution. You face a tremendous challenge in understanding and holding these new concepts in the face of widespread global thoughtforms to the contrary. This book grew out of a need to clarify some of the new paradigms that have been emerging as a result of this new consciousness shift. It also grew out of a need for a greater understanding of how the heart energies of love and compassion influence our personal growth, emotional well being and physical health.

Higher levels of energy have been impacting this planet for the past few years and they will continue to do so. The effect of this massive influx of new energies is to increase the personal vibrations of all that live here. Even within our own solar system, our sun has been undergoing tremendous energy surges and electromagnetic outbursts these past few years. All life on earth responds to this massive increase in electromagnetics across the spectrum. The vast majority of the sun's energy is invisible to us. Wave after wave of unseen vibratory forces pulse throughout our planetary system daily. Increases in this energy act as one of the catalysts in our expanding consciousness. You are now witnessing a major event in the evolution of human consciousness during which old energies and paradigms are co-existing with the new energies and the new paradigms. This is causing a tremendous upheaval in our world affairs and in our personal lives.

Our individual lives now change at a rate that has never before been experienced on this planet. Time passes much more quickly for us. With this rapidly accelerated passage of time, we also experience a very rapid rate of personal change. You will undoubtedly have experienced this yourself already, or you know of someone who has. Gone are the days when each year seems much like the one before it. Now, each year brings a multitude of changes, often massive changes, in our lives, perceptions, thoughts and in our desires.

The old paradigms are no longer supporting our life styles, nor are they supporting our growth. Many of us are unsatisfied with what we have accumulated in the past and have the feeling that there is more out there for us. In many cases, the new paradigm is not yet fully visible to us. This puts us in the uncomfortable position of being "between two worlds." This analogy is essentially a correct one. We now travel between the old energies of the past while simultaneously seeking out and being infused by the new energies of the new global shift in consciousness.

This influx of new energies is not raising the energy vibrations of all people at the same rate, however. The rate at which it affects us differs from person to person. You are becoming aware that some of the people you know are not tracking with these changes as rapidly as you are. The gap between you and them seems to be growing as your awareness of yourself and your spiritual growth needs continue to expand. You can see in these people a need and a desire to expand as well, but their ability to accept change, and the rate at which they are willing to accept change may be very much different than your own. They watch you and wonder what is happening to you. They may even comment on the changes, or they may be afraid to mention them. Fear of change and fear of the rate of change is one thing that they are definitely facing. The other aspect of these phenomena is that some of us on the planet right now are meant to be changing faster than others. We are here to act as facilitators of the change. This is a very important concept to grasp. If you have been drawn to this book, you are one of the facilitators. There is no doubt about that. You have felt that there is something different about you and about your path. Something has shifted, awakening in you both dissatisfaction with the old and a growing excitement for the new.

The Archetype of the Energy Facilitator

A facilitator is one who helps bring about a change through guidance, by living example and by direct teaching. There are many roles for the facilitator. Some of us are healers, directly working in the healing arts. Some of these arts take the form of physical healing practices, some take the form of subtle energy work. Some are a combination of different styles. Some of us spread light through our writing or artwork. Some channel higher energy sources directly and speak to many hundreds. Some work quietly and send their loving energies out into the world anonymously, but still achieving great benefits for others.

Some of us are working directly with the new energies and higher frequencies of light that are infusing the planet. Some of us are working as counselors, therapists or spiritual coaches. We work with the experiences of the mind, emotions or spirit. We are already helping others to cope with the massive changes coming into their lives. There is a great need for all of this type of work right now and this need will continue in the years to come.

The impact of the massive new energies and higher frequencies is to cause more people to have a shift in their consciousness into higher states of awareness. Because of this great influx of new energies, a new balancing of these energies is in order. The human energy field is expanding and taking on new dimensions capable of holding this higher level of energy. We are finding a greater need to interact with each other as we each experience these energies in a different way. Some of us are experiencing this calling to work together in a very powerful way. To some, this rapid shift is causing havoc in our personal lives as older energies and structures are breaking down. Compassion is replacing indifference. Love is replacing fear and ignorance. Activity is replacing complacency. A feeling of unity is replacing feelings of isolation.

This is a very profound transformation and our part in this process, as facilitators, is a key aspect of this new awakening. We are both participants in and catalysts for this change. This is a huge responsibility we must face. It is not one of onerous weight, however, rather it is one of lightness, growth and increased harmony of purpose.

You are a very special person. You are a being of light and higher energy frequencies that has agreed to be here at this time to help transmute old vibrations into the newer, higher vibrations. You are here to help others transition to higher states of awareness. You are here to facilitate growth as you grow yourself. Your capacity for love, compassion and sharing your heart energies has been increasing perhaps more than you even realize. Now, this ability is at a high enough level for you to interact with others on a wider scale and at a deeper level than ever before.

As you progress along this path of knowledge and awareness, you refine your skills as a facilitator. You will also recognize some major changes in yourself. Your chakra energies are now able to connect with and balance the chakra energies of others. You become a beacon of light that has a radius of influence far greater than you may have previously thought. Your own personal growth issues, problems and worries are no longer impediments to your ability to deal with others on a path of mutual growth and co-creation. Your own issues will resolve themselves as you work with others in helping them resolve their issues of energy, their growing capacity for compassion and their greater enlightenment on the path to creative responsibility. You will help bring about a greater understanding of the new paradigms that all of us are facing.

Now is the time for us to endeavor to make a loving connection with our fellow human beings— a connection from the heart that resonates with the energy of compassion. This can be done with our family and those closest to us. It can also be done with our neighbors, our daily interactions with people we know or do not know. It can be done with those next to us or with those half a world away. Distance is no barrier to the energy of compassion. We witnessed with the response to the world trade center disaster a wave of compassion spread across the globe in a matter of seconds. We are all on this planet together. We are all in this timeline together. It is no accident that we are together. It is no accident that you are reading this book. You have been drawn to its energies and its intent. Let us help each other to understand and evolve with the new energetic changes that we are experiencing. Let us embrace our roles as facilitators of the new energy and seek to expand our hearts.

Understanding the New Energies

A new level of vibrational energy is available on the planet at this time. This new energy functions as a catalyst in bringing about gestalt of consciousness with an ability to influence global though forms and individual experiences.

This book is designed to help bring clarity to some of the new paradigms and new way of thinking about the world.

As you read this material and connect with its loving content, you are becoming a more intimate part of the changes affecting us all. Understanding the Axioms will bring about a consciousness shift and a greater potential for you to raise your own vibration and the vibrations of others. This is a love connection. I thank you for being here and for sharing this experience.

How to Use this Book

Chapter One is titled "Human Energy Systems" and covers the human energy field and the Chakra System. This book focuses on the energy of the heart, which corresponds to the fourth chakra. It is important to have a general knowledge of the nature of energy and the chakras and how they relate to each other. That is the purpose of Chapter One.

Chapter Two is titled "Energy of the Heart" and deals with the heart center and its intimate energetic connection to spiritual, emotional, mental and physical bodies. This is where we begin to look in more detail at the heart as an extremely power energy center and what it means to have an open heart. We look at the power of the heart's energy flows and how to manage those flows. This chapter reaches deeper into the non-physical aspects of heart energy, its beauty and power. It also deals with actions and intentions that we can engage in consciously in order to open our heart energies to other people. This chapter also discusses the power of intention, the difference between giving and getting love, as well as the nature of fear and the power of forgiveness.

Chapter Three is titled "Silent Power— Energy Work and Bodywork" and deals with the power of subtle energy techniques such as Reiki and the EMF Balancing Technique, and gives specific information on the benefits to be gained from these modalities. It also describes many types of massage therapy and its benefits in addressing they physical needs of the body. This chapter also describes distance healing sessions as well as the various attributes associated with the Yin and Yang energies. Included also are several practical exercises and mediation suggestions for opening your heart center and raising your vibration. These practical exercises are included to provide an example of activities that will help integrate some of the material in this book into your understanding through the application of a physical activity.

Chapter Four is titled "Personal Experiences with Healing, Spiritual Growth and the Energy of the Heart" and contains personal accounts of working with subtle energies from various practitioners in the healing and balancing arts. These are powerful stories of compassion and service and reflect the very human aspect of energy work.

Chapter Five deals with the heart organ and contains a description of the challenges we are facing with the widespread problems of heart attacks and cardiovascular disease. Since we focus on heart energies in this book, it is important to be aware of how some of the physical problems of the heart are reflecting the inner struggles and imbalances facing so many people. This chapter introduces some medical terminology regarding the heart and circulatory system which is helpful in understanding the physical manifestation of the energetic imbalances we see in human society which is causing us so much heartache. Chapter Five also discusses the issue of depression in terms of an energetic imbalance.

Chapter Six is titled "Axioms of Higher Consciousness." This Chapter reaches into the realm of quantum physics and spiritual growth. It discusses our connections to our energetic selves, and our connection to our Higher Self. We do not specifically discuss the nature of God. Whatever beliefs you hold are yours and are respected. Our discussions of the self and the Higher Self are an important recognition of man's higher aspects and our connections to the divine. We are here together on an exciting journey of self-discovery and co-creation. As you explore this section, I sincerely hope you find some words and concepts that will help you on your personal journey.

In Chapter Six and throughout this book you will find a series of Axioms as well as material that expands on and builds around the Axioms. The Axioms are intended to provide a greater understanding of some of the new energy concepts as well as provide clarity of thought on many different aspects of personal growth and spiritual awareness.

When reading these Axioms, only accept what you feel is correct for your own experience and evolution. If you read something you do not agree with, just leave it alone. If you read something and cannot seem to grasp its meaning, leave it alone. Come back to it again several weeks or months and read it again. You may find that other aspects of your life have fallen into place sufficiently to allow you to assimilate the meaning of the Axiom into your belief system.

What is an Axiom? An Axiom is a fundamental principle or agreed-upon condition of reality upon which other aspects of reality seem to rely, or through which other aspects of reality can be better understood.

Intelligent, co-creative evolution of the spirit requires that we be conscious of our own belief systems. It is important to examine and understand the Axioms that underlie our belief structures. A greater understanding of the fundamental factors and components of our belief systems will provide us with a more holistic viewpoint as we take a more active part in our own evolution. In my previous book, *Energy Dynamics: Conscious Human Evolution*, (Unlimited Publishing, 2001) over 100 Axioms were presented that dealt with our energetic nature as beings of light, and fundamental principals of our interaction with others, and the nature of our existence.

The Axioms presented here build on those concepts and introduce new ones. The prior book's Axioms are not repeated here, and one should read the prior Axioms separately to experience their benefit. The Axioms that follow here are focused on a wide variety of topics that each has a place in our evolutionary process at this time.

The Axioms are not necessarily listed in any specific sequence. They can be read consecutively, or you can open to any Axiom and begin reading. Whatever feels comfortable to you.

They are all pieces of a larger view of existence than you may be accustomed to viewing on a daily basis. Some may seem very "matter of fact" to you. Others may challenge your consciousness to open to a wider view. However you perceive and absorb this material will be dependent in part on your own state of personal evolution and your degree of willingness to accept new information and new viewpoints.

These Axioms are not all inclusive. You will no doubt discover many other Axioms in your life experiences that will augment or replace those listed here. In a universe of infinite possibilities, any Axiom that becomes too self-limiting will fall away as its usefulness ceases. As we co-create our future, new Axioms will come into existence through the interplay of our intent with the forces of light in around us. The possibilities for creation are endless. Love and light all inextricably link us to together in some fashion. As our individual efforts to bring clarity to our own existence progress, we also bring clarity to each other on a universal level.

Bridging Personality and Spirit

"Mesmer and Mesmerism Reappear"

by Maurie D. Pressman, M.D.

> Communication— within each body, between
> ourselves and others, between us all and the
> cosmos— begins to be uncovered.

I was recently at the meeting of the International Society of the Study of Subtle Energies and Energy Medicine ("ISSSEEM"), and I confess that I am thrilled by the information that is making its way into mainstream thinking! The theme story is that we are truly beings of magnetic energy, and the discoveries which are now being validated by hard science and hard-minded scientists are breathtaking.

Some the things that emerged from the meeting are:

1. We are beings of magnetic energy.

2. These magnetic energies can be measured now by an instrument called the SQID (Superconducting Quantum Interference Device) which is far superior to electrical instruments such as the electro-cardiogram, the electro-encephalogram, and the electro-myogram.

3. By virtue of the magnetic emanation that we deliver—
and which delivers us, or makes us— there is a
validation of the inter-communication among all of
us.

One evidence of this is that the communication system arises
through connective tissue. This tissue connects everything in the
body from the coverings of the nervous system (the meninges)
down to the fascial and connective covering of every cell in the
body. If the connective tissue is a system of communication— and
it is— it follows that we are in communication within ourselves
from one cell to the other to the other, from each cell in the body
from those in the brain to those in the toes, and back and forth.
Every cell in the body knows everything about everything else
in the body. But this goes further, because each cell emanates
electrical and magnetic energy which surrounds us and which
meets with the magnetic energies of others.

The emerging energy therapies such as Reiki, Polarity, Hypno-
tism, Feng Shui, Qi Gong, and on and on, indicate that there
is an interfusing, intercommunicative system throughout our
world, throughout our planetary system, throughout our cos-
mos. Not only that, but this system communicates with us and
within us.

One of the most interesting findings of the new science is that this
connective tissue communication is carried on through electromagnetism, connecting every cell with every other. As the cell
itself is investigated, it is found that there is something within
it that is akin to connective tissue. What we thought was empty
space in the cell is really full of fibrils called integrins. These
integrins connect the periphery of each cell to its interior. Not
only that, they connect the interior of the cell with the nucleus.

Further: within the nucleus there are still other integrins. As we investigate the integrins themselves, we find a repetition of the same pattern, ad infinitum. This is interesting and exciting insofar as it indicates that there is this infinitude … not only of communication but of inner creation which matches outer creation, and is in itself consistent with, and an exact repetition of, the teachings of the Ancient Mysteries, the teachings of the core of all religions.

This work is marvelously summarized by James Ochsman, Ph.D., a highly credentialed academic scientist connected with The National Institutes of Health. His book, Energy Medicine: The Scientific Basis, tells it all. I had the privilege of attending an all-day workshop with Dr. Ochsman, and was alive with enthusiasm over the new knowledge which was given to us.

Ochsman has a lively and ever-inquiring mind. When he noticed that a fly was about to enter his eye but only hit the eyelid as he blinked, he pondered, "Why? How did it happen so fast? This was so much faster than anything that the neurological system can transfer and transport." The blink occurred in a quantum moment. So did another eye-sparing blink that occurred in a patient who had opened a flash furnace and in a moment suffered a severe burn of his face, losing his eyebrows and a good portion of his hair. But his eyes were spared. They were not burned! How? Why? It was too fast for anything known in our classical medical science. The postulate is that there is another, a separate, perhaps parallel communication system that is as fast as the speed of light, if not faster! Perhaps this system is in the acupuncture meridia that (Ochsman says) reside in the connective tissue of the body— which in itself is light bearing and light emitting. Perhaps it is a transfer and communication through the magnetic fields that surround us and which we can now identify and measure with our instruments. As Dr. Ochsman spoke, I could see a vision that was appearing in his mind and teaching about the communication system.

Is there any wonder why we may be so filled with marvel as we become aware of that energy self that we are; the energy self that is integrated with the body and yet is beyond the body!

Now to turn to Mesmer, for whom this column is titled. Anton Mesmer lived and did his work somewhere around 1775. He called this work Animal Magnetism, and it was the beginning demonstration of what is now known as hypnosis. He was able to produce some remarkable results. But when he called it Vital Energy, a term anathema to the scientific world of the time, he was excluded and ridiculed. As a consequence, Mesmerism became very unpopular until the late 1890s, at which time Charcot, Freud and others began to put it use again. It has remained in disrepute until recent years when it became the subject of scientific study and investigation. The important relationship with Anton Mesmer is that he called this energy "Animal Magnetism." Apparently, he sensed that it was a form of magnetic energy.

The work produced and validated in Ochsman's book and his research studies and those of other hard-line scientists such as William Tiller, demonstrates that we are made up of magnetic energy; that we emanate magnetic energy, that the technique of Reiki in which one transmits energy through the hands is, in fact a valid sending forth of healing and magnetic energies to the body surround, which will absorb (smorgasbord style) that which it needs.

An ancient painting of Christ, Jesus, shows that He carries his left hand over his heart while His right hand sends forth healing energy. Ochsman has pointed out that the heart is the organ that contains the largest field of magnetic energy. It has a brain

of its own which in many ways is superior to the cerebral cortex, and carries the functions similar to those of the right brain. The circuit of the heart to the right hand is a circuit of outpouring of healing energy, which is broadly demonstrated by the increasing popularity of Reiki, which now appears in some of the major medical institutions of the country. And so, after decades of being off limits in academic science and medical practice, there is now a major resurgence of interest in "energy medicine."
Biomagnetism is a new field of investigation of magnetic fields produced by all living things, with a focus on the effects of magnetic fields on living systems, and the effects of healing through the emanation of energy through the hands of the healers. It is a field of "magneto-biology" and "magneto-therapy" and thus shows that what was begun by Anton Mesmer continues. Anton Mesmer is alive and well in the twenty-first century.

Maurie D. Pressman, M.D. is the author of *Enter the Supermind* and co-author (with Patricia Joudry) of *Twin Souls: A Guide to Finding Your True Spiritual Partner*, republished by Hazelden in tandem with Transitions. (Available from Amazon.com)

Dr. Pressman is Emeritus Chairman of Psychiatry at the Albert Einstein Medical Center in Philadelphia and Clinical Professor of Psychiatry at Temple University Health Sciences Center. He is Medical Director at the Center for Psychiatric Wellness, clinics that operate in Philadelphia and Haddonfield, N.J. These clinics bridge traditional and spiritual psychotherapy.

Chapter One:

Human Energy Systems

The Nature of Human Energy Systems

Axiom

The energy of your biology comes from the energy of your spirit. Not the other way around.

At the subatomic level, the difference between "energy" and "matter," and the difference between "living things" and "non-living things," and the difference between "motion" and "non-motion" are entirely dependent on the level of responsibility you are willing to take for your own place in the universe when you view these things.

The Energetic Nature of Balance

You are an energy being of great beauty and vitality. You hold within your heart the powerful energies of healing and compassion. Your challenges are those of integrating your spiritual nature with your biology and achieving wholeness. Your challenge is the balancing of your spiritual, mental, emotional and physical energies.

What is balance? Balance is a state where energies flow smoothly throughout your system. Being "in balance" does not necessarily mean that you must be happy all the time. Being in balance allows you to deal with the challenges of life's journey more effectively and helps you relate to others in a more compassionate way. The four key elements of balance are:

- Relaxing the body
- Calming the emotions
- Quieting the mind
- Focusing on the spirit

The states of health and vitality are those where the energies of love are allowed to flow free and where one feels a connection to divine energies. Healing is a process of finding one's balance and of letting go of energy vibrations that interfere with the flow of compassion.

As you open your heart to the energies of love and compassion you also increase your connection to everything around you. You increase your ability to balance your own energies and the energies in your environment. The energies of love and compassion are the most powerful forces in the universe. Thousands of years of scientific study have taken us to the point where we now see that the physical nature of our world cannot be separated from the powerful energies of the heart. It is our heart-soul connection with ourselves and with others that actually creates the subatomic forces which shape our reality. In this book we will explore these heart energy connections and seek to gain a greater understanding of subtle energy forces so that we can achieve greater balance within ourselves and the world around us.

Quantum Physics, Metaphysics and Newton's Apple

These next few paragraphs may sound a little complex, but please bear with me and trust that this will all flow together. There are some basic concepts that must be introduced to help set the stage for what we will be talking about in this book. You are a beautiful being of light. You have a wisdom and depth of understanding far beyond what you even suspect. The analytical thinking portion of you, however, does not have immediate access to this great store of wisdom. Your intellect is engaged in a process of learning and discovery. It is engaged in a process of examination and integration of thoughts, feelings, concepts and symbols. Presenting information that helps break through the clouded veil of illusion and bring you into greater understanding is therefore a very worthwhile activity. It is with that purpose in mind that we touch on some basic terms and concepts that attempt to describe to your "thinking self" a world of knowledge which your heart already understands.

We know from Quantum Physics that everything that exists is a composite of matter and energy in a state of flux. But what is Quantum Physics? Quantum Physics is a branch of science that deals with discrete, indivisible units of energy called *"quanta."* The word quanta comes from Latin meaning basically "how much." The singular form of "quanta" is "quantum," thus we get the terms Quantum Physics, Quantum Mechanics and Quantum Theory.

Newtonian Physics is based on the works of Sir Isaac Newton (1643-1727) who drew upon the works of Galileo Galilei (1564-1642) and others. Newtonian Physics describes the actions of large bodies in the physical universe according to basic laws of motion and gravity. Newton's science explained well many of the observable phenomena of physical objects, gravity and the planets. However, Newtonian Physics was found to **not** hold true when one observed the motion and interaction of energy particles at the *subatomic* level. Subatomic physics is a field of study within the realm of Quantum Physics, since it deals with a view of the universe based on probabilities, energy quanta and the fundamental principles proposed by physicists such as Albert Einstein and others.

Quantum Physics is a collection of theories about the nature of the universe that have their basis in the principles of Max Planck (1858-1947), Werner Heisenberg (1901-1976) as well as contributions from other brilliant scientists. Max Planck's *Quantum Principle* is that energy is absorbed or released only in discrete quanta or packets. Heisenberg's *Uncertainty Principle* states that one can never be exactly sure both the position of a particle and its velocity at the same time. According to the Uncertainty Principle, the more we are certain about one, the less certain we can be about the other. Even more profound than this was the discovery that subatomic particles are really energy vibrations subject to influence by other vibrations, nearby or even at great distances. Subatomic particles (or quanta) are affected by subtle energies, and since we are essentially energy ourselves, we cannot observe subatomic phenomena without altering it. Our very act of perception changes the forces we are trying to observe. This discovery puts us in the position of co-creators of the universe in which we live, rather than objective observers. What subatomic quanta are "doing" depends on who is observing them and when they are being observed. This new understanding of physics is directly related to our discussion of subtle energy healing and why it has such profound effects. It is also why, as we continue to learn more about our universe, our personal knowledge and application of subtle energy modalities becomes even more important.

As you can see, Quantum Physics is a very different way of looking at the universe than what had been taught in Newtonian Physics for hundreds of years.

Metaphysics means literally "beyond physics." The underlying root of metaphysical thought is that all things are ultimately part of one main source comprised of energy and consciousness. Metaphysical thought holds that all things are interconnected and contribute to the existence of every other thing. Metaphysics has been considered a branch of philosophy that deals with the study of knowledge and wisdom. Up until recently, physics and metaphysics seemed worlds apart. Now that Quantum Physics is coming to the forefront and the classical teachings of Newtonian Physics are being increasingly viewed as a very limited perspective of the universe, there can be seen a definite parallel between many Metaphysical concepts and the principles of Quantum Physics. To the western mind, and to many across the planet, this is a paradigm shift of significant magnitude.

In brief summary:

Newtonian Physics *attempted to explain the large and the observable*

Quantum Physics *attempts to explain the subatomic, the unseen*

Metaphysics *attempts to integrate what we call reality with what we term "spirit"*

An understanding of Quantum Physics will give us a somewhat more formalized structure within which to align different fields of relatively esoteric study. Non-traditional approaches to how we view our bodies and how we view our relationship to the universe can be better understood if we view them from a Quantum Physics perspective. We know that answers to the nature of existence cannot come solely from splitting matter into smaller and smaller bits, hoping to get to the ultimate particle. It is evident now, even through western scientific channels, that the ultimate "particle" is not a particle at all, but a vibrational pattern which itself is has no ultimate characteristics independent of our observation of it.

Our Concept of Atomic Structure Has Evolved

Figure 1 shows the conceptual view of the atom that many of us learned about in grammar school science class. It gives the impression that atoms are composed of subatomic particles that swirl around a central nucleus much like the planets in a solar system. Figure 2, however, is the quantum physics view of the atom as a cloud of energy vibrations. The true (as far as we can determine what "true" is) view of the atom is a collection of vibrational energy forces in varying degrees of balance. The "matter" in an atom is infinitely small and has no definite stable location. It is always in motion. Always. Always.

Place your hand on a table. When one object in our world, such as a table, comes in contact with another object, such as a hand, the atoms exchange energy "particles" at a subatomic level. Parts of what were "the table" are now part of what we view as "the hand." This has powerful implications when you look at this from the perspective of energy work and energy healing. An energy worker or practitioner is exchanging subatomic particles with the client during an energy session. The unique difference between this activity and the interchange between the table and the hand is that the practitioner is using conscious intent to help sense and in some cases direct the energy interchange. In a *non-directive* energy interchange, the practitioner uses his or her senses to help allow and facilitate the natural tendency of the universal energies present to seek a condition of self balance. In a *directive* energy interchange, the practitioner uses conscious intent to direct energy to areas where balance is lacking and sort of "helps things along a bit." Energy therapies can be either directive or non-directive, and some can be both directive and non-directive in the same session, depending on what the practitioner's intent is at the moment.

We are co-creators of the reality that we perceive and are part of the energy and consciousness of all that exists, of "All that Is."

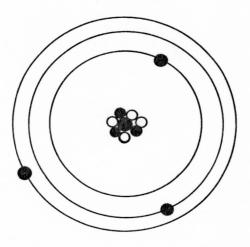

Figure 1 Old Concept of the Atom

The old concept of the atom, which still appears on many older science texts, give the appearance of particles (electrons) orbiting a nucleus of solid particles (protons and neutrons).

Figure 2 New Concept of the Atom

The new concept of the atom, which reflects the quantum physics view, depicts a cloud of energy vibrations where we do not know exactly where the electrons or protons are, and can only estimate their probable locations and estimated velocities.

The Nature of Our Physical and Energetic Bodies

Our bodies are composed of this energy-matter flux. As spiritual beings we radiate a field of energy. Remember early paintings of angels and deities and the glow around them? Remember seeing the halos around their heads? This was the artist's representation of pure energy. We radiate energy outward for a distance of several feet beyond the body. This is our bioenergetic field. This energy responds to our thoughts and intentions. We influence our own physical health through the thoughts and intentions that we radiate.

It is important to understand ourselves as energy beings. Our energy field is conscious and alive. The energy of consciousness affects matter. The physical body is a manifestation of energy. The molecules and subatomic particles of the body vibrate or resonate at certain frequencies, which are variable. An optimum vibratory range results in good health of the body. At lower energy vibrations the body can become susceptible to energy blockages. These blockages are impediments to a clean flow of energy within our field. In its unimpeded state, energy wants to flow. The vibrational energy of one being is different from that of another being. The precise vibrational level of a being is the "frequency identity" or energy signature of that being. Other people with whom you come into contact will recognize you because of your energy vibration.

With recognition comes the feeling of familiarity and knowingness. This feeling is the result of a harmonizing of vibrations at some level between you and the other person.

The Physical World Mirrors the Non-Physical World

The body has an inherent energetic pattern that defines its physical structure. Left to its natural energy flows, the body will tend toward health, vitality and creativity. When we impose our thoughts and intentions on the body's bioenergetic field, we can interfere with the flow of energies in the body. We superimpose energy blockages onto the body and bring about a disruption in the body's energy field. We can do this consciously and unconsciously. There are subtle energy pathways and energy centers in the body that conduct, generate, transmute and focus various energy fields and flows. In some respects, this powerful and beautifully intricate energetic circulatory system is the spiritual, non-physical counterpart of the body's nervous and circulatory systems. In the hierarchy of energies, however, the non-physical energy system is far more powerful and resilient than the physical systems of the body. Its subtle energy nature means that it responds quickly to changes in our thoughts, emotions and intentions. The body's physical systems also respond, but more slowly. Energy blockages in the body's subtle energy systems can eventually show up as blockages in the body's physical systems.

Our Cardiovascular System is a River of Living Energy

To some degree the heart and circulatory systems are a physical counterpart of the subtle energy systems that keep the body functioning and alive. When we look at the widespread problems of cardiovascular disease in the world, it should be a sign to us that there is a widespread problem in the subtle energy systems of many people. Our classic western medical approach to dealing with the problems of heart attack, arteriolosclerosis (hardening of the arteries), stroke and related problems are focused almost entirely at the physical level. When blood-carrying arteries become blocked the heart is not able to perform its job adequately. A quadruple bypass operation, for example, is essentially a retrofitting of the tubes carrying blood. This surgical process takes portions of internal tubing from the legs or elsewhere, cuts them, and re-attaches them to various parts of the heart. This is a highly complex technical process requiring a high level of skill on the part of surgeons. It has undoubtedly saved many lives, or at least prolonged them temporarily. In a crude sense, however, this technique is very similar to a pluming job. It is also a very time consuming, delicate, expensive and potentially risky operation for the patient. It does nothing to address the underlying energetic causes or blockages that may have caused or predisposed the person to having blocked arteries in the first place.

Cardiovascular disease kills more people in the world each year than any other disease. In my research for the non-intuitive sections of this book, I was amazed at just how widespread this situation is. When a dozen people die from a rare bacterial infection it makes national news. But when over 700,000 people die every year from complications relating to blood flow, it is barely mentioned. We will look at the physical side of the heart in more detail in Chapter Five. However, it is worth commenting at this point that operations such as quadruple bypass, angioplasties, and other physical approaches are after-the-fact attempts to remedy the symptoms of something which has multitude of causes, some existing in the realm of subtle energy flows. To maintain a healthy body, we need to maintain a state of balance in our energy systems. This means balancing our energies, including those at the spiritual, emotional, mental and physical levels. A holistic view is needed. A holistic approach to this problem means that all aspects of the person must be taken into account before true diagnosis and true curative actions can be taken that will actually have long-term benefit.

Essential Attributes of Balance

What Does "Being in Balance" Mean in Terms of Energy? Being in balance means that your energy fields and energy centers are open to the natural flow of energy in and out of your system as you interact with other people and with your environment. Being out of balance is a condition where the energies of the body are out of phase to a point where their natural and graceful flow is impeded. Disease is the result of an out-of-balance condition. Disease manifests as physical ailments when the imbalance is allowed to continue for too long a period.

An individual has many "energy bodies" and these can go out of balance causing a warping effect in the energy field. By the time the physical body displays the symptoms of an illness, the energetic "disease" has already been present in one or more energy bodies for a time prior to the physical condition. Western medicine spends the bulk of its time addressing only the physical manifestation of disease. Great benefits can be realized by addressing the energy bodies themselves and correcting imbalances at an energetic level before they manifest in the physical. It is also very helpful to address the balancing of energy bodies when there is no evidence of illness or disease. This strengthens the energy field, and helps keep bodies in balance.

The following is a list of the essential attributes of balance for the four primary areas of life, Spiritual, Mental, Emotional and Physical. These attributes are so basic that just reading the list can help you generate some of the vibrational patterns associated with these attributes. As you read the list, try to get the *feeling* of the concepts it is describing.

Essential Attributes of Balance

Spiritual Balance
- Acknowledgement of a higher source or divine guidance
- Having a sense of purpose and meaning to your life
- Cultivating spiritual goals and spiritual interests
- Experiencing a feeling of unity with other forms of life

Mental Balance
- Ability to hold high vibrational thoughts
- Ability to focus on pleasant memories not hardships
- Ability to avoid negative mental chatter and self criticism
- Ability to focus on the task at hand, in present time
- Ability to take a break from work and relax the mind

Emotional Balance
- Feelings of love and acceptance of yourself
- Feelings of love and acceptance of others
- Ability to overcome grief and loss
- Ability to feel compassion
- Ability to forgive

Physical Balance
- Feelings health, energy and vitality
- Feelings of connectedness to your surroundings
- A feeling of wholeness
- A feeling of centeredness
- Feelings of stability and strength

Table 1

Human Energy Dynamics and the Benefits of Subtle Energy Work

The existence of energetic healing techniques goes back thousands of years and is mention in many sacred texts. Many forms of hands-on healing and energy transference exist, some are somewhat structured, while others are more free form. The benefits of energy work are profound, however, and cannot be ignored in any of its forms. The following is a list of some of the typical benefits mentioned by those having received subtle energy treatments.

Benefits of Subtle Energy Work

- A feeling of greater balance
- Feelings of rejuvenation
- Recovery of past energies
- Release of blockages
- Release from specific past emotional traumas
- Release from patterns of repeating negative karma
- Relief from fatigue or upset
- Clarity and peace of mind
- Reconnecting with loved ones formerly estranged
- Improved ability to meditate
- Increased creativity and vitality
- A feeling of wholeness
- A feeling of lightness
- Expanded awareness
- Increased love for self and others

Table 2

The effect of energy work is to bring the individual into a greater state of self-empowerment. It usually follows as a consequence of this that the individual experiences greater health, vitality and zest for life. One also may experience clarity of purpose in life, and an unfolding of creative potential. Energy balancing allows for new energetic pathways to open up and new ideas can enter into one's consciousness.

Understanding Healing Energies

To understand how healing energies work, it is important to realize that all things are connected with one another on an energy level. Your feelings of love for another person are carried on an instantaneous vibrational wavelength to that person. Those who you love are aware of that love at some level of their consciousness. They are not only aware of it, they respond to it. Love encourages love. Love is an energy of acceptance that engenders a feeling of wholeness and unity. We can connect with others energetically at the level of love energy. When someone is working with healing energies, they are in essence working with the energy of love. The energy of love and acceptance is so powerful it can help return the body to a state of health. The lack of love and acceptance can, on the other hand, cause a person to fold inward on himself or herself. Lack of love and acceptance over a long period of time can be very detrimental to the body, mind and spirit. A healer or energy worker is someone who can awaken this healing energy of love and help another person restore his or her own energetic balance. We all use the energy of love and compassion to heal ourselves. An energy worker (lightworker or bodyworker) is really a *facilitator* of energy flows.

The Nature of LIGHT

Light is a form of energy. Light is a high vibrational state of energy that mirrors aspects of our own human energy field. The difference between visible light and non-visible light is *our* ability to perceive within a given rage of vibration, not an inherent difference in the light itself. Some people see a broader range of light frequencies than others do. Since light is a form of energy, it is possible to sense or "see" light with other senses than just the eyes. Although traditional physics states that light has a uniform unchanging speed of 186,000 miles per second, there are forms of "light" that travel faster that that. In the world of energies, the concepts of "speed," "distance," "time," and "space" are so closely related to our act of perceiving them that we cannot talk of independent characteristics of light or energy without making it clear that we are creators of what we are perceiving. Conscious aware beings can manipulate light in a variety of ways. *Vibrational medicine and energy balancing are manipulations of non-visible light through the application of conscious intent.* Discoveries in quantum physics in the past 80 years have significantly changed our understanding of light and its relationship to matter, as well as its relationship to our perception of the universe as we seek to understand it. We actually create our universe through creating light. Our act of perceiving light is part of this creation process. The universe does not exist unless we choose to perceive it. It is by perceiving light that we create light.

The Nature of ENERGY

Energy is a vibrational potentiality capable of being directed, transformed, transmuted and transferred. At a gross level, energy can be thought of as vibrating particles in constant motion. However, the particles themselves are not solid and do not have defined locations in space. Therefore, they are not truly particles, as we understand the term. Matter is a solidified form of energy, based on our perception of what it means to be solid. Matter and energy are relative states, which rely on our perception and interpretation for their existence. Light and all forms of electro-magnetics are energy. An energy field is simply a collection of energy patterns that are in a higher in vibrational state than the type of energy we normally refer to as "matter." All matter has energy fields; all matter is energy. There is no sharp dividing line between an object of matter and an energy field. One blurs into the other. Energy can be focused and directed through the conscious intent of an aware being. All forms of life have an energy pattern. When the pattern is disrupted by disharmonious energy wavelengths, physical, emotional or mental problems can result. Balancing energy is the act of removing obstacles to the free flow of energy within its basic pattern that allows the life form to more closely approximate its native state of wholeness, health and vitality. Evolution is an increase in the vibrational rate of an energy field over time, towards a higher state of being.

Different Types and Sources of Vital Energy

The preceding paragraph describes the nature of energy in general. When it comes to describing our energy systems as human beings, there are many different types of vital energy as well as different sources from which that energy comes. According to the ancient science of Ayurveda, we are each born with a certain amount of vital energy that is an inherent part of our physical make up. In addition to this, we take in energy through breathing and take in energy through all the various senses. We also take in energy from the food we eat, and from ingesting nutrients, certain herbs and vitamins. On the other side, eating foods that are unhealthy for us can deplete our body's energy. The process of thinking generates energy. Certain types of thinking can be an energy *drain* as well. If we think all day about problems or how things cannot be accomplished, we will feel drained and tired. If we think about succeeding in new projects or meeting our life's goals, or exciting new relationships, we gain energy.

Studying about the nature of our world, or learning new skills can increase our energy. We can create energy by "ingesting" information that helps us organize data into useful patterns.

We can also create energy through meditation. Clearing the mind of unwanted clutter helps put us in touch with universal forces of positive energy and has an uplifting effect on the body, mind and spirit. Acting responsibly in the use of our sexual energies is also an important way to maintain or increase physical energy. If we abuse our sexual energies by over use or mix our sexual activity with harmful drugs, we actually deplete our sexual energy reserve and can weaken the body's defenses. Sexual energies are extremely powerful and the body has an amazing ability to generate and re-generate sexual energies which can then be used to create new life, or to energize the entire being. Sexual energies shared through a loving relationship can increase the amount of energy available to both partners, so abstinence is not a requirement for maintaining healthy sexual energies. Probably the reverse is true. Learning to use our sexual energies responsively and lovingly brings us greater energy and vitality. Specific techniques for doing this are included in some forms of Tantra Yoga.

When our body's energy level is healthy, and our mental, emotional, sexual and other energies are active and strong, this is felt strongly in they body's subtle energy fields. The subtle energy fields, the electromagnetic and Biomagnetic energies surrounding the body, are very interactive when it comes to the energy levels of the physical body. One can sense, through the subtle bodies, whether there are blockages in the body's energy production systems, whether the energy is too low, or whether there is too much energy. The condition of the subtle energy bodies is a wonderful indicator of the current and future health of the physical body. One of the key words here is "future health" meaning that energetic problems in the energy bodies will show up before the physical body begins to manifest them.

Vital Energies and Reversing the Effects of Aging

Of interest to many people is just how far man's knowledge of science, physics and biology will take us in the realm of reversing the effects of aging. We know that given the proper conditions and given sufficient energy, some chemical reactions can be sustained almost indefinitely. Breakdown in the human body occurs when the biochemical processes stop functioning normally. Instructions on how to perform these processes are carried in the DNA. Damage to DNA can come from several causes, one of which appears to be free radicals (see Chapter Five). DNA has an energetic nature as well as a chemical nature. Subtle energies that strengthen and reinforce our electromagnetic field, balance and re-energize our physiological energies, as well as help integrate our mental, emotional and spiritual energies are a powerful influence in reversing the effects of aging. It appears that cellular aging is at least partly a response to faulty programming, perhaps due to damaged DNA, coupled with blockages in the human energy system.

As we evolve spiritually to higher levels of vibrational energies, we are less bound by the traditional paradigms of linear time and their associated expectations of aging and decay. Once we break free of such mental limitations as linear time, we enter a new realm of consciousness where we have a much greater influence energetically on our physiology than we might have ever expected. Revitalization of our physiology as well as retaining youthful energies in this higher vibrational state is not only possible it is a normal condition of this new existence.

Scientific Studies into Subtle Energies

The term "subtle" energy is used when we want to speak of those energy vibrations that are higher than what we view as visible light, or what we experience as electricity, for example. The term "subtle" should not be understood as being weak. These subtle energies are very powerful and can affect our physiology in profound ways. The human energy system is composed of a wide variety of energies, and energy centers. The chakras are one part of this system. Other parts are the meridians or pathways of energy flow, the energy bodies or energy fields, and the higher energies of thought itself. Because this energy is unseen, and its very existence has not been something that western traditional medicine has emphasized or even in most cases acknowledged, various scientific studies have been done over the years in an attempt to provide those with an objective western mind a more substantive scientific, physical validation of subtle energy's existence.

A number of scientific tests have been done over the years in an attempt to measure the healing energies associated with energy healing. In one example, Maxwell Cade, a British scientist in London, conducted extensive experiments in the 1970s. Cade used an electroencephalographic brainwave monitor in his experiments and discovered that the brainwave patterns of both the practitioner and the client altered simultaneously as the practitioner started the healing session. This showed an unseen connection at an energetic level.

In the early 1980's, Dr. John Zimmerman began a series of important studies on therapeutic touch, using a SQUID (Superconducting Quantum Interference Device) magnetometer at the University of Colorado School of Medicine in Denver. Dr. Zimmerman discovered that a large pulsating biomagnetic field emanated from the hands of a Therapeutic Touch practitioner. The frequency of the pulsation was found to "sweep" up and down from 0.3 to 30 Hz (cycles per second), with most of the activity in the 7 to 8 Hz range. The biomagnetic pulsation from the hands was found to be in the same frequency range as brain waves. In addition, scientific studies of the frequencies necessary for healing indicate that they naturally sweep back and forth through the full range of therapeutic frequencies, thus being able to stimulate healing in any part of the body. (Source: *"Science Measures the Human Energy Field,"* Reiki News, International Center for Reiki Training, 1999)

A more recent book on the scientific basis for energy work is *"Spiritual Healing: Scientific Validation Of A Healing Revolution"* by Daniel J. Benor, M.D., published in 2001. Dr. Benor has studied spiritual healing for two decades. In his research, he explores the history of spiritual healing, from medieval miracles to today's cooperation between doctors and healers. His book focuses on how spiritual healing is an effective factor in health care with the potential to become an essential part of tomorrow's medical practice.

For an in depth look at a very powerful energy balancing technique, known as The EMF Balancing Technique®, there is a new book available called *"Elegant Empowerment,"* by Peggy Phoenix Dubro, developer of the EMF Balancing Technique® and David La Pierre, a physicist. This book describes the underlying principles of quantum physics as they apply specifically to this new method of energy balancing. Published by Platinum Press, this book provides an amazing insight into the basis for this powerful new technique of energy balancing and provides detailed description of the energy lattice surrounding the human body, known as the Universal Calibration Lattice.

Specific Institutions for Organized Research

There has been an increasing interest in the formal scientific study of subtle energies, energy related body work and the energies of the heart in the western world. Organizations exist which have as their goal the exploration and understanding of these energies for the overall benefit of humankind. Here are several examples.

International Society for the Study of Subtle Energies and Energy Medicine ("ISSSEEM") is one of the leaders in the effort to synthesize traditional wisdom and shamanic knowledge about subtle energies and energy medicine with scientific theory and study it with scientific method. Designed as a bridge between scientifically-inclined intuitives and intuitively-inclined scientists, ISSSEEM supports experimental exploration of the phenomena long associated with the practice of energy healing. Through the sponsorship of conferences, the publication of its quarterly magazine, *"Bridges,"* and a scientific journal, *"Subtle Energies,"* the Society serves its members and strives to stimulate theory, research, and discussion in the larger scientific community.

The Institute of Heartmath® is a non-profit research and education organization which focuses on the energies of the heart. The goal of the Institute for Heartmath is to conduct research on the human heart and its role in establishing physiological, mental and emotional coherence. The Hearthmath organization works to develop effective interventions to improve learning, performance, behaviors, health and quality of life

The Touch Research Institutes focus their scientific research into the physical side of therapeutic modalities, specifically massage therapy, yoga and Tai Chi. These studies show amazing benefits from massage therapy (as well as from Yoga and Tai Chi) including specific benefits to those with cardiovascular disease, high blood pressure and stress and other diseases. The research shows that massage therapy is a very powerful therapeutic tool for a very wide variety of issues. (See Appendix D for contact information).

Who Can Be an Energy Facilitator?

Anyone can learn the basic techniques of facilitating energy flows. There are techniques and practices that you can learn to then apply and help yourself and your family achieve greater balance, health and harmony. At the very least, these techniques can help you and your loved ones cope more effectively with the rapid change facing all of us today. Like most things, to become highly skilled at energy facilitation requires practice, dedication and an intention to work consciously for the benefit of others. The key word here is *intention*. Intention, or application of your inner self in a focused direction, is what causes the energy to respond. Using intent and focus, you can direct healing energies to the areas in the body or in the bioenergetic field where they are needed most. This influx of energy, coupled with the energy of the person's own field, then works to restore optimum energy flow within their system.

One of the special skills that an energy facilitator needs is a sensitivity to energy itself. As a facilitator, you need to be able to sense energy blockages, energy flows, energy vibrations, as well as areas of balance or imbalance. One learns to sense this energy with practice and over time. Techniques that can be learned and practiced to help one learn more about energy sensing include meditation, yoga, tai chi and other practices. One of the first things that is needed is the ability to sense one's own energy and the energy of other people. We are with ourselves twenty-four hours a day, seven days a week. We go through all manner of energy shifts during that time period. If we learn to quiet our emotions and let our feelings flow, we will learn what it is like to experience our own energies. When we interact with others, we need to focus on experiencing *their* energies so that we are able to sense changes that are happening external to us. Whether you want to be a facilitator of energies for the benefit of others, or you just want to improve your ability to manage your own energy, a knowledge and awareness of your own energy as distinct from the energy of others is essential.

An emotion has a certain vibrational wavelength associated with it. A person who is relatively new to sensing energy on a conscious basis may find it difficult to distinguish between a strong emotion coming from an individual around him or her, and a strong emotion that they are feeling themselves. They may walk into a room and suddenly feel afraid, when in fact they may be sensing the emotion of fear that already exists in the room, caused by one or more people already there. This is an understandable occurrence and one that should be approached with patience. With time and practice, your skill at differentiating the source of emotional energies will greatly and rapidly improve.

Sensing Emotional Energies

Part of sensing energy in general is the ability to sense emotional energies. Energy enters or leaves our system primarily on an emotional level. We all know how exhausting powerful emotions can be when we are dealing with other people, or how energizing and uplifting they can be, depending on whether energy is entering or leaving our system. When we say that something is a "drag" or that someone is a "drain" on our energy, we are actually speaking factually not just figuratively. Individuals, places, events and circumstances can in fact either drain our energies or can contribute to our energies. As you learn more about your own energy management, you will realize that it is your choice whether your give up your energy to a situation, person or thing or whether you keep your energies to yourself. No one can "take" your energy unless you allow it to be taken. Most people are not up to this level of awareness, however, and it still makes sense to communicate to those people in terms of losing or gaining energy.

When someone is experiencing a "heartache" or is "heartbroken," it is the energy of the heart center that is most effected. The focus of this book is to shed some light on the connection between the energy of the heart center and the massive problems of heart-related illnesses facing our fellow human beings. Heart bypass surgery, heart transplants and artificial hearts are marvels of technology to be sure, but they do not begin to address the energetic causes behind the existence of physical heart diseases. Can we step up to the challenge of working with the issues of the heart on an energetic level? Can we take the next step to a higher level of responsibility for ourselves and our fellow humans to love them and love ourselves, with acceptance, compassion and a unity consciousness?

I believe that we *can* do this, and that the time has come to engage ourselves in a co-creative effort to bring greater love into the world. We know we are in need of it. We have seen where the lack of love can take humankind. We have also seen the winds of change blowing across the globe, bringing a greater awareness of the oneness of humankind.

Love is Active, Not Passive

Love is not a passive or "no action" state of being. Being a loving person does not mean you live a life of no impact on others. Conscious loving is a dynamic activity. To love is to focus on higher energy vibrations through conscious intent. When it is time to act, a loving person acts for the betterment of his fellow humans and the overall human condition. Sometimes hateful, destructive actions by a few can have broad impact on many. A loving person can take responsible action without adding hate or destructive anger to the process. When a child is prevented from engaging in a harmful activity, the act of prevention limits their freedom, but does so out of love and a view towards the higher good. Sometimes it is vital for the loving person to act decisively to help balance creative vs. destructive energies. Love energy is a powerful, creative force that can overcome lower vibrational energies. Ideally, it does this through raising the vibrations of surrounding energies and transmuting hate into compassion. A responsible, loving person does not fail to act when action is motivated by spirit.

The New Energy Facilitators

As the levels of the new energy available to us increase, we have a greater opportunity now to incorporate these into our lives and into our daily work. More and more people are becoming aware of subtle energies. Those who are already aware of subtle energies know that the power in the energies and the "feel" of the energy is changing.

Our primary task as New Energy Facilitators is to raise ourselves as individuals to a level where we can hold the energies of love and compassion and share these with our family, friends, and all those around us. As we do this, their energies will flow into ours and we will become stronger. Our individual sphere of influence energetically will grow and expand to encompass more individuals. This is part of the role of the energy facilitator. Our task at hand, and our challenge, is holding the light of increased vibrations and higher levels of love energy. Being able to hold such energies and direct them outward to others is at once a beautiful, powerful gift and a unique challenge.

In today's complex and rapidly changing environment, the energy facilitator needs a variety of tools in his or her tool bag in order to be successful. Addressing issues of balance in terms of the spirit, mind, emotions and the physical body requires knowledge of various modalities so that the most appropriate solution for any given person or situation can be brought to bear. Bodywork, energy work, meditation, spiritual coaching, all have their place in our world. We deal with each other and with the universe on multiple levels simultaneously. It is important to have a multi-dimensional approach to our personal and professional interactions with others. In this way, our give of service becomes more valuable and more effective.

The Importance of Formal Training

Some people ask whether a formal style or modality of energy therapy is required or if anyone can just "move the energy." There are two specific aspects of formal training in a specific modality that should be considered.

(1) Different types of energy work (e.g., energy therapy modalities) address the body's energy field in different ways. There are specific techniques that promote balance at a very profound level and when applied according

to the methodology of that practice can achieve greater benefits than if applied in a haphazard way. Training in a particular modality and adherence to a structured format ensures the continuity and purity of the techniques used.

(2) Formal training usually includes issues of how to deal with people who are undergoing therapeutic treatment and what some of the appropriate guidelines are for etiquette, interpersonal relationships in a professional environment, how to deal with issues of emotional or energetic release during therapy and other related issues. The better equipped a person is to handle such issues the better the sessions will go for both the client and the practitioner.

Some form of formal training in energywork or bodywork is also an acknowledgement to the universe that you are willing to be of service in the application of techniques to assist other beings in bettering themselves.

Vibrational Energy: The Quantum Nature of Our Reality

Axiom

> A **vibration** is a regular and continuous change in the position of a particle, between two different locations or states of being. The rate at which the change takes place is a multidimensional aspect of the vibrational forces involved and actually affects the nature of what the particle appears to be (its mass/energy structure), where the particle is likely to be (its probability), and when the particle is in a particular location (its existence in time).

The Nature of Universal Energy

Where does this energy come from? The energy we are talking about is all around us and all through us. Although it can be said to flow from one point to another, increase in strength and vibration and exhibit numerous other characteristics, it does not really *"come from"* anywhere. It is all pervasive and ever present. The energy is part of "All That Is." It has been given many names and descriptions down through the millennia of human history. In some cultures the energy is personified with humanlike names or forms. In quantum physics, the energy is an aspect of the "unified field." The energy can exist in many different forms, hold different vibrations, spin, flow, stretch, expand, contract, and exhibit multiple other characteristics.

The most important aspect to understand about the energy is that it is the basis for our existence and interactions with all things, including ourselves. We are an aspect of this energy and we share its intelligence. It responds to our intent. We are never separate from it. Our journey for a definition of energy ultimately takes us back to ourselves. Our journey to personal health and healing, and our desire to understand the body's energy fields, is a microcosm of the greater desire to experience all that is. We are love experiencing itself.

Multi-Dimensional Vibrations

All matter is composed of vibrations. Matter is composed of the shifting of position of "particles" or packets of energy. The term "matter" is misleading, since matter is really energy. How we perceive energy and its relative vibrational rate determines whether we view it as "solid" (such as a table) or as ethereal (such as light and electromagnetics).

The energy packets that comprise a table are of much lower frequency than those that comprise a beam of light.

The energy packets that comprise a quartz crystal are structured in a geometric matrix that is far more orderly than the arrangement of energy packets that comprise a piece of wood.

The vibrations of the energy packets determine the nature of the packets. To attempt to understand this, we need to remember that these are vibrations that are not just "back and forth." They are not two-dimensional vibrations, but rather multidimensional vibrations. The energy packets of any living or non-living thing are vibrating in multiple dimensions simultaneously. This means that we cannot view the entirety of something at any given time.

When we view anything, we see only selected aspects of that thing's existence based on the vibrational frequencies that we are able to attune to at that time.

Those who can sense and work with subtle energies, meaning the vibrational energy packets and energy strings that exist throughout all things, are in fact perceiving a higher vibrational aspect of "matter" than most people are generally aware of.

Higher frequency energy vibrations also have a tremendous uplifting and healing benefit. As Gary Zukav states in his beautiful book *"The Seat of the Soul,"* "A joyous person abounds with energy and feels buoyant, because he or she is running a higher-frequency current of energy through his or her system." We know these higher vibrational energies by the feeling which they impart to entire systems.

Wavelength, Frequency and Energy Flows

A "wavelength" is the distance between two identical points in the adjacent cycles of a wave. A wavelength can be measured from the top of one wave to the top of the next wave. The wavelength of waves can be large, such 20 meters in width, as in an ocean wave, or extremely small, as in a beam of light. The wavelength of a beam of light, for example, is measured in nanometers (billionths of a meter).

A shorter wavelength means higher frequency and higher energy. A longer wavelength is associated with lower frequency and lower energy. Wavelength and frequency are thus related. They have what is called an "inverse proportional relationship." However, it is not as difficult to understand as it might seem. A higher vibration is associated with a shorter wavelength. This means, for example, that a light beam is a higher energy form than the energy in a flow of electrons through a conductor.

A vibration occurs across a single wavelength. The term *"frequency"* is a measure of how many vibrations occur in one second. This is measured in "cycles per second" for which the term *"Hertz"* (Hz) is used.

- Sound Vibrations
In sound waves, Hz corresponds to the pitch of a sound. The higher the frequency the higher the pitch of the sound. Normally, people can hear sounds in the range of 20 Hz to 20,000 Hz (20 kHz). Amplitude is measured in decibels. Decibels provide a relative measure of sound intensity

- Electromagnetic Waves
In working with energies, it is helpful to know why rates of vibration and frequency differences are significant. Energy waves can interact with each other, producing specific phenomena. Electromagnetic waves permeate our environment. We are impacted by electromagnetic waves all the time. This includes macro-level waves from electrical power plants, television, radio, automobile engine (alternators) and computers. It also includes much more subtle sources of electromagnetics such as those emitted by living things.

A general understanding of the range of energies below and above the visible light spectrum can be gained from viewing the description of the "Electromagnetic Spectrum" in the Table shown.

Short Wavelength Means Higher Frequency and Higher Energy

Longer Wavelength Means Lower Frequency and Lower Energy

Electromagnetic Spectrum

Cosmic Rays

Cosmic Rays, which actually behave more like particles, are the highest energy radiation known to exist. At the highest energy scientists can measure today, Cosmic particles have been found that have 300 billion times the energy of a proton. Scientists have found no top end to the Cosmic Ray spectrum. Their origin is uncertain, but they appear to come from outside our galaxy.

Gamma Rays

Gamma Rays have been detected coming from deep space and from supernovas and deteriorating atomic particles and black holes. Both the Sun and the Moon emit Gamma Rays.

X Rays

X Rays are emitted by comets, pulsars, neutron stars, black holes, supernova remnants, and stars. The energy of the sun also energizes the Earth's magnetosphere, which interacts with the ionosphere and produces Earth x-rays.

Ultraviolet Rays— Near, Far, Extreme

Ultraviolet is classified into three types, based on wavelength. Near (NUV) closest to visible light; extreme (EUV) closest to X-rays; and far (FUV) between the NUV and EUV.

Visible Light

The entire visible spectrum of light exists in this band.

(continued...)

Infrared— Near and Far

Near Infrared rays are not visible and not harmful. They are used in electronic eyes and sensors, such as VCR remote controls. Far Infrared is longer in wavelength and is felt by us as heat. Sometimes heat lamps are Far Infrared, sometimes called Thermal Infrared. Objects that give off heat are emitting thermal radiation. Night Goggles are Infrared detecting sensors. Humans and all life forms give off Infrared, which can be detected by special detectors. Certain snakes sense Infrared, which allows them to hunt at night.

Microwaves

Short wavelength microwaves are used in sensing devices such as RADAR and Doppler (weather detection) devices. Microwaves are also used to transmit information over straight-line distances. Longer Microwaves (about a foot in length) are used in microwave ovens. The universal background noise contains microwaves, which can be detected coming from all directions.

Radio Waves

Television, Radio, Cellular Phones and other devices utilize radio waves, which can have very long wavelengths. Usually, the shorter the antenna used on the device, the shorter the wavelengths of the wave band it is using. Planets, stars, galaxies and other celestial bodies emit radio waves. This makes possible the science of Radio Astronomy.

Alternating Electric Current

Very long wavelengths are a characteristic of AC electricity. Household current is this type.

Table 3

Alternative Healing Therapies
and Vibrational Medicine

Axiom

Native State is the highest vibrational energy level possible before all vibrational motion stops. The Ultimate Native State contains no motion. All-that-is, before the act of manifestation, is the condition of Ultimate Native State. Ultimate Native State is beyond the duality of living and non-living. The Ultimate Native State is pure potential.

To achieve a state of balance, health and wholeness, it is often the case that we must remove obstacles to the free flow of energy, by raising vibrations and clearing pathways. A light worker or energy facilitator takes this approach of removing barriers to vibrational energies so that Native State can be more closely approximated. The return to Native State is a return to wholeness, health and vitality.

Alternative healing therapies that rely on the power of sound, light, crystals, essential oils, flower essences, or direct energy field work are based on the quantum principles of vibrational energy and frequency. Our native state of physical health is one where the body is resonating at a high vibration. Illness or disease occurs when a portion of our energy field and/or physical body begins to resonate at a lower vibrational frequency. Healing is a return to balance and a return to higher vibrational states. In his book "*Vibrational Medicine*," Dr. Richard Gerber noted that "Disease becomes manifest in the physical body only after disturbances of energy flow have already become crystallized in the subtle structural patterns of the higher frequency bodies."

Every object has an electromagnetic field to which there are no absolute edges. One object's electromagnetic field blurs into another object's field when they are in close proximity. If we talk in terms of electrons and subatomic particles for a moment, the electrons and subatomic particles of one object will share the space of adjacent electrons and subatomic particles "belonging" to the adjacent object. This applies whether the object is an organic living thing or a "non-living" thing. In the case of the human energy system, this sharing of electrons and subatomic particles can be influenced by the thoughts and consciousness of the person.

Taking things a step further beyond the subatomic level, research into the apparent differences in behavior between what we call "particles" and what we call "waves" has led scientists to a new paradigm model of the universe based on what is called the "Superstring Theory." Superstring Theory (or simply "String Theory") views everything in the universe as being made up of vibrating loops of strings. The old model of tiny particles in orbit around other tiny particles fell apart when scientists were able to go ultra-small in their experiments with cyclotrons, giant electromagnets that propel subatomic particles to fantastic speeds. The rules of the macro world, which have been viewed for hundreds of years from the Newtonian Physics perspective, do not work in the ultra-small realm of the subatomic. Quantum physics helps explain what appears to be happening at the subatomic level, but its description does not mix well with the Newtonian Physics view. The Superstring Theory has elements that help unify these two views of the universe. The essence of both the Superstring Theory and Quantum Theory appears to be the vibrational nature of energy.

Sound Vibrations, Geometry and Crystals

Sound can generate geometric patterns at a molecular level that help organize subatomic energy particles. The reason that a harmonious, high vibrational sound is pleasing and a discordant collection of noise is unpleasant is due to the inherent organizing pattern of the geometrical structures, which the sound is creating. Sound that creates a higher order of structured geometrical patterns will feel closer to our native state of high vibrational energy. Our physiology will respond to sound vibrations, since it will respond to the geometric patterns created by the subatomic energy vibrations. The structure of the subatomic energy patterns is a mechanism in our universe for storing and retrieving information. In the Tibetan practice of Tantric Meditation, for example, one meditates using a mantra and visualization to invoke wisdom. The vibration of sound is linked with the visualization of light and geometric images. A geometric pattern is an information module. It has an inherent intelligence, which is its structure. Because a geometric pattern is composed of vibrations of energy, the structure is not a static, unmoving picture. It is alive with energy and it is alive with the potential for influencing other structures in its vacinity. This is also why crystals have been known to have healing properties. They have a subatomic organizing power that can actually influence the subatomic structures of nearby objects and bring those energy fields into a higher state of alignment.

Gems & Stones

Specific to Heart Energies

- Emerald
- Ruby
- Tourmaline (green and pink)
- Malachite
- Green jade
- Green aventurine
- Chryoprase
- Kunzite (a.k.a. Evening Stone)
- Rose quartz

Table 4

For a very detailed online scientific reference covering gems, stones and minerals, see "*The Mineral and Gemstone Kingdom,*" at www.minerals.net/index.html.

Aromatherapy: Oils and Essences

Aromatherapy is the use of essential oils derived from plants, flowers, trees and herbs to increase one's vibration and achieve greater health and vitality and to achieve a rejuvenation of the body, mind and spirit.

Essential oils and flower essences have a very high vibrational energy frequency. When these substances come into contact with the energy field of organic living energy systems, they can quickly affect the living system's vibrational rate. They can be used to raise the vibrational energies of our physiology and facilitate a return to a more healthy, balanced state. The use of essential oils can be combined with various modalities of healing and balancing to provide greater overall benefit to those being treated.

Essential oils have been known for their therapeutic properties for thousands of years. It is likely that the modern tradition of women using perfume behind the ear, on the neck and on the wrists goes back to very ancient times when essential oils were widely used to raise one's vibration and promote health and increased energy. Those particular locations, behind the ear, on the neck and wrists, are specific areas where absorption of oils is more profound than in most other areas of the body. Many religious practices mention the process of anointing with holy oils. Perhaps the "holy" aspect of the oils is their higher vibrational energy which mirrors divine energy. Much of what we see today as "religious practice" has its roots in ancient times in the application of techniques to raise the energy vibration and electromagnetic frequency of devotional objects and even of the devotees themselves. When an enlightened spiritual being (e.g., bodhisattva, saint, avatar) bestows a blessing on someone, what is actually happening? There are thousands of stories throughout history of objects being blessed which then seem to acquire healing properties. Is a "blessing" a raising of vibration?

The following table gives examples of oils and scents that have a beneficial influence on heart energies. Oils oil blends have specific frequencies. Some people will respond better to some oils than other oils. There is a personal frequency attunement relationship here.

Oils & Scents

Specific to Heart Energies

- Rose
- Bergamot
- Melissa (a.k.a. Lemon Balm)
- Jasmine
- Marjoram
- Sandalwood
- Magnolia

Table 5

Achieving Balance through Subtle Energy Healing:

Calming Anxiety and Emotional Trauma

An individual who is anxious or traumatized has both energetic motion and emotion out of balance. This has a snowball effect. The sensation of emotions out of control can cause fear, worry, uncertainty, an inability to focus, nervousness, and similar reactions and can cause emotional feelings to increase. This increases the energy imbalance and increases the feeling of anxiety. This can become a spiral of increasing imbalance.

Prescription drugs marketed to treat anxiety often act as depressants that inhibit the individual's ability to feel the motion and emotion. They function in an attempt to break the spiral of escalating imbalance. However, they do not address the energy disorder at the root of the feelings. By masking the feelings, the individual may experience temporary relief from the associated sensations of motion and emotion. Therapies that address the energy centers themselves, and the associated motion of energy into or out of the system, will have a deeper and more profound effect on the individual's ability to overcome the feelings of being out of control, and thereby have a greater potential for lasting balance. There is also an important educational aspect associated with most energy work modalities that is beneficial to the person being treated. If an individual is given an opportunity to understand to a greater degree the mechanics behind what can cause an out-of-balance condition, he or she will be in a more stable place with regard to managing personal energies. Through learning one or more of the various modalities that promote balance and greater wholeness, an individual is put in charge of their metabolism. Prescription drugs, on the other hand, tend to influence the metabolism and provide no such opportunity for the individual to really gain mastery of their own energetic systems. In very severe cases where it appears to medical doctors that only western medicine can help, it is important to seek appropriate guidance.

Anyone who has experienced anxiety or emotional upset will know that it is a "feeling" that resides in the chest area. The heart is highly influenced by emotional imbalance and long term anxiety. *An "anxiety attack" is an energy imbalance in the Heart*

Chakra area and other energy centers in the body, usually including the solar plexus area. Balancing these energies is an essential step on the road to healing the heart.

Our individual consciousness focuses our energy in specific patterns that are highly unique to us. Getting in touch with what we are feeling and improving our ability to understand our emotional energies is a vital part of our growth process.

The Importance of Physical Touch

The trend in our society has been one towards increasing isolation at the physical level. In some ways, we have become a "touchless" society and many people are starved for physical contact. Higher primates that live in social groups exhibit more physical contact with each other than most human groups. In fact, studies have shown that in a normal day, people will go well out of their way to avoid touching another human being. A certain amount of energetic interchange takes place through physical contact. When we deny this basic need we create an additional layer of anxiety that is self-created and self-perpetuating. Our physical body is one of our primary communication channels to and from our environment. We need to be sensitive to these channels and to our interactions with others and our surroundings. Our journey to healing and balancing our energetic selves has a physical component that must not be ignored.

This may be especially true for those who have experienced a life trauma, or who are going through a serious physical illness. Enforced lack of human touch does not promote greater healing, it has the opposite effect. Along with subtle energy work that focuses on energetic interactions of unseen energies, we should also consider where appropriate the use of body work modalities to help achieve a greater overall approach to integrating these energies. Many example of this exist in the field of massage therapy and its numerous specialized approaches. We will take a look at these in Chapter Three.

The Importance of Personal Interaction

As you focus on healing and balancing, another important area to be aware of is the need for personal interaction, on a human-to-human basis. I believe that technology has given us wonderful advancements and educational aids but it can also be used to disassociate people from one another. The proliferation of broadcast television and the poor quality of broadcast content has contributed to our isolation from one another. Television can interfere with person-to-person communication by enforcing barriers of silence while "the TV is on" and causes people to focus on being spectators rather than being engaged in an interactive activity. Television is not only prevalent in our homes, but you will often find television screens in doctor's waiting rooms, some large grocery stores, bars and restaurants, gasoline pumps and even in health spas. I have seen people drive to the local health spa wearing headphones, exercise wearing the headphones and only take them off long enough to change clothes while watching the television mounted in the locker room, then back on go the headphones. One could spend all day at the health spa and never talk to another person, or even hear them if they tried to talk to you. Meeting places where potential conversation between humans might occur have often been turned into "viewing stations" where no human interaction is expected because television is available.

Sometimes people will use television as a means to avoid communication that might otherwise be uncomfortable. If we are uncomfortable with our own feelings, then we might be inclined to shy away from communicating with others where such communication might cause us to "feel" something. Because of its one-way direction, television, when carried to the extreme, has a numbing effect on the senses.

This phenomenon is important to understand since it is a growing part of our western culture, and in cultures around the world where technology is introduced. Technology has also given us the Global Internet, which has tremendous potential as a communication tool because of its two-way interaction. Still, person-to-person contact is limited through this medium also.

As you work towards achieving greater balance and in studying or applying subtle energy work or bodywork, it is important to understand the environment that many people are living in day to day.

Transmuting Energy vs. Absorbing Energy

From a metaphysical standpoint, it is worth mentioning that in the past it was not uncommon for people of a compassionate nature to seek to balance negative energies by absorbing them into their own energy fields. Such people often came down with physical maladies associated with taking on this negative emotional energy. Such people then exhibited many of the symptoms of the imbalance when in fact they were normally quite balanced individuals. Ideally one should be able to raise one's own energetic vibration high enough to transmute lower energies into higher energy wavelengths and thus promote balance in oneself and others. More people are learning to do this and fewer are taking on the lower vibrational energies on a personal basis.

The ability to transmute lower energies into higher energies is the essence of subtle energy work. The term "light worker" denotes someone who can take the darker energies of low vibrational emotional states and raise them "into the light" thus facilitating the individual's own innate balancing processes. As the dynamics of our modern age are causing more dark energies to come to the surface, we need more individuals who can understand and deal with the subtle energies and facilitate our evolutionary transition to higher vibrational states on a personal level as well as a global scale. This is not a task for the weak of heart. This is a challenging activity that requires commitment, persistence and an "unbending intent."

Part of our conscious awareness is intimately connected with our body's energy fields and with a system of energy vortices (spinning energy centers) called the chakras. There are thousands of energy chakras in the body and they act as bridges between the physical and the non-physical energies. There are seven major chakras in the body which focus energy in specific patterns and represent specific dynamic aspects of our existence. In the following section, we will introduce and explore these seven primary energy centers.

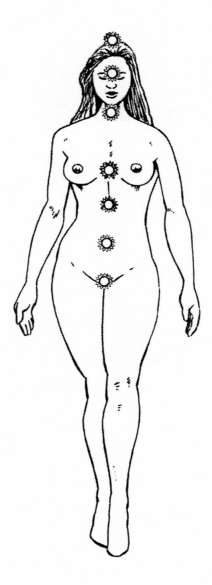

Figure 3 The Seven Major Chakras

The Seven Major Chakras:

Axiom

Each chakra is an energy vortex. Meditation on a particular chakra causes increased energy to flow to that chakra.

Chakras respond to intention and energy in its various forms. These forms include sound, light, emotion and vibration.

The human body is part of and is connected to the Universal Energy Field. We interact with our environment on an energy level constantly. How you "feel" at any given moment is at least in part a sensory translation of how you are doing "energetically" in terms of your relationship to yourself, to others and to your reality as a whole.

Where are the human energy centers? There are hundreds of energy centers or vortices of varying strength located throughout the body, and near the body, which interact with each other and our environment. There are powerful energy centers located in the hands, for example, as well in many of the joint areas. Seven of the most powerful energy centers lie along the vertical axis (spinal column) and are called "Major Chakras." The term Chakra comes from the Sanskrit word meaning "wheel," which is appropriate since these energy centers are spinning vortices of energy.

What Are the Chakras?

The chakra energy vortices appear to spin in a clockwise direction. They correspond in terms of location and influence with major nerve centers in the body and with the endocrine system. Their rate of spin is variable and their energy projects forward in front of the body as well as outward from the back. They are three-dimensional energy centers.

The chakras are very powerful energy centers that interact with a whole array of energetic systems running through the body and beyond it to the external energy bodies. The chakras are part of the body's overall energy system. There are thousands of chakras in the body. We will be looking at the seven major ones more closely.

The following table lists the *Seven Major Chakras* of the body.

	Chakras	Elements	Issues	Sanskrit Names
7	Crown	Thought	Understanding	Sahasrara
6	Brow	Light	Vision	Ajna
5	Throat	Sound	Communication	Vishuddha
4	Heart	Air	Love	Anahata
3	Solar Plexus	Fire	Power	Manipura
2	Sacral Plexus	Water	Sex	Svadhishana
1	Root	Earth	Survival	Muladadhara

Table 6

The chakras are significant in any study of the human energy fields since they have certain identifiable qualities that are associated with them. More importantly, energy blockages that affect the chakras can have a profound on the entire body.

How Do the Chakras Become Blocked?

From a causal standpoint, one of the ways that the chakras become blocked is through a misapplication of one's energy. Putting one's mental, emotional, physical or spiritual energies into activities, or thought forms that do not promote one's higher good can result in a blockage of energy flows. In terms of experiences, chakras can become blocked as a result of an emotional upset, trauma, severe stress, conflicting emotions, prolonged power loss, physical attacks on the body and other similar causes. A trauma that results in a person feeling that he or she cannot speak the truth in a given situation, or that their opinions are unworthy, can result in a blockage in the area of the throat chakra. Such a person may find it difficult to speak openly, or speak loudly due to an energy imbalance in this center. Blockages in spiritual, emotional, mental and physical energies all have a corresponding energy blockage in the related chakra or chakras. These blockages prevent the even flow of energy into and out of the chakras.

Chakra Energies Interact with Each Other

It is important to note that the energies of the chakras interact with one another and the functions of the chakras overlap in some areas. For example, the root chakra is associated with the earth and basic survival instincts, the second or sexual center chakra is associated with sexual interactions, the desire for food, and other things. The solar plexus chakra is associated with digestion and issues of power, control and vital energies. Blockages in any of these three can affect the nearby chakras. This is important to be aware of in energy work since you may be called upon to determine the areas in the body where primary blockages exist. A problem with digestion, for example, could be a blockage in the solar plexus region, but also have associated blockages in the two lower chakras.

When doing energy work to clear blockages, you will likely need to focus on clearing more than one chakra. It is important to remember that they all work together as a system.

Chakras and Colors

A color is simply a vibrational frequency of light. Different colors have different frequencies and therefore different vibrational energies. Studies of the chakra system seem to indicate that each chakra is associated with a particular color, i.e., vibration. This does not necessarily mean that each chakra is a different color. This means that from a vibrational frequency standpoint one of the things that distinguishes one chakra from the next is the level of vibration associated with it. Chakras can differ in color and intensity from one person to another depending on that person's energy level, state of consciousness and mental/emotional health. The colors, therefore, are indications of different frequencies. Working with light and color one is working with specific frequencies and one is actually changing energy patterns when doing this. The human energy field, including the radiated energy from all the chakras, is a beautiful mosaic of swirling colors and varying intensities. The light that emitted from these areas pulsates with life and vitality!

The Importance of Balance in the Chakra Centers

For most people in our society, a balanced chakra system is an ideal, but not a reality. In most people, the chakra system does not operate in a harmonious balanced fashion. The Chakras are not balanced individually, nor are they balanced one with the other. To find someone with all chakras in balance and operating from a position of wholeness and unity is usually rare. We have few role models for this, and the traditional medical teachings do not yet recognize the meaning or importance of balancing the subtle energies of the whole person when treating perceived disorders. We have a long way to go before this new paradigm of energetic medicine becomes the dominant underlying principle in our traditional healing professions. However, some progress is being made. On an individual level and on a global level, there is an increasing respect for the role played by subtle energies in the overall health of the body, mind, spirit and emotions.

Why is this important? Balancing chakra energies is important in many respects. Chakra energies are part of our energetic nature. Chakra energies come into play whenever we interact with other people. Energy blockages directly affect our interpersonal relations and are often the driving force behind many of our decisions. Unexamined blockages and imbalances can cause us to repeatedly make choices in our lives that are not in our best interests. On the positive side, balancing the chakra energies is something you can begin to take charge of yourself. You can learn to sense and work with your personal energies and learn to assist others in achieving greater balance. If you feel you are significantly out of balance, you may want to focus time on getting yourself in balance first. Then as you become more comfortable with these energies, you will want to reach out to others. This is a natural process.

A Description of the Seven Major Chakras

First: Root Chakra

The root chakra is our connection to the earth. It is located at the base of the spine, at the perineum. (see Appendix I— Glossary). This energy center is focused on our connection with powerful earth energies. Our ability to be grounded is our ability to be connected to the earth through this center. It is associated with nurturing and gives life force to the body. It is associated with materiality, survival and individuality.

This center is associated with the color red and is energetically connected to the functioning of the spine and kidneys

Characteristics of Chakra Blockages or Imbalance:
- inability to feel grounded with the Earth
- poor sense of direction
- difficulty connecting with others on a physical level
- issues of insecurity, instability, loss of power
- aggression, confusion
- lower tract physical problems, excretory and intestinal problems
- paranoia, fear
- defensiveness
- constipation
- hemorrhoids
- low back pain, sciatica

Second: Sacral Plexus,
also called the Sexual/Creative Center

This chakra is associated with sexual power, pleasure, sexual passion, health and family issues. The vital sexual energy flows through this center. It is located in the lower abdomen, sexual/genital area. This center is an extremely powerful generator of creative energies. The root chakra, sexual/creative chakra and the solar plexus chakra taken together represent the powerful physical universe energies interacting with one another as this energy moves up the spine to the higher centers. These energy centers are so powerful, that even minor blockages can create physical symptoms of disease or malfunction in one's physiology. The existence of clear and healthy energy flows in these three areas especially is associated with youth, vitality, potency, fertility and creativity.

This center is sometimes associated with the color orange. It governs the reproductive systems.

Characteristics of Sexual Center Blockages or Imbalance:
- tendency towards envy, possessiveness, jealousy
- overactive desire for physical sensation
- fear of sexual contact
- sexual guilt
- fear of any physical contact, dislike of being touched
- kidney, bladder or lymphatic infections
- obsessions with cleanliness
- lack of purpose
- impotence, frigidity

Third: Solar Plexus Chakra
This center is just above the navel. This is the center of personal power and will. This center is the seat from which many people interact with the world, using their force of will to accomplish what they set out to do. Overemphasis on this area is a cause of many problems and blockages in the overall flow of energy through all the chakras. We know instinctively that this is the seat of our competitive power. Professional boxers, wrestlers and other physical sports give their champions large belts with oversized brass or gold colored circular disks that fit right over the

Solar Plexus region when worn. For those who can visually see the chakra energies, this center does in fact emit a yellow/gold color especially when energized.

This center is associated with the color yellow. It governs the stomach, liver, gall bladder, and the nervous system.

Characteristics of Solar Plexus Blockages or Imbalance:
- anxiety, envy, greed
- obsession with power or control issues
- digestion problems
- poor metabolism, poor weight control
- liver, gall bladder, pancreas disorders
- anger
- victimization

Fourth: Heart Chakra
This is the center that is midpoint between the three lower chakras and the three higher chakras. This area is located in the center of the chest and is associated with heart energy, especially love, forgiveness, compassion, understanding, balance, openness, harmony, peace and other similar qualities. The Heart Chakra energy is extremely powerful. When the heart center is open, the love energy can flow from this center outward to connect with others.

A heart connection between two people is one of the most intimate and powerful connections that one can have. During Kundalini Rising the heart center can open up with tremendous volume and can cause life-changing events to take place. On the negative side, those with blocked heart energies are often subject to heart problems, sometimes resulting in a need for medical intervention, or so serious as to cause heart attack. Working with the heart center to help balance all the upper and lower chakras is a good way to facilitate clearing blockages and promote a healthy energy flow.

This center is associated with the colors green and pink. It governs the heart, blood, and the circulatory system.

Characteristics of Heart Chakra Blockages or Imbalance:

- selfishness
- inability to give or receive love or affection
- lack of compassion
- persistent relationship issues and difficulties
- heart, lung, circulatory problems
- immune system problems
- loneliness, isolation,
- hatred and condemnation of others
- disconnection

The High Heart Center

There is another energy center in the area of the heart. This is just above the primary Heart Chakra and is called the "High Heart Center." The High Heart Center is located just above the heart, between the Heart Chakra and the throat chakra. The High Heart Center corresponds to the Thymus gland. The Thymus gland consists of two separate lobes, which reside just above, and in contact with the heart. The Thymus glands are a vital part of the body's physical immune system. The Thymus is involved in the production of T cells which fight infection. The significance of the Thymus gland has become apparent in the last few years. Correlation between a strong immune system and a healthy Thymus gland suggests that this energy center is a key focal point for the body's self protecting mechanisms.

Fifth: Throat Chakra

This area is at the throat and is associated with speaking the truth, speaking one's inner feelings and being true to one's own spoken wisdom. Communication, expression and loyalty are some of the attributes associated with this center. A blockage in this center is characterized by throat problems, faulty speech, weak voice projection or other similar symptoms. People who are uneasy about speaking will often unconsciously grab their throat or rest their hand over their throat area, signaling that there is a suppression of energy in this area. Those who lie, suppress their own creative energy flow in this area. Sometimes, teeth, throat and mouth problems result from energy blockages in this area as the energy does not flow smoothly. On the positive side, those who are known for being strong, powerful singers usually have a clear open flow of energy from the lower chakras up to the heart chakra where the energy is amplified and directed to and through the throat chakra. To hear someone sing "from the heart" is a beautiful experience and these powerful energies have the ability to touch the hearts of others.

The fifth chakra center is associated with the color blue. It governs the bronchial area, lungs, and the vocal system.

Characteristics of Throat Chakra Blockages or Imbalance:

- inability to express oneself clearly
- inability to express one's truth
- too soft a voice
- muscular tension
- throat problems, such as laryngitis, sore throats

Sixth: Brow Chakra

This center is located in the center of the forehead, between the eyebrows. This is often called the "third eye." It is the center of intuition, imagination, perception and clairvoyance. It is also associated with self realization.

This center is associated with the color indigo. It governs the lower brain, left eye, nose, ears, and the nervous system.

Characteristics of Brow Chakra Blockages or Imbalance:

- inability to focus
- lack of clarity
- sinus problems
- eye problems
- fogginess
- dizziness

Seventh: Crown Chakra

This is located at the top of the head. It is associated with the connection between the higher states of being and the human energies, including the personality. The higher aspects of oneness, unity, wisdom, idealism, understanding, spiritual connections and service are associated with this center.

This center is associated with the color violet or sometimes white. It governs the upper brain, and the right eye.

Characteristics of Crown Chakra Blockages or Imbalance:

- psychological problems
- overly egotistical
- atheistic
- disconnected from higher sources

Chakra Energy and Consciousness

Axiom

Chakra Consciousness:

The energy contained in the chakra is conscious. This energy responds to our will or intent. It will flow outward to objects or persons towards which we have chosen to direct focused energy. Each chakra has an awareness of itself and its own energies.

The chakra energy responds to our intent whether we are consciously aware of the intent or not. Desires, drives, motivations, and needs, all create an intent which then acts upon the chakra energy, which in turn responds to that intent.

Creativity:

Exploring one's creativity is one of the best ways to raise one's vibration.

Even in the absence of conscious choice making in any area of our lives, there exists a process of choice making that exists below our conscious awareness. This is "unexamined" choice making. Unexamined choice making refers to choices we make which are based on our past intentions that are not consciously examined. These unexamined choices nevertheless affect the energy release and activity of the chakras. These same unconscious choices also impact our environment and our relationships with others. This means that there are motivations and intentions that we hold onto that affect our actions, decisions and choices at all times.

We make thousands of choices throughout each day. Many of our actions are in response to internal motivations or intentions that we have not consciously examined. Many of our actions are in response to an external stimulus. We may pride ourselves on being independent thinkers, but may not realize how much we react to the power of global thought forms and group consciousness. One of the ways that we take charge of our own spiritual growth and evolution is to advance upward from unexamined choice making into conscious and responsible choice making. As we become centered and whole, we disconnect somewhat from the influences of group consciousness and group thought forms.

Responsible choice making is the examination in the light of conscious awareness of the motivations behind why we make certain choices. Responsible choice making requires an examination of our intent. Transforming unexamined choice making into responsible choice making is the journey of becoming self-empowered.

As we merge our conscious awareness and intent with the energetic awareness of a chakra center, we can feel and understand what the chakra center is feeling, and what it has felt in the past.

Through empowered, conscious choice making, we bring a heightened level of power and creativity into the world.

We are responsible for the *quality* of the energies we send out into the universe, and we are responsible for *where* we send our Chakra energies. The quality and direction of our energies is determined by our intent.

The Energy Matrix: A Glue that Binds

Axiom

There exists an Energy Matrix which aligns the subtle molecular forces of all atoms and subatomic particles of the body into a specific pattern, and which holds that pattern as long as the energy matrix remains unchanged. This energy matrix is unique to each individual and holds the specific organizing instructions that make each one of us unique. This energy matrix is our energy personality to some extent and is comprised of the collective consciousness of all our cells and their subatomic parts.

The matrix holds the subatomic particles together in a cohesive but somewhat loose arrangement. It is cohesive in that our physical form appears to remain the same. It is loosely arranged in that all particles are allowed freedom of vibration and motion within certain parameters. The "form" is maintained by the imposition of the energy matrix upon the vibratory mass of particles that is our physical body.

This matrix extends outward from the body as well, and includes levels of the energy bodies surrounding our physical body. This unique energy matrix is our personalized vibrational energy signature, our personal symbolic representation of ourselves.

The body is a collection of matter and energy in a state of flux. The subatomic particles of energy that comprise the body each have their own attractive forces and energy field that interact with all the particles around them. These subatomic particles are in constant motion and their potential energy values fluctuate. There is a constant energy interaction between subatomic particles. They exchange energy with each other. They exchange particles with each other. Here are some interesting questions to consider.

Given that the body is composed of molecules, which are in turn composed of atoms and subatomic particles, and given that the particles involved are a vibratory flux state in constant motion, why then doesn't the body simply fly apart into trillions of tiny bits?

Why don't the subatomic particles vibrate themselves out of position and cause the whole body to morph into something else? When every particle in the body is in constant motion, how does the body keep its shape?

If our bodies are composed of matter, energy particles and fields, why is it when we walk under the powerful electrical field generated by a 50,000 volt power line we don't just explode into a molecular shower of sparks and particles? What holds the body together?

If the subatomic particles of the body are in constant motion, why is it we maintain the same physical shape down to the freckles on our backs or the number of eyelashes we have? With all this movement and vibration going on wouldn't we eventually change in appearance?

The answer is that the Energy Matrix is what holds the physical pattern of the body intact, despite external forces acting upon it. This matrix can be acted upon and influenced by our focused intent, and will respond to energy interactions. The pattern is responsible for the relative constancy of form. Within this relative constancy, however, is an undercurrent of continuous change. We are always changing and renewing our selves at an energetic level. Applying conscious intent to this process of change and renewal is one way we can play a more active role in the re-creation of our bodies and perhaps give us a reason why our intentions and thoughts are so powerful when it comes to determining our state of health or lack of it.

Present Time Power and Choice Making:

Choosing to Heal the Heart

Axiom

The point of power is in the present, in the NOW.

Conscious choice-making activates that power.

You are a being of unlimited potential. Your point of greatest personal power is in the present moment. The greater your consciousness can be focused in the present, the greater your ability to create your conscious reality with awareness.

All true power is concentrated in the present moment, in the Now. You can project your intent outward from your point of power into the future or into the past. You can also project it "laterally" into what you might call a parallel simultaneous reality. Although co-existing, that lateral reality has its own future, different from your personal future.

Understanding that your personal power exists in the Now is important. Any beneficial changes you want to bring about in your life will depend upon your ability to collect your conscious awareness and focus in the Now, and project this power through your intent, to bring about the desired changes.

The reality you perceive is a reflection of your beliefs and what you have brought about through your intent. If you are unaware of your intent, you are creating your reality from a condition of "unawareness." Such a condition presents a situation where you may be creating aspects of your reality on "automatic" rather than through conscious choice-making. When this occurs, you are not in a position of power. You are in a position of being affected by your own lack of power, or, more correctly, by the shadow side of your own power which is operating without your conscious, present time awareness.

You may be holding suppressed anger or resentment in your heart because of past events that have happened to you. Even though the event and its circumstances are long passed, you may be keeping parts of the energy of that event alive in your system. This is especially true of heart center energies. Emotional attachments, relationships, love and betrayals are all associated with the energies in the heart center. When you carry forward in time the trauma of past events, you suppress your own heart energies. This can not only affect your emotional outlook in present time, but can and does affect your physiology. Whenever you "hold" any energy, you create a blockage. Energy no longer flows freely. You can change this at any time however. It is vitally important to recognize your own power to do this. Your power of intention and conscious choice in the Now.

Critical aspects of this healing process are forgiveness of self and others. Forgiveness releases some of the "hold" on the harmful energies of the past and allows new energy to flow into and cleanse your system.

Our Higher Self and the Veil of Occlusion:

The Oversoul's Perspective

Axiom

The oversoul sees each of its life paths in totality, without occlusion. Each one of its individual "selves" proceeds along its own independent path of learning. The oversoul sees how one life relates to and complements all the others. A thin Veil separates one life's path from another's. The oversoul's task is to allow balance, harmony, growth and unity of all its "selves."

The oversoul is without judgement. It has access to the knowledge of the totality of our being. It provides us what we need to fulfill our mission of learning and balance. We need only ask with pure intent.

Christopher Bache describes the concept of an Oversoul quite well in his book *"Lifecycles: Reincarnation and the Web of Life."* He notes that the Oversoul exists outside of space-time and is our bridge to higher intelligences. We are an aspect of the Oversoul. The Oversoul is not God, and does not separate us from God. The Oversoul facilitates the learning experience by fragmenting itself into focused aspects of itself, which can then concentrate on learning specific life lessons. The experiences of each self are available to the Oversoul, although a veil separates individual selves from knowing all aspects of all simultaneous lives.

In order for you to focus your consciousness on your life's learning, without undue distractions, you have agreed to the co-creation of a curtain or "Veil" which clouds to some extent the direct perception of your Higher Self or Oversoul.

Look inward to your heart and you will feel this to be true.

You began the creation of this Veil before you came here.

The Veil serves us as both a memory barrier and a perception filter.

It is a self-imposed boundary that keeps us from viewing the entirety of the agreement (or contract) that we made before coming to the earth plane. The Veil can be thicker at some times and thinner at other times. When the Veil is thick, one feels isolated, and less powerful. One does not see the invisible connections to other things.

One cannot normally see beyond the Veil. However, through practice and intent, one can cause it to become "permeable." One can sense beyond the Veil and achieve an expanded state of awareness of one's own life and the larger picture of which it is a part.

The Veil can also be described as a "wall of occlusion." It is an energy barrier that we co-create and hold in place actively.

Sometimes it is necessary to see beyond the Veil in order to put ourselves in touch with a greater vision. Sometimes we need to see beyond it to give ourselves the clarity of direction that we are indeed on the "right" path, and that all paths are worthy. The oversoul can help us to see beyond the Veil. Guidance comes to us at each step as we need it. Every prayer, every question, every request is immediately heard and new knowledge is made available to us. We may not see the new knowledge immediately, but it will come. As we grow still and allow the Veil to grow thinner, this new knowledge will become integrated into our being and help provide the clarity and grace that strengthens us on our path.

Resisting or focusing on the Veil directly does not diminish its strength. That is like one fist battling with the other. Neither one wins, since such a battle is with oneself. To see beyond the Veil it is necessary to apply *intent* and *feeling* together. We must ask for guidance and assistance in lifting the Veil. Asking for guidance and assistance is not an indication that we are weak or incapable. It is an acknowledgement of the validity of the co-creation process and a recognition of the agreements we have made that allow the Veil to exist.

It is as if we hold the palms of our hands facing us, in front of our eyes. Looking off into the distance, we say "Why can I not see the mountains?" We then seek "gurus" to tell us what the mountains look like.

We read books that explain what it is like to climb the mountains.

We seek therapies that try to help us remember what the mountains might have looked like in the past. All the while, it is we who shield ourselves against the brilliant beauty of the mountains. If we develop the courage to slowly spread our fingers apart, we will gradually see the splendor that lies directly on our path. It is Love that gives us the courage to take this first glimpse of the near blinding beauty of the mountains that are our infinite and unlimited potential.

Through conscious loving, compassion and intent, we can make a conscious connection to the Oversoul through our heart center energies. Asking for guidance is a way to make this connection. When our hearts are weary with earthly troubles that seem insurmountable, we can seek help in the form of guidance from the Oversoul, who has a more intimate knowledge of the struggles and challenges we face than we even do ourselves. Intuitive Guidance is a powerful ally on the road to greater awareness, health and vitality.

Intuitive Guidance

Axiom

Your Oversoul, is a source of love, energy and direction. It has access to the totality of your being, and can provide a level of guidance that is beyond what anyone on the physical plane can contribute.

Your Oversoul or Higher Self has access to the knowledge learned by other aspects of yourself that are also engaged in their own journeys of personal growth. Many of these other aspects of your Self are learning things that will benefit you just as you are learning things that will benefit them. Your Higher Self is not limited by illusions of time. It has total access to all lessons learned, whether in the present, "past" or "future."

Asking for guidance from higher sources takes many forms. Prayer, intent, active meditation, visualization and verbalization are all valid methods of asking for guidance. When you ask for guidance, through your conscious intent, you are making an active connection with higher level energies that can assist you in your personal growth process. These higher level energies are intelligent, compassionate and conscious. Some of these energies are also entities that are on their own personal growth path. It is part of the natural order of things for higher level entities to help raise the vibration of lower level entities, so that all life progresses and evolves towards love and wholeness. You may seek to communicate directly with God, however you perceive God to be, or you may communicate with a variety of other energies or beings. Some people develop a special relationship with certain higher energy sources and these sources provide guidance over long periods of time, sometimes spanning more than one lifetime.

You send communication to these higher energies through your intent. You receive communication from them through your intuitive communication channels. "Ask and ye shall receive" is a powerful description of just how this process works. The quality and content of your daily thoughts and intentions has a great bearing on what you perceive daily in your life. If you consciously ask for guidance, through your intent, you will receive it. Many people are not in the practice of asking, or of seeking a response. Some people are good at asking, but are not attuned or centered enough to notice when they are getting a reply. This takes an understanding of the process, and it takes a quiet mind. In order to be receptive to a reply, you need to be attentive, patient and balanced. The more centered and balanced you are, the quicker you will notice when a reply is manifesting itself. The higher level energies will respond to the *intent* of your request, not merely to the words you are using. You must therefore be aware of what you are really asking for, and if that is what you really want. If you are asking for money, what is the intent behind your request? What do you intend to do with the money? Is there a more basic need that your soul is trying to fulfill?

Part of the spiritual path is the process of knowing ourselves well enough to understand what it is we really need for our own personal growth, and what we think we want to feel satiated. Our basic needs are areas where we can benefit from an increased flow of love energy. Our wants are fleeting, and will be replaced with other wants once they are met. We should therefore, intend to receive guidance for our higher spiritual good and for the good of others. Conscious loving intent will raise your vibration and make you more receptive and perceptive of replies from higher sources.

The Importance of Intent
in Evolution and Personal Transformation

> "Transformation of the planet begins in trans-formation of the self. Evolution starts with the commitment and intent to go higher."
>
> —Orin/Sanaya Roman,
> *Personal Power Through Awareness*

> "There are no limitations to the self, except those you believe in."
>
> —Seth/Jane Roberts, *The Nature of Personal Reality*

Axiom

Intent comes from the center of one's being. Intent is closer to who you are, than any other aspect of yourself.

What is Intent? Intent is not a "wish." Sometimes a wish is merely a statement of a desire for a different condition, while simultaneously acknowledging (reinforcing) the fact that the condition does not exist. There is nothing wrong with wishing, but is it not intent.

Creative vitality and passion for one's goals are released through the application of conscious intent. When you apply your conscious intent to achieving a goal, you open up pathways and potentialities that were otherwise dormant. Through intent you create your own NOW and your future NOW. Through intent you can place events, feelings and objects into the future time stream, so that you will encounter them in the NOW.

Visualization of a state of health and balance, coupled with conscious intent can help bring about that state in reality.

You are a multidimensional being with no limits to your creative energies other than those you create or agree to. Each step you take towards greater self-empowerment brings you that much closer to your true self.

Sensing Energy:

Intentions, Thoughts and Vibrations

Axiom

We connect with others at an energetic level long before we connect with them on a verbal or social level. We sense their energy vibrations and they sense ours.

Our intentions determine the quality and frequency of the energy vibrations of our thoughts.

Every thought we think changes the space around us.

Our thoughts have a vibrational energy pattern that exists within our physical space. High vibrational thoughts attract other high vibrational thoughts. When we "think" a thought, we set up a vibrational pattern in the universe. The phrase "Great minds think alike" could be restated more correctly as "Great minds generate vibrations of similar frequencies."

Thinking is a creative activity. When you think, you create thoughts that exist as real energetic patterns of specific vibrational frequency. The frequency of the pattern is dependent on the power and intent behind its creation. The vibrational energy pattern holds the intent. If you tell someone you wish them well while secretly harboring destructive thoughts against them, it is the vibration of the destructive thoughts that becomes the vibration of the thought pattern. The power of the thought, its frequency, is based on the intent behind it. Words spoken without intent have no power. Words of praise with no intention to praise behind them, are powerless and not of high vibration.

This concept is important when we are considering how we relate to other people and how they relate to us. Other people pick up our thought vibrations and intentions before they hear our words or see our facial expressions. Our thoughts radiate a vibrational energy around us, which we are not normally consciously aware of. We are aware of them nevertheless. We are aware of the intentions others have for us, even when they do not speak them. The intentions set up vibrations in the fabric of the etheric plane that instantaneously travel outward where we can perceive them. Again, we must understand the difference between being consciously aware of something, and simply being conscious of something.

Conscious Awareness and Selective Focus

Your consciousness is fully aware of all the signals it is receiving from anyone in your vicinity and anyone who may be thinking about you, even in remote locations. However, you are not fully aware of your consciousness. This may sound like a nonsensical play on words, but it is not. Your consciousness is fully aware of and is interacting with far more than you are individually, personally aware of. For example, your full conscious mind is aware of the different temperatures in different parts of your body at every instant. YOU, however, have selectively chosen to not focus on that aspect of your awareness during most of your daily activities. Nevertheless, the conscious awareness of that information exists, is recorded in memory and forms a part of your overall experience.

Practically speaking, you therefore have a record of what others have thought and intended for you and about you, even though you do not consciously focus on that knowledge. Part of your higher consciousness has access to this information, however, and can use this information in influencing how you interact with those people at a conscious level. You can contact this higher consciousness "database" so to speak, through your intuitive abilities. You already do this to some degree already, but again, it is without your full awareness that you are doing it. Intuitive information, hunches and feelings about various people are flooding into you system all the time. The amount of detailed information you are receiving about any given person or group of people at a given time is not only astonishing if you were made aware of it, it would also be completely overwhelming.

We are dealing here with a sliding scale of awareness along which we are seeking a range of balance. As you become more evolved, your awareness of the higher range of this scale will increase. Along with this increased awareness of higher ranges of the awareness scale will come an increasing sensitivity to subtle energies. This is an extremely important part of the growing awareness that is now opening up within you. You will need to understand what it is like to *feel* these subtle energies in your environment and you will need to learn how to process these sensations in a way that complements your rational and intuitive abilities. We each have a unique vibrational pattern that no one else has. It has been said that Helen Keller, author/lecturer/teacher who was both blind and deaf for most of her life, had the ability to recognize people just by their energetic vibrations. She was sensitive enough to spot the subtle differences in the energy fields of those she came into contact with.

In order to relate to another person in a conscious, empowered manner, you need to be aware first of what you are feeling, in your own space, about yourself and your immediate environment. This is where meditation techniques as practical applications of awareness expanding methodologies provide great potential benefit. Meditation techniques allow you to train the mind to calm itself amidst the noise of external stimuli and the incessant internal stimuli of mental chatter. Once you have successfully attained a familiar quiet state of mind, it becomes easier to get in touch with your own energies and how they feel. You can focus on your own feeling centers, chakra by chakra if you wish, and become familiar with your personal vibrations.

Chapter Two:

Energy of the Heart

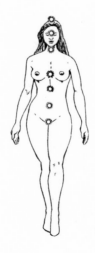

The Heart Center and the Energy of Love

Axiom

The greatest Earth School lesson we all have in common is to learn to love ourselves and each other; To learn to give from the heart, through the heart and with the heart. When we achieve this, everything else falls into place.

The greatest gift you can give to yourself is to open your heart center.

The greatest gift you can give to another is to love them.

It has been said that the Heart Chakra is the seat of the soul, the place in your body that coincides with your essence and truth. On a physical level, it corresponds to the thymus gland, which is located just above the heart organ, in the center of the chest. The heart center is one of the main energy portals through which we give love and receive love. The love energy in the heart center is the most powerful energy there is. When we give love to another, our heart opens, expands and reaches outward. When it is open, our heart radiates high intensity, high vibrational energies. We connect with others through our heart center. We use the terms "heart and soul" together since the heart and soul are so very close. We are our soul, and we are love energy. An individual soul is the embodiment of the energy of love. If you want to be a more loving person, connect with the energy of your soul and reach out to others.

When we feel a close loving connection to another person, it is through the heart center. The heart is the center of our emotions. When we feel that we have been hurt by another, or feel that our attempts to give love energy have been rejected, we often carry that hurt in our heart center. The heart is capable of holding a great deal of pain and sorrow, but it does so to its own detriment. The heart is meant to be open and free. It is meant to be a center of light and a source of free-flowing energies.

The human heart generates a bioelectromagnetic field larger and more powerful than the electrical field generated by the brain. The lungs and our breathing processes fall within the heart's magnetic sphere of influence. The breath or "prana" is associated with this area and is influenced by the heart energy.

The Fourth Chakra: A Link Between Worlds

As described in Chapter One, the Heart Chakra is the fourth of the seven major chakras. It is situated in the middle between the three lower chakras (Root, Sexual and Solar Plexus Centers) and the three higher chakras (Throat, Third Eye, and Crown Chakras). As one follows the earth energies from the Root chakra up the spine, the Heart Chakra is the point where we start to function in the higher vibrational energies of love for others and love for higher beings. Having a balanced Heart Chakra is a vital part of our energy anatomy since the heart can help direct us in making choices that will affect our interaction with others and ourselves. The Heart Center is a gateway, a center of transformational energies. The consciousness below the Heart Chakra is Earth focused. The consciousness of the energy centers above the Heart Chakra is focused on the universal nature of life— expansion, divinity, and unity. The heart is also in tune with all the other energy centers. It has its own wisdom. It knows your deepest inner thoughts, desires and goals. Nothing you think, feel, intend or experience escapes its sphere of influence and knowingness. It can reflect this vast collection of wisdom back to you when you ask for it. When you are on the right path, you "know it in your heart."

The Evolution from Third Chakra

to Fourth Chakra Energies

Because the heart center sits in a pivotal location between the lower and upper energy centers, its opening to the flow of increased energy is a vital part of one's transformational process. While living on the earth, we are connected to both the lower and higher chakra energy centers. The Heart Center is the focal point of awakening consciousness from its earthly focus into an increased awareness of the higher realms. At the third chakra level, just below the Heart Chakra is the center of energy for earthly power, ego and power struggles. When we do battle, we do battle from the third chakra energy center.

People who have had long term power struggles are likely to have problems with the solar plexus area of the body, such as digestion problems, ulcers, hernias, stomach cancer and other intestinal problems. I have personally seen people who have been engaged in long term power struggles develop hernias in the stomach area. A hernia of this type is where the intestine comes through a break or whole in the abdominal muscles. It begins to protrude just like an energy fiber protrudes from the chakra. Although a hernia can be caused by physical injury, it can also be caused by trauma. The correlation between what is happening physically (traumatic abdominal hernia) and what is happening energetically is striking.

Figure 4 Heart Center Energy Vortex

Third Chakra Power Struggles

and the Survival Instinct

A power struggle is an attempt by a person to control his or her environment by force of will. Force of will comes largely from the third chakra. The third chakra center is not evolved enough on its own to hold the higher concept of "allowing" and feels that it must control the process and the outcome of events in order to safeguard the individual's survival. The survival instinct is an energetic pattern or blueprint that is superimposed on the cells of the body that calls for individuation from external energy sources. The survival instinct sees external beings and forces as completely separate from itself. The survival instinct is present to maintain a sense of individuality so that the body can exist independent from, but interact with, the other energies of creation. The survival instinct is necessary to perpetuate the functioning of independent creatures in a realm where energetic forces would otherwise tear the system apart. Since the soul or spirit does not have a finite life span, it never ceases to exist. The survival instinct is a way to maintain the illusion of a single lifetime as something to protect and defend. As we evolve and begin to recognize at a deeply personal level the divine and immortal aspects of ourselves, we gain the perceptive ability to view the survival instinct as a necessary part of the game of life, but not as the end goal of the game. It is a step on the ladder to higher states of awareness.

All the lower chakras are concerned with physical survival on the earth plane. Although the entire chakra system functions as a holistic system, when taken individually, one can see that the lower chakras are not "aware" of the higher chakras. It is the love energy of the fourth chakra that brings together the upper and lower chakras in a communion of energies. The fourth chakra (heart) brings a dynamic equilibrium and energetic balance to the entire system. The Heart Chakra "understands" the lower chakras and helps align their powerful, earthy energies into the higher energy systems of the upper chakras.

During a power struggle, energy leaves the third chakra and goes out to other people, places or entities in an attempt to control them. We also receive energy back from those we are in a power struggle with and it hits our third chakra center. The consciousness associated with the third chakra does not see itself as in unity with other beings. It sees itself in a struggle for power, control and survival. It is a very powerful energy center, but not one that has a consciousness of what it means to engage in universal love.

A person focused primarily on the energies of the third chakra expresses "love" through control. In relationships, when one person is controlling another, their love energy is going through the third chakra more than the fourth chakra. If the energies of the individuals are not allowed and encouraged to evolve, there will be no advancement to the next level, that of fourth chakra energies.

Kundalini Energies and the Heart Center

According to ancient yoga teachings, a massive reserve of spiritual energy is located at the base of the spine. This reserve of energy is known as the Kundalini. The word "Kundalini" comes from Sanskrit, the ancient language of Hinduism and the Vedas and the classical literary language of India. Kundalini means "coiled serpent." The Kundalini energy is sometimes envisioned as a coiled serpent at the base of the spine. The full potential of this powerful reserve of energy is usually dormant in most people. At very special times, however, it comes to life and causes a massive surge of energy to flow upward within our body, and the chakra system.

When the Kundalini is aroused, it travels up the spine through the six chakras, or centers of consciousness, finally reaching the seventh or crown chakra. As this energy reaches the higher centers it produces various degrees of enlightenment.

The phenomena known as "Kundalini Rising" is a spiritual growth process in which the energy centers of the body begin to vibrate at a highly increased rate. For some people, the Kundalini Rising process is like being plugged into a high voltage power line. As the energy rises from the root chakra up through the body, any blockages in the other Chakras are hit by the rising tide of electromagnetic energy and profound reactions can take place in the body's energy centers. The massive influx of energy is the body's way of clearing itself out to adjust to the higher vibrational energy it is now connecting with at the higher spiritual levels. This affects not only the physical body, but the other subtle energy bodies, Chakras and the body's normal analytical thinking processes.

The series of events brought on by Kundalini Rising has often been linked to what has been called "mid-life crisis." However, the rise of this energy has less to do with physical age and more to do with a bioelectromagnetic energy shift that signifies a spiritual evolutionary change. It helps greatly to recognize when this event is occurring, since it marks a turning point in one's awareness, and when approached properly can be a source of immense spiritual growth.

The Kundalini Rising is part of a conscious evolutionary step. During Kundalini Rising, all spiritual and energy processing centers of the body are re-energized. This often opens the doors to formerly unrecognized talents and abilities, as well as the ability to achieve a greater connectedness to others. In Hindu tradition, the Kundalini is the serpent goddess that travels from the root chakra to the crown, piercing each energy center along the way. At some point during this process, the Kundalini energy reaches the Heart Chakra, which is the midpoint between the three lower chakras and the three higher chakras. If there have been energy blockages in the area of the Heart Center, the

Kundalini energy will infuse them with new energy and blow the blockages apart. This is much like blowing an electrical circuit breaker. The Heart Center then begins to open up like the blossoming of a flower. The Heart Energy radiates out ward and upward. For some people this is a gradual process. For others it happens very fast. When it occurs rapidly, it can take a while for a person to adjust to the new energy.

During Kundalini Rising, the heart center can open up with tremendous volume and can cause life-changing events to take place. On the negative side, those with blocked heart energies are often subject to heart problems, sometimes resulting in a need for medical intervention, or so serious as to cause heart attack. Working with the heart center to help balance all the upper and lower Chakras is a good way to facilitate clearing blockages and promote a healthy energy flow.

The rising of Kundalini energies from the root chakra up the spine encounters the energies of the fourth chakra as well as any blockages that reside there. The blockages in each chakra are opened up since they cannot withstand the direct power of the Kundalini energies. This rising of the Kundalini and the opening up of the Heart Chakra energy blockages is usually associated with some major trauma or major energy shift in a person's life. A traumatic or energetic event can trigger a Kundalini rise, and once started, the Kundalini can spark further energetic shifts as it moves up through the system. Such precipitating traumatic events or energy shifts can include the death of a loved one, a serious accident, a divorce, an encounter with a powerful spiritual healer, or other forces.

Once the shifting starts, the person may be drawn to make major changes in their life style, personal interactions and/or be drawn to move to another physical location. The transformation from being third chakra centered and becoming fourth chakra aware is a major turning point in a person's spiritual evolution. There is no going back from this point. Old paradigms and control mechanisms will no longer work for the person. A new consciousness is born out of the Heart Chakra energies and it creates new energetic pathways all through the energy body. This is an extremely powerful energy redistribution within the entire being, including all subtle energy levels and levels of consciousness. This is an evolutionary process.

If one attempts to block the awakening of the Heart Center Chakra, or suppress these new energies of awareness, growth and creativity, this can cause a feedback within such energies which can be destructive to the body. The physical heart area is usually one of the first areas so affected.

The Evolution of Our Physiology

This new energy of the heart also affects our physiology and creates new brain pathways, giving us greater access to subtle energy centers in the body and greater access to our inherent creativities. New talents can emerge and often do. New goals begin to replace older, more third chakra centric goals. This transformation can wreak havoc in a person's life as it will turn relationships upside down. Personal relationships, work relationships and love relationships will be affected. Some relationships will be transformed, others will end and new ones begin. This is a time of tremendous change and growth. The speed and power of these changes can be unsettling for the person involved and for those around him or her. Most people do not recognize a spiritual awakening of these energies and only perceive the shift in third chakra energies into something else as a change, sometimes unsettling, sometimes mysterious, often frightening.

There is another interesting phenomenon in the human condition and that is that people tend to be aware of the energy interchanges and reality level of the chakra they are primarily operating through, but not consciously aware of the chakra immediately above it. Those who are focused on third chakra energies operate at the worldly level of power, acquisition, judgement and control do not "understand" someone who is operating from the heart center energies. Third chakra-focused people view fourth chakra-focused people as an oddity, or weak or even threatening. People who operate primarily at the third chakra level see the world through the eyes of self-centric power. They are closely tied to the lower vibrational energy of fear.

Fear, Anger and Power

Fear, anger and power are closely associated. Fear is energy going out from us in a dispersal pattern. When we experience fear, we lose our sense of focus. We feel out of control. Fear is a loss of power from the whole chakra system, but most significantly from the third and lower chakras.

When one feels that his or her power is being drained from the third chakra, they immediately descend into the level of fear. Their reaction is to fight back against a perceived attack, or to flee the attack. They are unable to take the quantum leap in awareness to the fourth chakra level where they will see relationships and interactions with others as mirrors of inner struggles and growth processes within themselves. When they can eventually make this transition to the heart level energies, they will find the heart energies will *transmute* the fear they have into a feeling of unity. They will be able to transcend the need for daily power struggles and will be able to relate to other beings on a higher vibrational wavelength.

A fascinating aspect of the chakra energies is that they can at times seem to interact with each other on a bypass of the Heart Chakra. An example is the third chakra's ability to focus energies in a power struggle and tap into the intellectual energies of the mind quite effectively. Operating at the level of fear and power, the third chakra energies focus the intellect to calculate responses and courses of action without input from the heart. Carried to its ultimate extreme, however, these energies of power and control, driven by fear, will focus the intellect into perceiving the world as dangerous, and will warp the intellect into perceiving all other beings as things to be controlled or destroyed.

This is how mankind can produce the "evil genius," "heartless killer" or "criminal mastermind." The heart energy is blocked or bypassed while the third chakra energies dictate actions that this lower chakra believes to be in the survival interests of the personality. A serious disconnect happens and the person begins to act in a heartless way, often causing great damage to others, with no regard for the feelings of other people. Anger and hatred are energy flows that have become stuck and rigid. Hatred is a dark energy which is real and tangible. When energies of the heart are shut down and not allowed to flow, anger and hatred form a dark energy "blockage" that affects the entire energy system.

When people kill others in the name of religion, they are attempting to link sixth and seventh chakra energies with the third chakra power center, and bypass the heart center of compassion, love and unity consciousness. They feel that in order to survive as a spiritual being, they need to kill others who are not of the same spiritual background. This is a highly distorted view of the world and represents an extremely unbalanced energy system. Such individuals wreck havoc in any society, as we have seen in our current world scene, and in past centuries. Our most difficult challenge in this arena is to bring the energy of love back into the system and reestablish a balance and sense of compassion for all beings.

The Anatomy of Fear

"Fear is the little death..."

—Paul Atreides, from *Dune* (Frank Herbert)

Axiom

Whereas the vibrations of love energy represents wholeness and unity, the vibration of fear makes the universe around us appear unsafe. However, in a larger sense the energy of the universe is us. When we fear the universe or feel uncertain of our position in it, we cut ourselves off from the larger part of ourselves. The vibration of fear is a separation from the whole. Fear is a step backwards from unity consciousness.

If you feel the energy vibrations of fear encroaching on your life, calm your self by visualizing your center. Visualize your center of energy in the solar plexus (just below the navel). Then visualize a full column of light extending downward from your solar region, into the earth. Visualize that same column of energy also extending upward through your body and to the energy center above your head. Holding your core energy in this way is also one of the steps in the EMF Balanc-

ing Technique®, a powerful process of calibration, balancing
and self-empowerment.

> "One of the attributes of the new energy will
> be the absence of fear-based decision mak-
> ing.... Once the truth is known and the path
> validated, fear will cease to be a player in ev-
> eryday life... This is indeed the Alchemy of
> the human spirit! Going from fear to Love is
> the Alchemy process...."

> "Fear-based decisions will bring poor results in
> the new energy... over and over. Love-based
> decisions will elevate a person into new areas
> of discovery. Therefore the evolving human
> (who takes responsibility for all that happens
> to him) may try both, but it won't be long be-
> fore the results speak for themselves and the
> fear-based decisions are discarded."

> —Kryon/Lee Carroll,
> *Alchemy of the Human Spirit*

If the energy of fear causes you to want to retreat into yourself,
or to run away, instead greet the universe as part of yourself,
as a familiar friend. Talk to it. Co-create it in the NOW. Fear
will vanish if you talk to your surroundings. This may sound
odd, but it is not. If you communicate with your surroundings,
through touch, sight, sound, smell, even singing or talking, you
create an energetic link with the energy of the universe and an
immediate calming will being to engulf you. If you feel fear, you
have disconnected parts of yourself from parts of the environment. Reconnect these parts through live communication and
fear dissolves into love.

How Anger Affects Our Physiology

Anger and hate are known to be disharmonious and not conducive to a healthy state of body or mind. On a personal level, the emotions of anger and hate cause the heart center to accumulate negative energies. By negative energies, we mean energy that no longer flows in harmony with the rest of the person's energy system. Anger and hatred held over long periods of time manifest on the physical level as diseases of the heart and circulatory system. Suppressed anger and hatred, "hard heartedness" can translate into a physical hardening of the internal organs and vessels. This may sound too far-fetched to be believed and too simplistic a view, but consider the following. We know that individuals will heal faster in an environment of love and compassion, than in one of anger or hatred. We know that the presence of loved ones and the warm energies of compassion can help physical and emotional healing. Even the presence of loving animals can help lower anxiety, stress and blood pressure. Something happens to our physiology when we express love to another. This is real, not imaginary. Thousands of songs, poems and books have been written on the power of love to heal. You know this in your heart, because you have felt it.

What about anger and our physiology? There is a direct correlation between holding anger in our hearts for long periods of time and the long-term health of our *physical* heart. This is not to say that anyone with physical heart problems is a hateful or angry person. This is not meant to be a statement of judgement, blame or condemnation. The knowledge that strong emotions affect our physiology at a cellular level opens the door to preventing or healing diseases and conditions that plague many thousands of people.

How can anger and hatred affect our body's cells? Anger, hatred, resentment and similar emotions are energy vibrations that can disrupt the normal flow of life energies. Anger is an outward push of these vibrations. Hatred is a holding onto of energy flows in an attempt to stop the motion of the energy. Resentment is an attempt to pull back energy. All three of these emotional energies represent some aspect of control. Not control in a benevolent sense, but control motivated by fear— fear of losing, fear of dying, fear of pain, fear of darkness.

We know from quantum physics that our physical bodies are composed of energy vibrations. This of course includes our cells and all body organs. When we allow the lower vibrational energies of anger, hatred and resentment to permeate our thoughts and feelings, we change the bioelectromagnetic resonance of our entire energy field. This energy field passes through all our cells and tissues. The bioelectromagnetic field affects the atoms and molecules of each cell, just the way a bar magnet affects tiny iron particles. The cells are influenced by this bioelectromagnetic energy. If your thoughts and emotions are loving, the cells will respond to this. There is a consciousness that exists at a cellular level that interprets bioelectromagnetic energy as a communication to the system as a whole. When you are loving, you are telling all your cells to be loving. When you are angry, you are telling all your cells to be angry. This is not science fiction, this is what is really happening. Thoughts and emotions directly affect your physiology and the body will respond according to the signals you are sending out.

Cellular Imbalance and Cellular Anarchy

Equally important to realize is that the thoughts and emotions you are sending out may, over a period of time, slip below your conscious awareness. You may be carrying around anger and resentment that you have "forgotten" about. You have not really forgotten, however, and some part of your energetic anatomy is still creating this resentment energy flow. The body at some level is still responding to these lower level vibrations. When bioelectro-magnetic messages of resentment, anger or similar emotions are transmitted to your cells over a long period of time, the cellular processes can be affected at a molecular level. Normal cellular function goes awry. Cellular activity becomes imbalanced. Electrochemical exchanges between cells becomes abnormal. Some cells die when they should not. Some cells multiply out of control when they should not. Some cells fail to fend off outside viruses or bacteria, or may even attack other cells themselves.

The result of this entire tendency towards energy imbalance is cellular anarchy— cellular rebellion. Actually, it may sound like chaos, but the cells are very intelligent. They know how to cause internal damage and destruction if that is what your energy field is communicating to them. Have you ever wondered why people who intensely hate other people are often depicted in stories as being ugly, and people who are loving and kind to others are usually depicted as being beautiful? Remember the ugly wicked witch, the beautiful fairy godmother? Granted, these are archetypes, and not everyone fits these images. However, the archetypal views of goodness and beauty, versus evil and ugliness may have their historical roots in how we manage our energy fields and their resulting affect on our physiology. More importantly, is the fact that how we manage our personal energy field, through our conscious choices in the types of thoughts, emotions and actions we engage in *does* affect our physiology.

Distinguishing Anger from Aggression

Anger and hatred are unhealthy emotions from the heart's perspective. Anger and hatred are not the same as healthy aggression, although we sometimes confuse these terms. It is wise not to confuse long term anger and hatred with healthy aggressive energies.

Anger and hatred are energies that we are holding onto. They are an *inward* focus. Aggression, on the other hand, is an *outward* focus. Although angry people often display their anger outwardly, they also hold a great deal of the anger internally. In contrast to an expression of anger, a momentary outburst of aggressive energies may be appropriate and healthy for a given situation. Fighting off a threat against your family's well being, or taking effective action to stop someone who is actively suppressing your energies can be a very healthy and positive use of energies. Overcoming a difficult challenge often requires a focused and aggressive use of our energies. Healthy aggression can break through stuck energy and allow creative energy flows to take their place. The act of creation, such as bringing a new life into the world, or building a city is an aggressive expression of positive energies.

It seems that a certain amount of aggression clears energy blockages and can increase the power of one's immune system. A team of researchers at Penn State and the University of Nebraska conducted a study, which suggested that differences in people's aggressive behavior influences how their immune systems are prepared to deal with infections, viruses and bacteria. A moderate level of aggression was found to increase certain specialized types of lymphocytes in the white blood cells, that played a part in the body's overall immune response. However, higher levels of aggression did not show increasing benefits, and increased aggression and aggressive behavior presents its own series of problems. The intent behind your activity determines the nature of the energy vibration.

Suppressed Emotions and Unexamined Beliefs

Our conscious emotions, intentions and thought forms affect our bioelectromagnetic field. Because we are complex creatures and hold many suppressed emotions and unexamined beliefs about our world, and ourselves we also have the ability to generate energies based on these things. Unexamined beliefs are those ideas, considerations, viewpoints, and judgements that we have created in the past, or have incorporated into our belief systems without consciously examining them, that still have an effect on how we perceive the world on a daily basis. Our awareness is like the layers of an onion. Each layer is functioning and alive, and aware of all the other layers. However, our daily conscious awareness is focused on a narrow part of our experience and is not fully aware of all the hidden beliefs in the various layers.

It may take time to reverse older, lower vibrational energy patterns and beliefs that we have held for long periods of time. Self-examination of our deeper intentions can be beneficial in uncovering negative or self-limiting beliefs we have about our selves. Focusing our energies on our higher spiritual growth will help bring some of these unexamined beliefs into the light, and eventually into alignment with our goals. Our energies, thoughts, beliefs and values are highly fragmented. Bringing these fragments into alignment is part of our journey into wholeness. We are responsible for the quality of that journey. By focusing on higher vibrational energies we can make it a wonderful journey of self-exploration and learning.

The Archetypal Warrior and the Eternal Battlefield

In our daily lives, it is very easy to get pulled down to the third chakra level of power struggles. The third chakra is the home of the consciousness of the "Eternal Warrior."

The nature of the Eternal Warrior's energy vibration is one of eternal struggle. There will *always* be another battle to wage in order to prove the validity of that energy's existence. You only win the third chakra battles by transcending that vibrational level into the higher levels of heart energy, the fourth chakra.

As beings on this planet we have lived for many millennia within the energy sphere of the third chakra. It is the cause behind our wars, our battles over territory and our battles over food, resources and power. Some of these archetypal struggles were a necessary part of our evolution as beings, but we must not make them the focal point of our future energies.

When someone who is operating at a third chakra level challenges you, it is an attempt on his or her part to bring you down to a lower vibrational energy level. Once you come down to the level of third chakra power struggles, there is no ultimate win or loose to that game. The playing field of this game is the "Eternal Battlefield." The biblical message "Love your enemy" does not mean ignore violence and become passive. It means do not play the game of returning hatred and violence with more hatred and violence. From an energetic standpoint it means transmute the energies of hatred and anger into higher vibrational states. You never win by hating your enemies. You only win when your enemies cease to hate.

This viewpoint of third chakra energies and fourth chakra energies should not be taken to mean that one does not confront evil in the world. It is important for loving beings to act together responsibly for the betterment of our world conditions. The challenge is to do this from a higher vibrational level and not from a level of judgment or hate. This is an extremely difficult challenge at this time.

Heart Energies and the Global Consciousness

Just as individuals operate from different levels of consciousness and different chakra energies, the nations of earth also operate from different levels of group consciousness and group energies. Many poor nations on the planet today are at the first or second chakra consciousness of basic survival and procreation. Many other nations are at the level of the third chakra consciousness in their evolutionary growth. These third chakra nations see all other nations as being in a potential power struggle with them. They build armies either for protection or for expansion. They focus their energies on maintaining extreme nationalism, enforcing boundaries, zealous control or slaughter of their own internal populations, and exploiting or even wasting earthly resources. None of this is reflective of fourth chakra energies. It is important for the eventual survival of humans on this planet that nations are able to evolve through and beyond the third chakra energies into the fourth chakra energies. It is at the level of the fourth chakra consciousness, that nations will act in brotherhood with other nations, and will recognize that all nations are partners on the planet. The fourth chakra consciousness will bring with it the ability to understand one-another through love and compassion, and a realization that conflict harms both sides.

With the fall of the Soviet Union we saw the collapse of the Soviet communist paradigm which came from a third chakra level of power and control. The political structures supporting this level of energy simply could no longer maintain the vibrational energy needed to hold that thought form together. The system fell from the inside as people on an individual basis and as a group were able to come to a new level of awareness where this old paradigm no longer was appropriate for their future growth. Walls and barriers came down, both metaphorically and physically. Energy of that old system was released into the global energy stream and affected the future directions of many other smaller nations as well as the large ones.

This global paradigm shift caused a tremendous upheaval and confusion, but this is part of the confusion of growth. As new paradigms come into being, we feel very uncomfortable with our loss of the old familiar ones, even if the old ones were painful and constraining. Between the act of throwing off the old worn coat and putting on the newly woven coat, we stand for a time naked in the exposure of our shifting belief patterns. It is a very awkward and frightening time for many, but it is a temporary phase that comes as a necessary part of the evolutionary process of change.

The Archetypal Struggle of "Good vs. Evil"

There is no doubt that the earth is still in the midst of the powerful good vs. evil archetypal battle. Old power struggles and hidden forces are coming to light and being exposed on a global scale. Bringing dark energies into the light will raise their vibration. Those that can transmute to higher levels of energy will do so. There will be some that cannot change at this time. One of the goals of the energy facilitators we talked about in Part One is to raise the vibrational energy and consciousness of those trapped in this archetypal battle so that they can evolve beyond it. This is a global consciousness shift that will be unlike any previous era in human history.

As part of this shift, social structures and conditions will be affected on a broad scale. Things will simply not be the same as they have been in the past. The perspective from which we view these changes will be a reflection of our level of consciousness at this time. There will be times of confusion as old paradigms cease to work and old social values are brought into focus for re-examination. People will be challenged to look at their own individual life priorities and make conscious choices on how they want to live their lives. People will need to make choices as to what mental thought forms they want to hold in their minds and in their hearts.

We are moving into an era where the compassion and wisdom of the heart will be sought out and valued as a means to balance the lower energy vibrations of fear and control.

The Wisdom of the Heart

"Open your heart. Let it show you what it knows. Learn to trust what you know. You're wiser than you think."

—Melody Beattie, *Journey to the Heart*

Because of its vast interconnected web to other energy centers in the body and to the body's energy field itself, the heart has a greater depth of wisdom than you will find in the intellect alone. The heart and the head (intellect) do not speak the same language.

Rational Center vs. Heart Center

When faced with a decision, your intellect or *rational mind* will speak to you in these terms:

- It sounds ok.
- It seems logical.
- It makes sense to me.
- I think it is fine.
- It seems rational enough.
- I think it will work.

On the other hand, when faced with choices, the *heart center* often speaks to you in these terms:

- It feels right.
- I can connect with that.
- I am uncomfortable with that approach.
- I have a yearning to do that.
- I feel called to do that.
- I love that idea.
- I feel pulled in that direction.

Table 7

The wisdom of the heart runs deeper into your psyche than does your intellect. It is very important to achieve a sense of balance between the head and the heart. Many people who have ignored or suppressed their feelings for years have a difficult time listening to the heart. For them, this is a new and different approach. It may take some getting used to. This is part of the modern paradigm of the new energy, which is to "think with the heart."

Anahata

The Heart Chakra is the middle chakra in the system of the seven primary chakras. The Heart Chakra symbolizes the two polarities of body and spirit as in perfect balance.

The Sanskrit name for the Heart Chakra is Anahata. The symbol above is the 12-petaled lotus, the symbol of the Heart Chakra. It contains within it two intersecting triangles forming a six pointed star. The upward pointing triangle symbolizes matter rising into spirit. The downward triangle represents spirit descending into manifestation.

The Fourth Chakra and Sound

The fourth chakra is referred to as the Anahata-Chakra, which is Sanskrit for "the wheel of the unstruck sound." This translates roughly to the sound that is produced without mechanical means. What the word Anahata is trying to convey is the concept of the universal sound that is ever-present when one achieves a state of balance within the heart center and becomes resonant with its vibrations. When the mind is still and the heart center is activated, one can hear the subtle inner sound called the *nada*. This is referred to as an "unstruck" sound, since it is a cosmic vibrational pattern, not a physically produced sound.

An Open Heart and the Power of Healing

When the Heart Chakra is open, a person has a heightened ability to sense energy flows from other people and other living beings. A person with an open heart can also send heart energy (love energy) outward to others to help them heal and achieve greater wholeness. On open Heart Chakra is an energy vortex that can be used to focus energy and connect with the energy fields of others. When your heart center is open, there is a definite feeling of deep warmth in this area, a deeper warmth than any other you have known. As your heart energy expands out from your heart center, it has a radiating quality that can be very healing to other people. This is a very real energy, not an imaginary feeling.

Those who can see energy can see the glow of the heart center in a person with strong heart energies. A "cold heart" is a heart center with darker, clouded energy around it. An open heart radiates energy, sometimes interpreted as a greenish glow. More significant than the color is the feeling associated with the heart energy. The powerful feelings radiating from this center can deeply touch the soul of another being. This energy can transcend the physical plane and connect us with divine energies as well as beings who are not currently locked into our physical reality. This energy center is also a gateway to connection with all nature and life in general— plants, animals, everything.

Those who do energy healing know the tremendous power that the Heart Chakra holds. One makes an energetic connection with another through the heart center, and expands their love energies into a powerful healing, radiating flow.

Heart Energy Blockages and the Relationship to Physical Health

Axiom

The ease of blood flow through the physical heart region is directly influenced by the level to which the Heart Chakra is open. Physical heart problems are a biological manifestation of non-physical energy blockages in the vortices of the Heart Chakra.

What we call the physical heart organ is only the small visible portion of a complex, multi-dimensional energy center, part of which exists outside of our physical perceptual range.

The heart is the center of balance between the energies of day to day survival, power, and sexual creativity on the one hand, and the centers of truth, wisdom, and spirituality on the other hand. The heart processes energies of the entire being and provides a constant stream of information back to you in the form of emotions or feelings. Because the heart can process vast amounts of information from sources we do not see, the feelings and sensations from the heart area do not always appear to us to have a logical foundation. We cannot always explain what we are feeling or why we are feeling it. The western mind has been trained to have an explanation for everything. Applying the logical, rational mind to those things that are unseen is an uncomfortable approach for many people who are unaccustomed to following their own intuitive senses or inner feelings. At times, the rational mind and the feelings of the heart seem to be directly at odds with each other. If your rational mind says you should take a certain trip and your heart tells you not to make that trip, you have an internal conflict. This type of conflict will not necessarily be resolved with more analytical data, which is what the mind seeks. There may be intuitive factors at work which the heart is attuned to, but which the mind cannot comprehend or even sense. Balance is essential to integrating mind and heart. Maintaining too heavy a reliance on either one, to the exclusion of the other, will lead us into difficulty.

For many people who have ignored or suppressed their feelings for years, listening to the heart is a new and different approach. It may take some getting used to. For people who have relied on their intellect to tell them what they are "feeling," the new approach of listening to the heart will feel strange at first. It will take some practice to be accustomed to getting in touch with the "heart mind" as distinguished from the logical mind. This is part of the modern paradigm of the new energy, which is to "think with the heart."

Millions of people die each year of heart-related diseases. Over a million coronary bypass surgeries are done each year. As a society, as a planetary population, we need to do more to open our hearts to ourselves and to each other. When heart energies are blocked, the Heart Chakra is not fully functioning. Parts of its energies are closed down. Heart energy blockages are directly related to physical maladies of the heart. Factors of diet, structural defects in the body's physiology, and one's activity level (exercise/life style) are not to be ignored. However, the energies of the Heart Center are superimposed on structure and at some level actually create and influence the structure. Remedies that focus only on the physical structural level will not have long-term success. Whether or not you feel you have love in your life has a tremendous bearing on how healthy your entire emotional and physical bodies are. Feeling disconnected from other people, feeling unloved, feeling sad, lonely or isolated are very energy draining to the heart center. Your life force literally drains away from your system.

When the energy of the heart is not replenished from your connection to spirit, and from your connection with others, your life energy is at low ebb. Energy related problems arise such as anxiety, depression, chronic tiredness, lethargy, rapid aging, disorientation and a feeling of no purpose. This energy drain at the spiritual and emotional level will also manifest at the physical level. This is extremely important information. It is not coincidental that a person with a "broken heart" over a long period of time will actually develop physical ailments, whether these are in the form of depression of the immune system or large scale physical collapse of the circulatory system itself. Long term blockages of the heart energies will eventually result in congestion of the physical circulatory system.

If we can open our hearts, we can become more highly connected with our world at large, and with the healing energies of the earth.

If we are fully in touch with our heart energies and the signals our body sends to us, it is less likely we will engage in eating habits and lifestyle habits that promote unhealthy conditions. In many cases, diet and lifestyle that result in self-destructive behavior have their roots in a lack of self-love and self-esteem.

At a personal level, there are practical steps that we can take to help realize the goal of achieving balance. From a high level perspective, attaining balance is a four-fold process involving these key activities:

- Quieting the Mind.
- Relaxing the Body.
- Calming the Emotions.
- Focusing the Spirit.

We focus on these from a practical activity perspective in other areas of this book. Before entering those topics, let us look further at the energies of the heart and its various aspects.

The Importance of Self Love

in Maintaining a Healthy Heart

Loving oneself is a very important part of developing a healthy, loving life style. We cannot claim to really love others if we let our own bodies deteriorate under abuse or neglect. Love of self is an honoring of the heart energies and ultimately benefits all those you come in contact with.

Low levels of self-love and low self esteem manifest in behavior patterns of excessive eating, drug abuse, excessive smoking, alcohol abuse and a lack of physical motivation. All these behavior patterns work to influence the physical/biological systems of the body. When the body's physical/biological energy systems are weakened, this creates a downward spiral of energy loss. When the physical body is in need of energy to function, it draws on the energy of the spirit and the emotions. If the connection to spirit is weak, and the energies of the emotional body are partially blocked, there is no support system for the body and it breaks down. Blockages in the arteries mirror blockages in the energy flows. Arterial blockages are one of the physical manifestations of what is occurring on an energetic level.

When energies are unable to flow and replenish themselves, the body breaks down, internal systems fail, cell tissue deteriorates, aging speeds up, illness and eventually mortality results. A stroke is a physical manifestation of a blockage, which is occurring at the subtle energy level.

Managing Your Energy Flows

You are responsible for the management of your own energy flows. Our unique gift of the power of conscious choice-making allows us the freedom to determine much of our life's direction. It also gives us a level of responsibility that puts us in a causal position with regard to our own spiritual, emotional and physical health. It is through our own intent, our conscious choice-making, that we affect our energy flows. We send energy outward into the world. We connect with others and with our environment through an energetic, vibrational field. We determine the quality of our own energies. If our energies are blocked, we are to some degree responsible for this blockage. We may not realize specifically how we are doing it, but we are in some measure *creating* the blockages ourselves.

Animals do not have the same conscious choice making ability as we do. Also, animals do *not* suffer from massive rates of cardiovascular disease. Animals do not have the same ability to consciously interfere with their biological rhythms and energy flows that humans do. As humans, we consider ourselves more intelligent than animals. We are able to affect our energy production and energy flow through our conscious choices. If we harbor negative emotional energies, such as anger, hatred, resentment, jealously, we create a resonance pattern in our energy field that works to influence our biology. There is a direct correlation here. In fact, the power of our intent to influence our energy field is so great that our energetic blockages can affect not only our own bodies, but the bodies of those around us. This applies to people and to animals and other life forms.

The Quantum Nature of the Heart's Energy Field

Your energy field has tremendous reach and power. The quality of your energy field influences the environment around you at a greater distance than you probably realize. Have you ever met people with multiple persistent illnesses who also have pets that have multiple persistent illnesses? Animals who live with humans can pick up energetic disorders and physical disorders that are counterparts to our human illnesses. The energetic fields of animals are sensitive to our energetic fields. They can pickup on excess energy imbalances that their owners have, and their biology reacts to that. Since animals are generally more in tune with nature if left to their own ways, it is unlikely that their energetic patterns are causing similar disturbances to people. In fact, the mere presence of animals in recovery areas has proven to be very beneficial to humans.

Animals can, by their close connection to the biorhythms of their particular species and their connection to nature itself can help alleviate human energy imbalances, to some extent. Certainly the loving affection of a dog or other pet has a very beneficial effect on our heart energies. As we give love to our pets, they resonate with this vibration and give love energy back to us. This increased flow of energy is highly therapeutic to our systems. If we truly understood the level of service that the animal kingdom provides to us on this planet, we would have a much greater respect for them.

Have you ever noticed that couples who live together for many years sometimes have similar energy disorders? When you live in close proximity to another, the quality and vibrational levels of their energy field influence you. This is simply a phenomenon of quantum physics. We are not living isolated lives. We are an intimate part of our environment. At the energetic level and the molecular level, our physical bodies have no well-defined edges. They are energy vibrations in a state of vibratory flux. They appear to be solid, well defined structures with definite boundaries. That perception, however, is merely a function of our selective perception of reality. A more correct view is that we are all energetic beings whose size and scope of influence is not limited by the reach of our arms. Our energy fields extend out at least several feet from our physical bodies. In fact, quantum physics tells us that we are connected with our environment at even greater distances. Through the phenomena associated with non-locality, our thoughts, emotions and intentions can have an energetic effect on people and things at remote distances, instantaneously. This is a tremendously different paradigm than the traditional western view of the body as a machine with limited range of operation and influence. This new paradigm opens for us a whole world of possibilities. With it, brings a new awareness of our responsibility as co-creators of the energies and realities of our world.

Responsibility is Not Blame

We are responsible for our energy flows, and ultimately for our spiritual, emotional, mental and physical health. Being responsible does not mean we are "to blame" for any illness or malady that befalls us. Blaming yourself is the exact opposite of the type of energetic vibration that is needed to restore health and harmony to all our energetic bodies. There are many reasons behind the manifestation of illness or disease in the body. Physical challenges, whether minor or life threatening are not an indication that one is a bad person or that one has evil intentions. Such challenges are an indication that some area of imbalance is being manifested. This manifestation is sometimes a necessary part of the learning process that provides us with an opportunity to more closely examine our own inner world. When faced with challenges at the physical level, we often finally take the time to examine our goals, value, intentions and choices. This inner exploration is an extremely powerful and valuable part of the human growth experience. Our development on the spiritual plane is augmented by our experiences on the physical plane.

Physical illnesses and disabilities also provide us with an opportunity to experience and express the energy of compassion for other beings. This too is a very valuable and honorable gift. Our responsibility for our own choices is reflected in how we choose to engage our hearts in the service and support of our fellow beings. Love and compassion are the most powerful energies there are. As we choose love and compassion in our daily lives, we will see the results of our intentions reflected in our own view of the world. We change our personal reality to match our higher vibrations. This is a tremendously powerful process of continued growth in awareness and consciousness. We are extremely fortunate to have such a wealth of other beings of diverse energetic patterns with whom we can share this journey of self exploration and discovery.

The Power of Giving: Opening the Heart Center

When we give to others, we conduct an energy interchange. It creates an immediate flow of energy from ourselves outward to the universe. Our giving can be in the form of energy itself, such as love or compassion, or in the form of kind words, thoughts or prayers. Giving can also be in the form of physical objects.

The giving of energy to another is truly a gift of high vibration. You can give energy to another through direct energy work, such as Reiki or one of the other subtle energy modalities described in this book. You can also send high-energy vibrations to another person just through the intent to do so. If you have not had direct experience doing this, it may sound too simple to be true. It is simple, and it is true. When you give the intent to send energy, through the focus of mind and heart, you actually cause energy to be transmitted to the person to whom you are intending the energy go. This is a gift of spirit. When you say to someone "I wish you well." You are actually sending them a bit of energy along a wavelength of high energy and compassion. The stronger and more focused your intent, the better you ability to send energy will be. Practice comes through continued use of your conscious focused intent.

Giving kind words, thoughts or prayers are another way of sending energy. Again, it is the intent behind the words, thoughts or prayers that is the key impetus for the energy. A weak intent, or no real intent at all, will not generate an energetic flow to the other person. Similarly, negative thoughts (resentment, anger, impatience, etc.) will also not result in you sending high energies, even if you use high sounding words of good will. It is the intention behind the words that always holds the greater power. Words and thoughts of higher energy, coupled with the intent to send such energies, is very powerful. In this case, the words, thoughts or prayers act to focus the intent even more strongly.

The giving of objects is another way of sending high vibrational energy. Objects are condensed energy. Every object has its own vibrational frequency. Objects can also hold higher vibrational frequencies if they are endowed with energy through conscious intent. If this sounds far fetched, or something out of science fiction, remember how man religious practices and spiritual rituals around the world hold the concept of blessing objects, thus making them "holy" or "sacred." What happens during a blessing? The conscious focused intent to raise the vibration of an object to the highest level possible does have an effect on that object. When you do this, you infuse some of your spiritual energies into the object. The gift becomes one from the heart. Sacred objects are those that have been recognized as having had some exposure to divine energies. Those objects with which you have an emotional connection are those objects with which you have made an energetic connection.

There is an interesting human phenomenon when it comes to the subject of giving. When we give from the heart, we create an energy flow outwards into the universe. We contribute energy in this way to another person, to a group of people, we can even contribute energy in this way to a thought form or an idea. However, when we give with the simultaneous expectation of receiving something in return for what we give, there is a "pulling back" type of energy flow that inhibits the full energy of our giving.

Axiom

Layers of Mind

The Heart is part of the Mind. Overemphasis on the value of analytical thought has created a collection of mind chatter that interferes with the ability to feel the thoughts of the Heart. The Heart Center energies are part of the overall Mind of an individual, which is not the brain, but a collection of multidimensional energies stored in an energy field around the individual and in both physical and non-physical space.

Humankind's evolution and integration into the physical world required at some point in the past an emphasis on the development of analytical thought, somewhat independent of the body's intuitive feeling and instinctual drives. That analytical development has been largely achieved and a re-integration of that function into the larger overall mind is now required for the human to advance into the next stage of evolution as a new being. That is happening now across the planet.

Right now, we live as a planetary species with two distinctly different evolutionary states. Two "kinds" of human. One consists of a fragmented mind where the layers are not integrated one with the other. The new emerging being is one where the layers of mind are integrated with each other and with spirit. This is an evolutionary leap. Right now, both the new form and the old form are co-existing on the planet. We are entering a period of major adjustment and change on the planet as more people transition to this new level of being and the old paradigms of existence fall away. We are weaving for ourselves a new and expanded consciousness at each moment. Those of like-mind seek each other out in order to co-create this new level of reality and to assist others who are ready to make this transition. This is accomplished through raising the frequencies of light and vibrational states. This is the role of the new artisans of the future. This is your role now.

Open Your Heart by Finding Your Passion

One of the key ways to open your heart to the power of love and the vitality life is to discover your passion and follow it. Each of us has a deep inner passion that drives us toward meeting our life's goals. Following your passion is the difference between living a full and joyous life and merely existing. Passion is what gives vitality to our thoughts, actions, dreams and activities. Passion is what infuses our relationships with others with the energy to expand and grow together. Knowing what our passions are is vital to our expressing our creativity openly and fully. You have this power in you now. It may be lying untapped or unacknowledged. It is time to awaken your passion and bring it into your life.

If you have not yet discovered your passion, discovering it should be one of your primary goals. Once you have tapped into this incredible resource of internal energy, you will be able to unleash tremendous internal creative energies. Finding and following your passion is what focuses your creative energies towards expression in the outer world. Your passion and creativity is how you share with others the power and vitality of your life. Many people seem to live lives of repetition and mundane activities. Many seem to live in the future, waiting for a better day or better opportunity to come along. They put their lives on hold until this or that happens. They fail to see the tremendous power that exists in the NOW. They put their emotional expressions on hold while they saturate themselves with "busyness" and unfulfilling tasks. Doing so, they are starving the heart by denying the energies of passion that it dearly needs to grow and expand. Heart disease is precipitated by a failure to allow the vitality of your inner being to flow through your system unimpeded. Loving yourself and taking care of yourself are the kindergarten steps on this path. Finding your true passion and expressing it takes you into the graduate school of the heart.

What is your passion? It may be working with other people on a one-to-one basis. It may be creating beautiful music, artwork, sculpture, writing, singing, dancing or the creativity of teaching or leading others. Only you can determine what your personal passion is. Look inside and examine what your heart wants to do. What gives you pleasure and joy? What thoughts seem to lighten your energies and give you a desire to move into action? This is the key. Your passion will be that thing or desire that brings you a higher energy vibration and calls you to action. Your passion may be hidden under layers of what you think you are "supposed" to do in life. We are told what we should be doing by friends, family, parents, media, co-workers and so on. It is time to listen to *you*. Finding your passion will unlock the energies you have been suppressing for so long and will open your heart to the beauty around you. When you follow your passion, you will meet others who are also following their passion. It takes you into a whole new realm of experience.

Your heart calls to you. It is time to listen. Open your heart and soul to your inner desires. Discover your passion *and follow it!*

Forgiving Others as a Process of Spiritual Growth

The act of forgiveness is directly related to the energies of the heart. The act of forgiveness is directed towards someone who we have designated as the cause of some unwanted effect. We are holding someone else responsible for some action or inaction that we interpret as having been harmful to us. When we refuse to forgive, we continue to hold that person in a negative energy framework in our mind and heart. The low energy vibrations of blame, resentment, and hatred that we hold in connection with this energy framework then become part of our personal energetic system. We reduce our own vibrational energies by holding onto negative frameworks or negative images of others. If we attribute the source of actions we dislike to other people, we then hold both the person and the action in that framework of dislike. The more we perceive someone as the cause of our pain, our discomfort or our problems, the more difficult it seems to be to forgive them.

The process of forgiveness is a letting go of a negative framework— letting go of lower vibrational energies. You are actively holding onto such energies very strongly. The state of being unforgiving is the continuation of holding such low vibrations in place.

Making a conscious choice to forgive someone who has harmed us will cause a release of the negative energies and a raising of our vibration to a higher level. This process is highly cleansing to the heart and soul. It gives us back a great deal of our own energy. The act of consciously forgiving someone allows the energies in the heart center and related areas of the body to be released and lightened. It allows the energies of the chakras to once again flow more harmoniously.

When we forgive others, we take an active step towards healing ourselves.

Heart Chakra Sensations

- "My heart reaches out to you."
- "He touched my heart."
- "My heart lit up with joy."
- "Her heart was warm."
- "My heart sang with joy."
- "His heart expanded."
- "Our hearts were moved."
- "His heart was closed."
- "Her heart was shut down."
- "We held it in our hearts."
- "Their hearts were entwined with love."
- "My heart opened up."
- "Her heart swelled with grief."
- "The heart burns with passion"
- "His heart cries out in longing"
- "My heart tingles with excitement"
- "Their hearts were moved to action"
- "My heart bleeds for them"
- "Their heartfelt thanks"
- "His heart was heavy"
- "His heart soared in exhilaration"
- "Their hearts were joined in friendship"
- "Her heart was light with laughter"
- "His heart melted with love for the child"
- "Her heart grew cold with jealousy"
- "She wore her heart on her sleeve."
- "His heart nearly burst with excitement"
- "My heart jumped in surprise"
- "Follow your heart."

Table 8

Love and Compassion

Axiom

To "Love" means making a conscious choice to move the heart towards compassion. Compassion flows from the heart center of one, to the heart center of another.

The energies of the heart can serve to open a doorway to other dimensions, times or places. Heart energies and longings are the catapults for our dreams.

The energy in the Heart Chakra area swirls in a vortex of powerful currents of warmth and vibration.

Heart Energies, when activated through our focused intent, can open the blocked passages of the body's meridians.

The ease of blood flow through the physical heart region is *directly* influenced by the level to which the Heart Chakra is open. Physical heart problems are a biological manifestation of non-physical energy blockages in the vortices of the Heart Chakra.

What we call the *physical* heart organ is only the small visible portion of a complex, multi-dimensional energy center, part of which exists outside of our physical perceptual range.

As we evolve along our path of spiritual growth, we expand our ability to sense and interact with the energies of others. We expand our ability to love.

"Spiritual growth assists you in creating loving relationships. As you grow spiritually, you
will connect with people in higher ways. Your
growth will allow you to trust more, keep your
heart open, and reach new levels of sharing
and intimacy. You will have deeper, more
meaningful connections with your loved
ones."

—Orin/Sanaya Roman, *Spiritual Growth*

Exercise: Raising Your Heart Energy Vibrations

Words symbolize concepts and impart meaning. The following
list of words describe states of being or characteristics that represent higher vibrational attributes. Reading and understanding
these conceptually will prompt our energetic vibrations to raise to
higher levels. Read this list over slowly, pausing just long enough
to get the concept of each term. Cycle through this list several
times. You will feel your energies strengthening and your vibration increasing as you resonate with the meanings represented
here. This is best done as part of a personal meditation process.

Higher Vibrational Attributes

Acceptance	Forgiveness
Affection	Freedom
Appreciation	Happiness
Balance	Harmony
Beauty	Love
Bliss	Peace
Care	Sincerity
Clarity	Tranquility
Comfort	Unboundedness
Compassion	Unity
Creativity	Wholeness

Table 9

The Energy Dynamics of Balance

The illustration above is an ancient Celtic symbol. The following interpretation came to me as I studied its design. The four primary circles may signify the balance of four aspects of the self: Spiritual, Mental, Emotion, and Physical. Each interlocking circle is a symbol of unity, wholeness and completeness.

The intersection of the circles represents the interconnectedness of the four aspects of the self. At the points of intersection, the loops become one with each other, creating a unified whole.

The twelve open spaces within the circles indicate storage places of knowledge and wisdom.

Opening the Heart: The Intention to Love

Axiom

When we give love, we extend the energy of ourselves outward toward another person, or outward toward any thing. Loving is a conscious act of extending part of ourselves outward, encompassing gently the energy of another.

By extending love energy outward, more is created.

The power of love is activated through intent.

Love is energy that resonates at specific vibrations.

Love is not something separate from ourselves, that we either have or do not have.

Love is part of ourselves— Love is ourselves.

We each have an infinite capacity to generate love. To achieve balance, we must also be willing to accept and receive love from others and from the universe. Giving it away does not deplete love energy, it is increased. Through giving love with intent, we increase our volume of love energy. This expansion is a very real event, not simply a metaphor. Therefore, our total amount of love energy *increases* as we give it to others.

If we love unconditionally, but do not receive love because we cannot accept it or recognize it, we may in time create an imbalance in ourselves. Our "selves" nevertheless, will then take steps at some level to correct this balance in order to restore harmony in our lives. We witness this in the action of spirit orchestrating life events and energies to urge us to disengage from the source of our imbalance. The feeling of dissatisfaction, the gentle longings or strong urges to act are all manifestations of aspects of our selves that seek to restore balance. Because this direction from spirit is specific in nature, this is called "guidance." The direction most often comes in the nature of "feeling" rather than words.

This is also the essence of life changes and the essence of spiritual growth.

We can express love of others by sharing our space and our energies with them, consciously. In the physical world, we have often used the giving of gifts to express love or affection. The giving of gifts or "things" is a symbolic representation of the act of giving of ourselves, our own energies, to another person.

A physical gift or "thing" is condensed energy in the form of matter. It is a higher level of giving to give of oneself, one's energy.

Law of Attraction

Axiom

The ability to focus our feelings and our intent influences the quality of our learning experiences on the physical plane. As we work to develop our ability to focus, we nurture the growth of this skill. As we do this, we will attract into our lives other people who are on a similar path of learning.

We see in other people, reflections of ourselves and reflections of areas that need healing, nurturing and love. The universe operates on a law of attraction. It orchestrates our coming together for our mutual growth and the balancing of our heart energies.

Giving Love vs. Getting Love

Many times we are caught up in wanting to be loved, wanting to have love or feeling the need to have someone give their love to us.

To engage the circle of love, we must give love. If we focus on being a loving person, giving of ourselves, connecting with our own love energy and projecting this out ward for the benefit of others, we begin a circle of love.

When our circle of love is engaged, it continues to flow and eventually comes back around to us. We will experience the love we have been sending outward. It may not always come from exactly the same source that we sent our love outward to. It may come from another direction. It will eventually flow back to us.

The energy of love that we send outward will touch many others as it flows from heart to heart, often increasing in intensity, power and fullness. When it finally returns to us, we may sense its familiar warmth, along with the increased warmth and added energies it has absorbed on its journey through the circle.

Receive it, accept it, be nurtured within it, and let it flow outward to another again. Activate the flow. Engage the circle once more.

Love is an act of creation. Feel the birth of love in your heart center. Feel the burning as its energies unfold and give birth to vibrations that seek out others to connect with. This is Spirit in action. Ride the wave. Be the love.

Shadow Selves

Axiom

The term "balance" implies that there exist opposing forces at work. What we call our "personality" is a mosaic of individual energy dynamics at work, constantly interacting with one another. Some aspects of our personality are actively at work, but we are not fully aware of them. These we can call our "shadow selves."

As we grow in spiritual awareness, we will and must eventually become aware of our shadow selves and what they represent energetically in our path of evolution.

We can encounter some aspects of our shadow selves through focused meditation. However, one of the most effective ways to experience our shadow selves is through other people and our relationships with them. When we are involved in the dynamics of personal relationships, the energetic forces that comprise the shadow selves will come to the surface and interact with the energetics of other people. This will happen without our conscious involvement, but as it happens, we can become aware of this interplay.

Bringing the shadow selves into the light provides us a unique and valuable opportunity to view and understand what aspects of our personality need to be examined to achieve balance and wholeness. The shadow selves are also a window to our past intents. Strong intents in the past are energetic patterns that have been set in motion by us and which can tend to persist without conscious examination. Shadow selves are not necessarily evil, they are simply areas that are not fully integrated into our conscious personality. They nevertheless have an influence on our behavior because they hold pieces of our own energy, which they use to interact with us and with others, thus causing thoughts, feelings and actions to occur.

By consciously experiencing our shadow selves without denial of their existence, and by viewing our past intents and patterns, we can bring forth areas in our selves that need healing and balancing. If we can learn to love our shadow selves and those aspects in other people that represent our shadow selves, we make a major leap forward in our progress towards wholeness.

Laughter

Axiom

Laughter is a vibration that re-tunes the vortices of the Heart Center, allowing all to resonate together. As it does this, it clears old blockages and infuses new vitality into one's whole being.

Laughter releases bioelectromagnetic charges and frees residual energy storage pockets and raises one's vibration. Laughter helps open the energy centers as it pulls energy upward from the base chakra up through the higher chakras. It rises from the earth to the heavens. The ability to laugh is a unique gift, which few species possess. It is simultaneously grounding and uplifting, allowing the intellect to experience the freedom of joy as opposed to the restraints of logic.

Laughter frees the soul from the bonds of seriousness.

Laughter is the sound of life's incongruities bubbling up from the depths of sadness into the light. Releasing and energizing, like bubbles bursting in the open air.

Shared laughter is the sound of one soul touching another soul, each allowing the other to let go… experiencing the priceless joy of the moment with unfettered abandon.

Laughter clears the dust out of the organ pipes as the songs of rapture fill the Heart.

Laughter is at once both grounding and uplifting. It is grounding since the Earth resonates with your laughter, and laughs with you. Your personal energy field and the energy field of the earth are woven together at the smallest subatomic levels. The earth cannot help but laugh with you.

Laughter is uplifting in that its energy wants to flow upward and outward. Laughter seeks to shoot forth and echo into the night sky.

Laughter re-energizes the vitality of one's being.

Deep, honest laughter is the sign of an open and joyous Heart.

Laughter turns heavy energies into light energies.
Laughter is an anti-focus. Ever try to thread a needle while laughing?

Chapter Three

"Silent Power"

Energywork and Bodywork

Balancing the Energies

Subtle Energy Balancing

In Chapters One and Two we discussed the human energy anatomy and why subtle energy balancing techniques work from a quantum physics perspective. In this chapter several specific modalities are described along with how they can be applied to achieve a greater sense of balance and integration of your body's energy fields.

Reiki

Reiki is a Japanese name for a specific type of energy work that has origins thousands of years ago in Tibet. Specific details of its origins are not known, but various techniques of energy healing in existence probably have their roots in the very early techniques practiced in Tibet and elsewhere on this planet, under different names, over many millennia.

Reiki is the application and facilitation of universal life force energies to help aid and balance the energy fields and chakras. The technique was rediscovered by Dr. Mikao Usui, a Japanese Buddhist in the early 20th century. He called this form of healing "Reiki" and taught it throughout Japan until his death around 1893. His original teachings are referred to as the "Usui Method" or the "the Usui System of Natural Healing." Reiki can help bring the body's energy centers into greater alignment and facilitate energy flow.

Reiki is a simple and natural technique that anyone can learn and use. The term "Re" generally means "universal," while the term "Ki" translates to "life force energy." The Reiki technique involves a Reiki practitioner focusing energy on the client, either through direct hands on contact or with the hands several inches away from the client's body. The universal energy is either directed to an area of the body or energy field, or it is simply "allowed" to flow to where it seeks a balance. A typical Reiki session lasts around 45 minutes to an hour and a half, but there is no firm time restriction. Very short Reiki sessions can also be given to address a particular aspect of a client's energy field or to address a physical manifestation of some kind. In a very short session, the client may be seated in a chair or on the floor, or may be lying down on a Reiki table (massage table) as is done for the longer sessions. Reiki is can also be given over long distances, through a remote session or distance session.

Reiki is taught through a process of education and attunement by someone who is already an attuned Reiki Master/Teacher. There are three primary levels, Reiki I, Reiki II and Reiki III

(Master/Teacher). Reiki also employs the use of special symbols drawn in the air by the Reiki practitioner (and/or visualized) to help focus energy during a Reiki treatment. Each Reiki level introduces new symbols and educates the practitioner in new applications of intent and brings about an increased ability to sense and work with the energy.

Reiki has been known to have many important benefits. It helps bring about deep relaxation, removes energy blockages, detoxifies the system, increases vitality and raises the vibrational frequency of the body. Reiki is excellent for addressing physical, mental, emotional and spiritual issues. A Reiki session can induce an extremely comfortable state of being in the client and can also bring about an alteration in the consciousness of the client which can have a profound beneficial effect in the energy balancing process. Reiki is also very powerful when done in group sessions, such as a "Reiki Circle." In a Reiki Circle, several practitioners work together on a client simultaneously. The "client," who is often another practitioner, can, after receiving a treatment from the group, then switch and begin working on one of the other practitioners until each practitioner has his or her turn receiving the Reiki treatment. A Reiki Circle is a beautiful way to share this powerful loving energy. Reiki treatments on people recovering from heart operations or other physical difficulties have been known to be very therapeutic.

Reiki has been gaining acceptance in the western medical field over the past 15 years and some continuing education programs recognize Reiki training as a qualifying modality under a CEU (Continuing Education Units) program.

Reiki was introduced to the Western world in the mid-1970s. Since that time its use has spread widely throughout the world.

The following information is provided courtesy of Doven Starr, a Reiki Master. It is a beautiful description of what Reiki is and how it works.

What Is Reiki, and How Does It Work?

Reiki is a Tibetan form of Energy Healing, rediscovered and promoted by Sensei Mikao Usui of Gifu, Japan. Usui Reiki is a gentle, non-invasive Tibetan tradition of healing yourself, each other and the earth using Spiritually Guided Life Force Energy. Reiki is Love, and therefore 'Helps ever, Harms never'! Reiki is provided to you through the hands, heart and mind of a Reiki Practitioner. *Given your conscious and subconscious desire and permission,* Reiki stimulates your Inner Healer at the root of whatever most needs healing at that time. The root of an issue may lie in the Spiritual, Mental, Emotional and/or Physical Body, *and it's possible to experience healing miracles at any level* if that is what is in your Highest Good! *At the very least* the healing leaves you relaxed and peaceful which enhances your perspective on any circumstance.

To become a Reiki healer, you receive a Reiki Initiation and Class from a Certified Reiki Master Teacher. Then, for as long as you want Reiki in your life, it will work with and for you. One of the greatest benefits of delivering Reiki is that as it passes through you, it speeds your own healing as well! Reiki is easy and natural! It's an exhilarating means for you to gain a richer understanding that your physical existence is but a tiny part of what we call Reality.

The Life Force Energy is of the Creator, it permeates our universe and everyone/everything within it. Its limitless abundance can be accessed and used to create balance and wellness in every aspect of our lives. Just as there is "Medicine" with its various specialties, there is "Spiritual Healing" with its various modalities. Just as there are different radio frequencies, the same is true of healing energy. Reiki is a particular, gentle, non-invasive frequency.

The Reiki Tradition is a Sisterhood / Brotherhood of those committed to healing themselves, each other, and our planet. Those who perform Reiki have been 'attuned' to access the Reiki wavelength of healing energy. From receiving and giving attunements, I can testify that they are truly miraculous, a gift of healing empowerment from Spirit.

Reiki energy makes direct contact with and stimulates your Inner Healer, that part of your Self that knows exactly what you need to be healthy in every way. Because it's guided by Spirit, Reiki is rooted in Love, has Divine intelligence and is always gentle, always helpful. Reiki works to heal and harmonize all the energy systems in all of your bodies (spiritual, mental, emotional and physical)! Reiki goes to the *root* of whatever most needs healing at the time of it's application, and the root may lie in any one of those 'bodies'.

Some people come for a Reiki 'tune up', which leaves you feeling peaceful, relaxed and better able to manage life in general. Another person might come asking for help with a particular problem, let's say with their heart. In this instance their physical condition relates to the Heart Chakra which contains our love, loss, grief and forgiveness issues (to name a few). In this case, the energy will go to the root of what is causing the heart condition, and begin to heal the client at the root level. With heart issues, it's common during a session for the client to recall something that hurt him during his life. Entirely guided by Spirit, the memory is gently processed then reintegrated with a more objective perspective, effecting great relief and a 'healing' of that memory! **Your Inner Healer is responsible for achieving results and in a direct and perfect manner, Reiki stimulates and boosts your Inner Healer.** Reiki is guided by the Intelligence Most High, for the Highest Good of both the healer and healee. You can trust Its intelligence, Its power, and It's gentle nature. You can trust the process!

'Healing' and 'curing' are different things!

There have been times when one Reiki session eliminated a client's long-term back pain. Other clients instead receive the spiritual, mental and emotional tools to better manage their physical condition. What determines whether a client is 'cured' or not is Spirit. Sometimes a person is learning soul lessons from their physical illness, and it's not meant to be 'cured', with our excellent medical technology or with energy healing! Although we can ask for a particular result from the sessions, it's then best left in the hands of Spirit… "Thy Will Not Mine". If a healer tells you they can cure your dis-ease, I offer this word of caution: If your spiritual, mental and emotional bodies aren't cleared of the root of the problem, it will LIKELY recur, either as the same condition, or something else in your body. Be aware of those who promise specific results.

Doven Starr is a Spiritual Advisor, Meditation instructor and Certified Reiki Master Teacher. She also teaches Laying-On-Of-Hands healing, and is a Certified Master Teacher of Magnified Healing and Universal Spiritual Healing. Visit her web page at www.usui-reiki.org.

The Reiki Principles

Just for today I will give thanks

for my many blessings.

Just for today I will not worry.

Just for today I will not be angry.

Just for today I will

do my work honestly.

Just for today I will be

kind to my neighbor

and every living thing.

Table 10

Karuna Reiki®

Reiki training and advanced techniques are also available in the form of Karuna Reiki®, a system developed by William Rand, at the International Center for Reiki Training. (Rand, *Reiki for a New Millennium*). Karuna translated from Sanskrit means "to take compassionate action to diminish the suffering of others". Karuna Reiki is different than Usui Reiki. Some practitioners of Karuna find it more powerful than the traditional Usui Method. Some practitioners have stated that the energy has a more definite feeling to it and works on all the energy bodies at the same time. Some people report a feeling that the energy simply surrounds them and the client instead of simply flowing through them.

What Does a Reiki Session Look Like?

If you watch a Reiki session you may not think that very much is happening. Most of what occurs energetically is not visible to most people. However, here is a general description of what may occur during a Reiki session.

The person receiving a Reiki session (also called a Reiki Treatment) is typically lying on their back to start, on a massage table. The client is comfortably clothed. The knees or feet may be slightly elevated, depending on the client's comfort wishes. A very light sheet is usually available to cover parts of the body to keep the client warm and comfortable.

The practitioner sets the environmental conditions of the room so that it is comfortable and ensures that there will be no external interruptions during the session. Light music, incense and candles may also be part of establishing the session's comfortable relaxing atmosphere. A general time frame is agreed upon with the client. The practitioner assesses the client's energy field and may discuss gently with the client any areas of the client's physical body or energy field that the client wishes the Reiki practitioner to be particularly sensitive to. The practitioner often begins with a few minutes of silent meditation and may ask for guidance during the session from higher sources. Then the Practitioner begins. With the hands gently raised several inches over the body, or in light contact with some part of the body, the intent is given for the Reiki energy to flow.

Normally, discussion during a Reiki session is kept to a minimum, but talking is perfectly fine. It is especially helpful when the client is experiencing a physical or emotional cleansing of some kind and wishes to share what is happening with the practitioner. Talking is fine. The client is always gently encouraged and never criticized for anything they share during the Reiki session. (See "Light Worker's Oath" in this section).

The Practitioner moves around to various parts of the client's body letting the Reiki energy flow from higher sources through the Practitioner and into and around the client. The Practitioner usually feels this energy flow quite distinctly at this time, and the client usually starts to feel it also. From this point, the Practitioner can follow a set pattern of addressing each area of the body in turn or can respond in a more free-form fashion and go to wherever the Practitioner feels guided to go. At some point about half way through the session, the client is asked to turn over on their stomach. This is not mandatory, but is usual practice to address all areas of the body.

When the Practitioner feels that the energies have been balanced and the client is ready, the session is brought to a close by gently "sealing" the client's energy field and letting the client know that the session is completed. If the client is in the middle of releasing an emotional or physical energy blockage, or feels uncomfortable about ending the Reiki session at that time, the Practitioner may continue for a while longer until the client reaches a good point.

The client is allowed to relax a few moments on the table before getting up. The Practitioner ensures that the client is comfortably back in their body and helps with grounding the client as needed. The client sits up slowly and may discuss with the Practitioner what occurred during the session. It is a good idea to give the client some water to drink as well. Water helps flush the toxins out of the system that have been released from the body's cells and tissues during the energy session. As Reiki energy causes a shift in the person's energy field, old energy blockages are released and energies are balanced. This causes a release at the physical level of toxins that have accumulated over time in the cells and tissues of the body. By drinking water (several glasses as an example) the toxins are more easily carried away without being re-absorbed into the body.

After the treatment, the client should be advised that they may notice some energy field adjustments taking place in the next few days or weeks after the session. This is particularly true if the session has been one of major cleansing or releasing of emotional or physical energy blockages.

Distance Energy Sessions

What is a "Distance Energy Session"?

One of the blessings of this universe is that we can bring about positive influences and create beneficial effects even at a distance. This fact has very profound ramifications in the area of human-to-human energy work.

A *Distance Energy Session* is when the energy worker (practitioner) and the person receiving the treatment (client) are not physically present in the same location. The practitioner gives the treatment and the client receives the treatment, even though great or small distances may separate them. Distance Energy Sessions operate on the quantum physics principle of non-local energetic interaction, sometimes called the principle of "non-locality." A Distance Energy Session is an energy treatment across a distance.

"By Any Other Name…"

A *Distance Energy Session* can also be called a *"Remote Session,"* or *"Distance Treatment."* In modalities where the term "healing" is used, the sessions are sometimes referred to as *"Distance Healing," "Remote Healing,"* or *"Absentee Healing."* Various types of energetic interactions can take place during a Distance Energy Session. A person does not have to be sick, injured or in difficulty to experience the positive effects of a distance session. Since to some people the term "healing" suggests a pre-existing state of illness, injury, or lack, the term Distance Healing is sometimes inappropriate. These sessions can provide very beneficial results even if no illness or injury exists. It is therefore preferable to use a term such as *"Distance Energy Session"* or simply *"Distance Session,"* in describing the overall activity.

How is a Distance Session Performed?

Here are some general guidelines for performing distance energy work. When you work with a specific energy modality, you should first determine if that modality has a specific approach for distance work, and follow that procedure with your clients.

(1) Before performing the session, the practitioner obtains the agreement of the client. This is an important first step.

(2) Next, the practitioner and client usually agree on some form of exchange for the session (i.e., payment, or a trade of some kind).

(3) The practitioner and client, where feasible, may discuss the overall intent for the session, which is usually along the lines of achieving and allowing the energy flows that are for the client's greatest good.

(4) The practitioner sets aside a specific time and place in which to perform the session. The practitioner must have full attention and concentration on the session, and not be in a situation where they might be interrupted. The client does not have to stop what he or she is doing to receive the session. The client may want to be aware of the exact time the session is to be performed, and to be in a quiet place for receiving the session but this does not appear to be a requirement. The client can also agree to receive the sessions while he or she is asleep.

(5) The practitioner carries out the session through visualization of the client and all the energy movements, intents, affirmations and other aspects of the session. The practitioner may also, if they wish, use a surrogate item that represents the client. The surrogate (or substitute form) can be a doll, teddy bear or two-dimensional depiction of a client. This helps the practitioner focus on the techniques involved in the application of the

energy work being done. It is not mandatory that the practitioner uses a surrogate. The purpose of a surrogate is to assist the practitioner in focusing. The practitioner may also elect to do the entire session through visualization, i.e., visualizing the session and all its various components, movements and energy flows. The practitioner decides how to best approach the performance of a distance session.

(6) The practitioner concludes the session at an appropriate time, with a formal intent that the session is now concluded.

Why Does a Distance Session work?

A distance session works on three principles:

(1) **The principle of interconnectedness.** As energy beings, we co-exist with other energy beings in a vast interconnected web of energy. At the sub-atomic level, the tiny vibratory energy quanta that make up all matter and energy are in fact part of the universal consciousness. These energy quanta respond to our intent. They respond to our focused intention. Our focused intention is a faculty that exists outside of space-time but can have effects in space-time.

(2) **The second principle is that of non-locality of events.** This means that the energetic forces at work during a distance energy session can create effects at a remote location simultaneously with the intention at the source point. The energy does not have to "travel" a specific distance away. It is capable of bringing about a resonant effect instantaneously at the point of reception. The quantum physics principle of non-locality describes how under certain conditions, actions directed

to subatomic particles in one location can create responses in subatomic particles in a different location. The effects are instantaneous. Distance does not seem to be a barrier. We are all interconnected at many levels so it is not surprising that we can generate effects at a distance, and that distant actions can also have an effect on us.

(3) **The third principle is that of soul love**. During a distance energy session, the practitioner connects at a soul level with the person receiving the treatment. This is a love connection at the heart level and at other levels. This is a beautiful and powerful connection that responds to the loving intent of the practitioner, regardless of the distance involved.

Healing and balancing energies respond and resonate like the strings of a musical instrument. Physical proximity is not required, since the energy of love transcends space-time. Experiments in Quantum Physics have shown that certain particles can effect each other at great distances, with no apparent connection between them. One can also send positive energies into future space-time events or past space-time events, since the intent and the energies exist outside the human construct we call time.

Getting the Client's Permission First

Since a distance session is a way of intensifying the interconnection you have with another person, it is a sign of respect and honor to first ask permission from the person you intend to work with. If it is not possible to directly communicate with the person, such as in the case of a coma or other severe trauma, or a lack of any traditional communication methods, you can seek permission from their higher self, on an intuitive basis, and follow your response that you get. In some cases, you will feel that the timing is not right to proceed with a distance session. That is fine. Trust your intuitive guidance in this area.

What is a Phone Session?

A phone session is another type of distance session where the practitioner stays in touch with the client over a phone line. With this method, there is a verbal interchange possible between the practitioner and the client. This adds another dimension to the session, and gives those involved an opportunity for verbal interchange before and after the session as well. It is not mandatory, but does provide another avenue of communication as an adjunct to performing distance sessions.

How Long Does a Distance Session Usually Last?

Like a traditional "in person" session, the length of a distance session depends on what is being done, and may be based on agreement between the practitioner and the client. The exact session length is probably best described as an estimated time length, so that the practitioner can feel comfortable flowing with the energy of the session, and not having too much attention on the passage of time. In some cases, a distance session may seem to go faster than a traditional "in person" session, since everything is being done at the energetic level, with no physical restrictions.

Can Distance Sessions be Repeated?

Just like "in person" sessions, distance sessions can be repeated as often as needed, based on the desires of the client and the guidance received by both the client and practitioner.

Should Specific Goals be set for a Distance Session?

Depending on the modality you are using, having a general goal or intent for the session is a good idea. However, having specific detailed goals (like healing a broken finger in the next 2 hours) may not be the best focus for client and practitioner, as it may set up false expectations or might serve to restrict the focus to tightly on a specific outcome. Goals that seek to achieve what is for the highest good of the client are usually the best approach.

Should the Client Give Feedback?

If the client and practitioner feel it is appropriate for the client to give feedback on how the session went, this is fine. Having the client describe his or her feelings and experiences (verbally or in writing), can sometimes help put things in perspective for the client, and help them as they interpret their own experiences. If the client does not want to give feedback immediately following the session, the client can do this at a later time if desired.

What are Some Basic Guidelines in Distance Sessions?

Here are some suggested guidelines:

- Seek permission from the client
- Honor and respect the client and the process
- Have a quiet place, no disturbances
- Set aside a specific time for you as practitioner to do the session
- Establish an exchange with client (with family and close friends the exchange may be less formal)
- Respect the client's boundaries, confidentiality, and sensitivities
- Do not judge, evaluate or interpret the client's experiences for them. Listen with compassion to their feedback and experiences. Provide encouragement always. Facilitate the experience, but do not attempt to control it.

Can Distance Sessions Be Performed on Children?

Yes. All the above guidelines still apply, and of course parent's permission should be obtain if working with a minor child, either in person or in a distance treatment.

What are Some of the Benefits of Distance Energy Sessions?

Just like "in person" sessions, some of the benefits of distance sessions can be very profound, while others can. be more subtle. It always depends on the individual and their personal experiences, and what they are willing to experience at any given point on their personal path of growth. Practitioners and clients should refrain from passing judgement on the content of a session, and should avoid comparing sessions between one client and another. Each person's experience is unique.

Many people have reported a wide variety of beneficial effects of Distance Energy Sessions. Here are just a few. These are essentially the same benefits that can be realized through in-person sessions. (see Table 2)

Typical Benefits of Energy Sessions

- A feeling of greater balance
- Feelings of rejuvenation
- Recovery of past energies
- Relief from fatigue or upset
- Clarity and peace of mind
- Increased creativity and vitality
- A feeling of wholeness
- Expanded awareness
- Increased love for self and others

Yin-Yang

In our universe, balance is achieved through the manifestation of opposites. Things are often measured against and defined by what they are not. "Good" is defined in part by describing what "evil" is. Light is the absence of darkness. Darkness is the absence of light. In the seemingly polarized attributes of male and female, neither one is completely "good" or completely "bad." They are complimentary energies which have a whole series of manifestations that are associated with one or the other. The concept of Yin and Yang describes this duality of energies and demonstrates how together these energies provide a balance that is essential to all life.

Yin is known as the female energy. Yang is known as the male energy. In human beings, all females have some Yang energy and Yang attributes. Also, males have some Yin energy and Yin attributes. Yin and Yang exist together and balance each other. The Yin-Yang symbol represents the eternal changing and movement from Yin to Yang to Yin and so on. The symbol shows a small circle of the Yin inside the Yang, and small circle of the Yang, inside the Yin. It represents an eternal wheel of change and transformation. Forever in motion, forever balanced. A Yin-Yang balance achieves harmony.

A male with female energies out of balance, or a female with male energies out of balance are equally potentially at risk for emotional, physical or other issues brought about by such an imbalance. In energy work, the practitioner seeks to bring all energies into a state of balance in accordance with what the client receiving the treatment needs at any given time. The goal of the practitioner should be to facilitate the client's ability to achieve balance at whatever level or to whatever degree the client can accept. The practitioner should not set "healing" as a firm goal, even though if and when healing occurs it is something to be gratefully acknowledged. An illness that is being manifested in the body may be part of a larger process at work which neither the client nor the practitioner are capable of seeing in its entirety. Seeking balance, however, gives credence to the power of the energy work and also respects the intelligence of the universal energies in their movement towards the balance that is most appropriate for that client at that time.

The following tables provide further detail on many of the attributes associated with either the Yin or the Yang energies.

Yin

Associations and Key Words: Moon, Water, Tamas, letting go, Mother Nature

Essence & Essential Qualities: Female egg, one, still, waiting, cyclic, attracting, selecting, receiving, nurturing, patient, subtle, looking for essence, pull, empty, endurance, romance, words, feelings, intuition, right brain, fear of loneliness, wants to be filled, wants to be valued, wants to be fulfilled by higher quest, wants to be safe from attack, wants to experience emotional intimacy, longing, expression, companionship, colder, softer, lighter, smoother.

Strengths: Attraction, reflection, scope of vision, sensing, seeing whole

Challenges: Contentment; to be true to self while accepting yang imperfections; to give effective and appropriate feedback

Situations: Child, student, employee, etc.

Danger: That it will block yang energy, or distort or withhold reflection

In Failure: Doormat; martyr, enabling or critic; nagging, judging

Pain: Waiting, feeling alone, love addict

Disease: Emotional; emotional pressuring, fear of being shut out, reacts by being perfect, trying to please, critical, distorting, vengeful

Body problem areas: Digestion, lymphatics, cancer

When the want becomes a weapon: Hurts emotionally

Needs: To empty, to express feelings and be heard; to seek larger meanings

Desires: To have union, to fill space, know higher power, share love

Language: Non-physical connection, words

Healing: Attract: be aware of what you attract; Select and choose your arena; Recognize your power and value; Say no when necessary, face loneliness; Reflect clear statement of feelings; Reflect no blame or demand for immediate solutions; Support the positive; See mistakes, but continue to reflect

Give: A safe place

Table 11

Yang

Associations and Key Words: Sun, Fire, Rajas, Action, Time, Outgoing, self-knowledge, to manifest, project

Essence & Essential Qualities: Male, Sperm, many, active, determined, competitive, goal oriented, aggressive, persevering, constant, self-propelled, concerned with timing and direction, adaptability, hotter, harder, heavier, drier, rougher

Strengths: Action, impulse, spark of movement, concentration

Challenges: Responsibility, to be open and responsive to yin feedback and the results of its actions, admit mistakes and be vulnerable

Situations: Parent, teacher, boss, etc.

Danger: That it will obliviously overwhelm the yin or become paralyzed by the yin

In Failure: Tyrant: arrogance, accepts little feedback; Wimp: denial, won't look at reflection or gets lost in illusion

Pain: ...aholic, avoiding reflection, compulsive, exhausted/depleted, addict

Disease: Shutting down; avoidance; denial; controlled by fear of emotional reaction; reacts by being too forceful or indecisive, paralyzed

Body problem areas: Heart, eyesight and back problems

When the want becomes a weapon: hurts physically

Needs: To act and makes mistakes, be open and vulnerable to criticism, be recognized, see its reflection,

Desires: To know itself, understand relation to world through projects, challenges, adventure accomplishment

Language: Physical, action

Healing: Act, be decisive; watch for effect, ask for reflections, be open, say yes, face criticism and limits, listen, hear truth, stay neutral, don't defend, active listening, respond, learn and adjust

Give: Time and attention

Table 12

EMF Balancing Technique®:

The Path to Self-Empowerment and Growth

There are powerful energy balancing processes that can be used to bring an individual's energies into alignment, and help relieve the energetic causes of disease as well as improve our mental, emotional and physical well being. One such process is the "EMF Balancing Technique®"developed by Peggy Phoenix Dubro. This technique directly addresses the balancing of the body's energy fibers. EMFs or "electromagnetic fields" surround and permeate our entire physical body. These fields also extend outward for some distance around the body and interact with the fields of other people. The EMF Balancing Technique® is the energy system designed to work with the *"Universal Calibration Lattice"*,a model of the human energy anatomy. It is a simple, systematic procedure anyone can learn.

Part of the tremendous healing benefits of EMF Balancing is the human-to-human interaction that takes place when an EMF practitioner performs an energy balancing session on another individual. This technique is both powerful and greatly beneficial in bringing about a state of emotional, spiritual and physiological balance. This technique is extremely uplifting and the results can be life changing.

At this point in time, there are four phases in the EMF Balancing. Each Phase takes about 45 minutes to an hour to perform. Each phase has a specific focus. Each session results in a strengthening of the Universal Calibration Lattice, allowing it to carry a greater electrical charge. While the procedure for each session is the same every time, the calibration (or strengthening) is unique to each person receiving the session. The calibration is determined by their inner wisdom, an expression of their unique electromagnetic configuration.

During the session, the client is invited to speak about anything that is important to them, or they may remain silent as the practitioner observes the energy patterns. Each session has its own set procedure. The balancing of the energy field begins as you lay comfortably on a massage table. First, the field is "prepared" as universal energy flows from the practitioner's hands and through your energy anatomy. This may create a warm, tingling, relaxed sensation. Then the "clearing" process begins as the fibers of energy are stretched. A feeling of strings of energy being gently pulled is not uncommon. This is part of the calibration process within the energy system of the universal calibration lattice.

Next, during the "balancing" process, the practitioner places their hands on several energy centers (chakras). This touch often creates perceptible temperature changes within the body and leads into the final adjustments of the energy session. A unique feature of this non-invasive procedure is a cool or cold energy flow that often accompanies the more traditional warm or hot "healing" energy.

The Four Phases of the

EMF Balancing Technique®

- Phase I— Wisdom and Emotions
  This session releases stress and establishes a new
  pattern of freedom and well-being. Experience the
  energetic balance between head and heart.

- Phase II— Self Direction and Support
  This session gracefully releases the energy restraints
  of what we call the past, and promotes awareness of
  Self support and Self direction.

- Phase III— Radiate Core Energy
  The radiating of core energy encourages the increased
  flow of spiritual intelligence into your daily life.
  Experience new understandings and insights into
  your soul's unique expression.

- Phase IV— Energetic Accomplishment
  In this balancing, a connection and communication
  with future Self is established through the Future
  Potential Prism, channeling future potential energy
  into the co-creation of present reality.

Table 13

Mastery: The Posture of Balance

As Peggy Dubro says in her description of the EMF Balancing Technique®, a major focus of the EMF Balancing work is the posture of balance in everyday life. This golden posture of balance is challenged repeatedly as we, our Earth, and the Universe continue to calibrate to the new structures of energetic reality that are in development. As you hold this posture, and gain the higher vibrations associated with it, you will find that conditions that are out of balance may simply fall away. Then you have what many people call healing. As you hold your individual sacred balance, you also contribute great peace and stability to the collective whole. This balance, then, is a key to the expression of grace.

Remember, we have been asked to practice mastery. To gain mastery is to hold the full charge of our being. Think for a moment about what living in mastery might mean to you: an always peaceful countenance, a joyful heart, complete lack of judgment of others, patience, humor, kindness, humility, quiet, grace, and so forth. Practicing mastery includes gaining the wisdom to know when to give and when to receive. By gaining mastery over ourselves we help others achieve their mastery so that we can all hold the energy to reach Ascension. This is a loving process

(See the new book *"Elegant Empowerment,"* by Peggy Phoenix Dubro and David La Pierre, published by Platinum Press, 2002. For contact information see Appendix D.)

The Lightworker's Oath

I will always respect and value the work itself.

I will always respect and value myself and my contribution to the greater good.

I will always respect and value my client.

I will always focus my intent on raising energies to a higher level.

I will dismiss critical or negative thoughts from my mind. I will transmute such energies to higher vibrations of harmony and balance.

I will listen attentively and be supportive to my client, but not tell them how they should be feeling, or try to interpret their personal experiences for them.

I will respect the sacred confidentiality of the practitioner-client relationship.

I will keep my personal boundaries intact, but be available for my client and supportive to them as they undergo their personal growth and adjustments.

I will attend to my own personal growth and continued training as I share my gifts with others.

I will remember the ever-present connection I have to the divine and I will practice gratitude, forgiveness, compassion and prayer in my work and in my daily life.

Table 14

My Healer's Creed

To Live Deliberately and Consciously

Honoring Myself and Others, Knowing that Each Is Doing
Their Best at Any Given Moment in Time

To Understand that We Bring to Ourselves All that We Need
in Order to Discover Who We Are

To Take Responsibility for Our Actions

To Believe that All Things Are Possible

To Not Restrict the Journey by Seeking a Specific Outcome

To Remain Humble as We Find Our Universal Power

And Know that It Is the Power of All

That Our Actions Affect the Whole

To Have Faith that if We Live with Unconditional Love
All that We Truly Need Will Reveal Itself

This Is a Life of Service to this World
And All of Its Creations
Knowing We Are One

Table 15

Massage Therapy

History of Massage Therapy

Massage is the gentle, rhythmic, structured manipulation of skin and muscle tissue for therapeutic purposes. Massage as a healing art has been practiced for over 5,000 years. There are records in China dating back 4,000 years, and pictographs showing massage being done in early Egypt. Massage, in conjunction with healing oils and incense has been known for its powerful calming and rejuvenating abilities for millennia. Since it comes from our natural desire to touch and be touched in a loving way, massage in truth has probably been around almost as long as there have been humans on the planet. Today, there are over 400 different types and variations of massage, and its popularity as a healing modality has been increasing.

Despite the availability of information on massage in its various forms, our western life style today is very touch-starved. Studies have shown that on a normal day-to-day basis people seem to go out of their way to avoid touching each other. We suppress our basic needs for the touch of other humans on a regular basis. This suppression creates an "touch anxiety" which we further suppress by engaging in distracting activity such as eating or watching television. We flood our senses with sensory input in an attempt to drown out the unwanted feelings generated from a lack of intimacy with our fellow humans. Even some of the apes and chimpanzee groups that have been studied show a natural inclination on their part to touch and groom each other as part of normal social interaction. We have largely isolated ourselves from the fulfillment of this basic need. Our bodies and our hearts have paid the price for this touch deprivation. It doesn't have to be that way. We can learn to appreciate the value of therapeutic touch in our daily lives, as a method of calming and rejuvenating ourselves and as a way to help prevent the stresses and anxieties that seem to underlie many of or modern heart-related health issues.

Massage and the Heart

Massage, therapeutic touch, is good for the soul and good for the heart. It causes the body to release substances in the body, which settle our nerves and make us feel more relaxed and whole. It provides us with an increased feeling of well being, reduces blood pressure and improves circulation. As part of an overall approach to taking better care of our bodies, massage is a wonderful way to show love to others and ourselves.

There is an organization called the Touch Research Institutes which have conducted scientific studies into the benefits of massage therapy (as well as Yoga and Tai Chi) including specific benefits to those with cardiovascular disease, high blood pressure and stress and other diseases. The research is extremely strong in showing that massage therapy is a very powerful therapeutic tool for a very wide variety of issues. (See Appendix D for Contact Information).

Massage Training and Certification

Courses in massage range from 6 weeks to 6 months, depending on the depth to which you want to study particular techniques. A typical body massage lasts from 1 hour to 1-1/2 hours, and the rates vary from $50 to about $85 per treatment. The therapeutic benefits last for days or even weeks. In most areas, a massage license is required to practice. Some people work and share offices with physical therapists, chiropractors or others in the healing arts.

Benefits of Massage

The benefits of a massage can include relieving muscle pain and stress, increasing body awareness, or bringing a sense of balance and relief to someone in a stressful situation or life crisis. The benefits of massage are well known and include:

- relaxation of the muscles
- improved blood circulation
- improved functioning of the lymphatic system
- relaxation of the nervous system
- improved elimination of metabolic waste
- stretching of connective tissues
- reduction in emotional and physical stress
- increased effectiveness of the immune system
- shortening of recovery time from muscular strain
- brings about an increased feeling of calmness
- brings about an increased feeling of connectedness
- stretches the ligaments and tendons, keeping them supple
- stimulation of the skin and connective tissue
- reduces risk of premature births in pregnant women
- reduces anxiety among those smokers wishing to quit
- reduces anxiety before surgery in heart patients and others

Table 16

Massage has also been known to help alleviate a number of conditions, including such things as Fibromyalgia, high blood pressure, migraine, cluster or tension headaches, depression, insomnia, irritability, and chronic fatigue. In some cases, heart patients are given a foot massage before surgery to calm and relax them.

Massage Training and Certification

Courses in massage range from 6 weeks to 6 months, depending on the depth to which you want to study particular techniques. A typical body massage lasts from 1 hour to 1-1/2 hours, and the rates vary from $50 to about $85 per treatment. The therapeutic benefits last for days or even weeks. In most areas, a massage license is required to practice. Some people work and share offices with physical therapists, chiropractors or others in the healing arts.

Massage and Other Therapeutic Modalities

Massage can be used along with other forms of body work and energy work including Reiki. Reiki can be given before or after a massage, or even during a massage. Reiki after massage is an excellent way to balance the body's energies and open the energy system to greater inflow of higher vibrational energies. I have often used the EMF Balancing Technique® after giving a client a massage, since it is an excellent "next step" to greater calibration with the person's electromagnetic field. Massage is an excellent complement to other forms of therapeutic healing and balancing since it has a physical relaxing component and promotes grounding. It helps the client feel more comfortable in his or her body and helps calm the emotions. The benefits last long after the massage is finished and many people experience a lightness and feeling of well being that lasts for days or even longer.

Massage and Pregnancy

Massage for women who are pregnant can be a great for relieving fatigue, aches and cramps. Massage can also help the mother prepare for the birthing process in several ways. Regular gentle massage to the lower back, abdomen, and inner thighs can release chronic tension in these areas for help reduce resistance during birthing. Massage also increases the mother's awareness of tension in her body and helps teach her how to release it. Massage can help increase her confidence, strength and control during labor. Pregnant women should check with their health provider to be sure that massage is recommended for their particular set of circumstances.

Massage can help a new mother deal with the increased physical demands of caring for a newborn baby by reducing tension and increasing energy. Massage can speed healing of an episiotomy by increasing circulation. It greatly eases cramping of muscles. If the mother is nursing, a relaxing massage can help since too much muscle tension can interfere with milk letdown. A general, soothing massage is also a great way to just relax and calm the emotions and get in touch with your body again.

Baby Massage

Yes, babies can get massage too! In India it has been a custom for many, many years.

Massage is very healthy and therapeutic for babies. A video covering the technique is available, based on the book, "Infant Massage: A Handbook for Loving Parents" by Vimala McClure. (See Appendix D for Contact Information)

Massage and Those with Immune Deficiency Challenges

Therapeutic massage can be very beneficial to those with immune disorders and immune system challenges. See Appendix C, "Providing Care for People with Immune Deficiency" for guidelines.

Types of Massage

There are many varieties of therapeutic massage. Here are just a few to give you an idea of the many styles available to choose from.

• Swedish Massage

The Swedish Massage technique probably looks familiar to most people when they think of massage. It was introduced to the United States in around 1856. The Swedish massage technique employs vigorous movements to help tone the skin and muscles and stretch contracted tissue. It works to stimulate the blood's return to the heart.

• Lymphatic Massage

Lymphatic massage is a recommended treatment for many stress related syndromes including depressed immune response, digestive disorders, skin problems, edema, allergies, headaches, sinus infections, sprained muscles, and joint inflammation. Lymphatic massage's effectiveness is in facilitating the movement of lymph fluid through the body's natural filtration system as well as revitalizing the visceral organs. There are nearly twice as many lymphatic vessels in our bodies as there are blood vessels. The lymph system plays an active role in the removal of wastes and the health of our auto immune system. Lymphatic massage typically has a sedative or deeply relaxing effect where Swedish massage, depending on the techniques employed, can either be stimulating or sedative.

• Deep Tissue Massage

Deep tissue massage is more than just a deep massage. It is specifically designed to address deeply held emotional energies that have become fixed and locked within the body's physical and energy systems. Deep Tissue Massage attempts to release these stuck emotions, helping to cure such ailments as migraines, colds, gall bladder and kidney related diseases

Deep Tissue Massage is often employed to release chronic patterns of muscular tension using slow strokes, direct pressure, or friction.

Often the movements are directed against the grain of the muscles using one's fingers, thumbs, or elbows. This is applied with greater pressure than typically used in Swedish massage. Deep tissue massage usually focuses on a specific problem area.

• Trigger Point Massage/Neuromuscular Massage

This is a form of deep massage that uses concentrated finger pressure applied to specific individual muscles. The purpose of this technique is to increase blood flow and to release trigger points, intense knots of muscle tension that refer pain to other parts of the body

Trigger point massage therapy is essentially a pain-relief technique to alleviate muscle spasms and cramping. The practitioner locates and relieves or "deactivates" trigger points. The major goal of this type of massage is to reduce spasms by inducing new blood flow into the affected areas.

• Esalen Massage

Esalen Massage was developed at the famous growth center, Esalen Institute in Big Sur, California. It is a marriage between classical Swedish massage, with its precise manner of working with muscles and circulatory system, and the deeply personal sensing work brought from Germany by Charlotte Selver. Esalen techniques began to fully take shape in the early 1960's. To some, Esalen massage is more of a philosophy than a specific massage technique. The focus of Esalen Massage is on creating deeper states of relaxation, beneficial states of consciousness, and general well-being. Esalen focuses on the whole mind/body system.

• Ayurvedic Massage

Ayurveda is a holistic system of health that dates back many thousands of years. The word "Ayurveda" means essentially the "science of life." Ayurveda teaches that there are specific body types and that a knowledge of these body types is of great benefit in dealing with issues of health and healing. There is a vast amount of information in the field of Ayurvedic medicine and its various treatments and techniques are very powerful. An understanding of body types (called in Ayurveda "doshas") is also important for understanding the mind/body connection and the are of nutrition. One of the techniques available in Ayurvedic therapies is the two-person synchronized massage, which is a unique and fantastic experience.

• Sports Massage

Sports massage is designed to address the physical needs of particular athletic life styles and is different from other forms of massage. A runner, for example, would get more specific attention directed at the leg and calf muscles, whereas as swimmer might focus on upper body muscles. This can be tailored to individual needs.

• Shiatsu

Shiatsu is a Japanese style massage that focuses on the acupuncture points through the application of pressure. This type of massage can be received with or without clothes. It is often done on the floor or on a surface suitable for applying pressure to the appropriate points. It can also be done with the client on a table.

• Reflexology

Reflexology is a scientific foot massage that addresses specific areas primarily on the soles of the feet. Reflexology is based on the principal that the feet contain the end points of hundreds of nerve channels that go to all parts of the body. Every body part and organ corresponds to an area of the foot. When working with pressure on these specific areas of the foot, the energy blockages can be freed up and the corresponding area of the body can obtain the benefits of this. Reflexology eliminates tension, improves the circulation, as well as stimulates the body's natural healing processes.

• Aroma Therapy Massage/Essential Oil Therapy

This technique focuses on the use of naturally occurring essential oils applied to the skin by a trained practitioner to raise the body's vibration and promote health and well being. Different essential oils have specific healing and rejuvenating properties, especially when applied to certain parts of the body. There is a lot of material available for study in the field of aroma therapy as an adjunct to massage.

• Sensual Massage

This is a special technique specifically designed as an avenue for sensual and often sexual intimacy between couples.

• Tantric Massage

Tantric Massage is a special type of sensual massage where the emphasis is on the understanding and sensing of the human energy centers. Specific attention is placed on increasing the sexual and other energies in the human energy system. There are specific techniques for this and Tantric massage requires specific training and an understanding of the human energy anatomy. Tantric massage includes subtle erotic stimulation that improves hormonal regulation and provides unique benefits in the area of freeing up trapped energies and energizing energy centers.

Massage Therapy Preparation Checklist

1. Establish an agreed-upon time frame and place for the massage.
2. Prepare the room, ensure it is clean and comfortable.
3. Ensure that there will be no interruptions.
4. Lighting should be soft and preferably adjustable.
5. Temperature should be warm enough for client.
6. Have small fan for circulation if needed.
7. Have background music available, suitable to your client's tastes.
8. Use continuous play on CD or tape player. (no radio)
9. Check client's tolerance and preferences for incense or oils before using.
10. Incense or oil diffusers to help set atmosphere and cleanse room.
11. Gently warm the massage oil to be used.
12. Have table clean with clean sheets and towels available.
13. Headrest should be clean and paper inserts used if possible.
14. Have knee/leg rests available for client if needed. Chair for practitioner if desired.
15. Have a non-ticking clock available to check time.
16. Have water available for client and practitioner.
17. Turn off phones, pagers, etc.
18. Practitioner's hands should be clean, nails cut short, hands warm.
19. Practitioner avoids using perfume or cologne.
20. Check breath and personal hygiene.
21. Ensure oils have nothing in them to which client may be allergic or sensitive.
22. Allow clients to remove clothes in private. Come back in when they are ready.
23. Oils are put on hands, never squirted or poured on client's body. (No turkey basting.)

Table 17

Interpersonal Relationships and

the Dynamics of the New Energy

"Every Drama in your outer life is a reflection of a drama in your inner life. Every person you are interacting with in your outer life symbolizes an interaction of energy going on within you."

—Orin/Sanaya Roman,
Personal Power Through Awareness

"Only in relationship can you know yourself, not in abstraction and certainly not in isolation."

—J. Krishnamurti

Axiom

It is through relationships with others that we learn to understand the nature of our energy flows, and discover the impact that our daily intentions have upon our reality.

We will always draw to ourselves what we have focused our intent on. The universe responds to our intent. It shows us what we are projecting, what we are creating. It is a reflection back to us of our deepest feelings, fears, desires and expectations.

We are energy beings. That is our essential nature.

At any given time, each of us has a multitude of human-to-human energy interactions taking place where we interact with others at an emotional, psychological, physical and spiritual level. These we call our relationships. Relationships and their various dynamics are what we use to explore the mysteries of ourselves and our world.

It is through our relationships that we connect with our world. We create and project an energetic sphere around us, which holds the emotional resonance of our inner intentions, feelings and desires. Emotion is the key. An "e-motion" is energy in motion. When we "emote" we create an energy atmosphere around us that corresponds to our intent. If our intent is for a loving, heart connection, then our energetic atmosphere will be one of high vibrational energy that resonates with love energy. If our intention is only to "get" things from the world, whether it is possessions, money, fame or control over others, our energetic field will resonate in accordance with these lower level vibrational patterns.

Difficulties we experience in our personal relationships, especially those relationships that are both intimate and intense, are reflections of areas in ourselves where we are struggling with issues of understanding our own inner intentions.

It is astonishing to discover that most of the time we do not even know what we are intending. It is as if we have put our tremendous power of "creation through intent," on "automatic pilot." The universe is still responding to what we are intending in our daily lives, even if we have momentarily lost sight of what we are intending. In many cases, we have let our desires, wants and expectations slip just a notch below our conscious awareness. We then wonder at the difficulties we encounter in trying to relate to others. We wonder why our love relationships do not seem to go as smoothly as we would hope. Some of us wonder why we cannot even seem to get started in a relationship. Others, repeat the same relationship patterns over and over and over again, even though they realize the unhealthy nature of the patterns and can even predict their own upcoming "failure." If we are powerful, creative beings, and we have the ability to create our own "reality," why is all this happening? Do we wake up each morning and say to ourselves "Today I am going to create relationship difficulties and emotional tensions so that I can discover my hidden inner intents as they manifest in my outer world." I don't think so.

The problem is not that we are powerless in the face of cosmic fate or some kind of hidden karma. The cause of many of our difficulties in relationships is our lack of awareness of our own intent. We project conflicting intents. We project intent with our feeling centers, and then expect the universe to match what we desire to see manifest with our rational, thinking centers. The two do not usually match. We often demand that the universe provide us with what we desire in exactly the form we want it to appear. The universe, however, responds at a much higher vibrational level. The universe provides us with what we "need" in order to understand, heal or balance our energies at any given time. We are always being presented with opportunities for growth at every moment in our lives. When these opportunities do not match our analytical expectations, i.e., what we "think" we should be getting, we often dismiss these opportunities for growth.

What can we do to better understand our own deeper intentions and achieve greater balance in our relationships and our lives? I believe that it is highly beneficial for us to focus our conscious intent on the higher vibrational energies of love, in all our human-to-human interactions. This means we should focus our conscious intent on the highest good for others. As we focus on higher level concepts (love, light, balance, unboundedness, harmony) we actually create real, tangible energetic vibrations that resonate with these higher ideals. This is not imaginary thinking. This is a real, physical universe manifestation of energy, which is under your direct conscious control.

What does all this have to do with the dynamics of the new energy? What can we do on a practical, physical level? The "New Energy" is the influx of higher vibrational energies that have been coming into the Earth system for some time. (See Lee Carroll/ Kryon, *"Letters from Home"*). It is the energy of responsibility and of conscious awareness of our roles as co-creators of our experiences. It is important at this period in our evolution to work at a conscious level with others, on a human-to-human basis, so that we may adjust to and thrive in this new, higher vibrational energy. Working to align ourselves with this new energy "lattice" is a vital part of the balancing process that is key to our personal growth and human relationship growth that provides us the loving energy that feeds our soul.

What does "being in balance" mean in terms of energy? The New Energy Dynamics requires that we have a greater understanding of ourselves as energy beings. Being *in balance* means that your energy fields and energy centers are open to the natural flow of energy in and out of your system as you interact with other people and with your environment. Being out of balance is a condition where the energies of the body are out of phase to a point where their natural and graceful of flow is impeded. Anxiety, depression and emotional trauma are the result of an out-of-balance condition. They are manifestations of an imbalance in the body's use of energy or power. Physical ailments may manifest if such imbalances are allowed to continue for any length of time. It is highly beneficial to seek out techniques that help you to balance your personal energy frequencies, to balance your body's electromagnetic fields with the new spiritual energies now becoming available to us on a global scale. On such method is the EMF Balancing Technique® (Peggy Dubro).

In addition to your own personal energy frequencies, you tend to develop resonance frequencies with people that you spend a lot of time with, such as friends, family, co-workers, that are familiar to both you and them. In your daily relationships, you co-create these energy wavelengths in order to have a familiar frame of reference. Some people are only comfortable with certain wavelengths of energy. They may not be comfortable with your natural, basic energies. If you have to interact with such people, both you and they tend to create other energies that appear to be compatible, so you can use theses as a common frame of reference. This is the energetic equivalent of the "social persona" that masks the person's true wavelengths. You may have heard people say, "I just can't be myself around him (or her)." They cannot comfortably exhibit their own basic wavelengths. Therefore, they create a false energy wavelength as a "cover" so that others can interact with them more comfortably. Doing this too often or too intently is unhealthy for the person doing it. If we are to experience life's beauty and interact with others in a meaningful way, we need to feel comfortable exhibiting and residing in our own energy wavelengths.

Remember that you are a beautiful energetic being of light and love. Your heart energies and your interactions with others on a human-to-human level are directly influenced by the nature and quality of your intent. Through your own intent, and with guidance, you have the ability to co-create a higher level of energy, vitality and quality of life in all your interactions with your environment. Your personal relationships will directly reflect your progress on your path to self empowerment and understanding. Your conscious choices in accepting opportunities to love that the universe presents to you, will determine the quality of your experience.

The most important aspect to understand about the new energy dynamics is that they are the underlying framework for our relationships with ourselves and with others. The power of our intent, how we use and direct this energy, is both a blessing and a responsibility. We are an aspect of this new energy and we share its intelligence. It responds to our intent. We are never separate from it.

Making a Heart Connection— Radiating Heart Energy

As you focus on your heart center, put your attention on the feelings of love that resonate in the center of your being. As you maintain your attention on this feeling, it will grow and expand. Radiate this feeling of love outward to another person.

If you are alone, visualize someone you know and send them love energy from your heart. This is a real energy that will travel outward from your heart center to the heart center of the other person. They do not have to know you are doing this, but you both will benefit. At some level, even at great distances, they will know this is occurring.

Radiating heart energy is a skill you can develop and use to improve your relationships with others and especially your relationship with yourself.

It is often helpful to visualize heart energy traveling like a beam of light outward from your heart center in the middle of your chest. Some people can visualize this in their mind's eye, to others it is just a "feeling." To some people it is both an image and a feeling. Whatever works best for you is fine. You will increase your ability to generate and radiate heart energy as you practice this on yourself and on others.

Radiating Heart Energy works on the Quantum Physics principle of non-locality. Your love energy exists simultaneously with the love energy of another. Your conscious intent to focus on increasing your love energies will cause a simultaneous increase in the vibrational state of the one you are focused on. Time and distance are no barriers to this transference. It is a simultaneous resonance

The following exercise will help you sense, feel and radiate heart energy to another. Try this exercise at least once a day for a week and see how your ability to focus on heart energy increases.

Practice this Activity: Radiating Heart Energy

Steps:

1. Go to a quiet, comfortable place where you will not be disturbed. (Note: someone can also do this exercise in a hospital or recovery environment quite easily.)

2. Visualize in your mind someone you want to make a heart connection with.

3. Mentally focus your intention and your sense of feeling, on the Heart Center in the middle area of your chest. You may experience this as a feeling of warmth. Like a thick, warm cloud of energy. There is a definite feeling associated with this center. Focus on that area until you sense the feeling. It is a feeling as if you have touched something non-physical, but alive. Focus your awareness on this center. Feel its warmth.

4. Draw into your mind the visual image and/or sensations of someone that you know, someone you want to share your heart energy with. As that image grows stronger in your mind, gently pull that image down into your Heart Center. Hold it gently and lovingly in your Heart. Feel the warmth of your Heart Center connecting with the heart Center of the other person.

5. Feel the heart energies of the other person. Focus on their energy merging slowly with yours. Feel the melting and merging of the energies of your heart and theirs, coming into resonance. Feel them vibrating together, in rhythm, in harmony, in perfect equilibrium and balance.

6. To maintain this visualization, it is often helpful to focus on the following concepts, by repeating these words to yourself silently. Doing so will actually increase the energy vibration of your heart center as your intent generates the energetic patterns associated with each of the concepts represented by the words. Go through this list several times slowly, silently. (See Table 4 for an expanded list.)

- Love
- Peace
- Beauty
- Unity
- Compassion
- Wholeness

7. As you progress through this process of making a heart connection, you will feel as if your hearts are both resonating at the same vibration. You may feel other emotions as well, as your heart centers are activated. Focus on the highest vibrations possible. Hold this feeling and let it build and rise higher and higher. Remember to breathe comfortably, stay relaxed.

8. You may hold this feeling for as long as it is comfortable. Several minutes, perhaps longer. When you feel the energies are stable at a high level, you may acknowledge the depth of the link, and ease off. To end of, send a strong "Thank You" intention to the heart center of the other person. Then send the same "Thank You" intent to your own heart center.

Relax and breathe normally. You may want to further close this exercise by taking a short walk silently and alone, noticing your surroundings. You may experience a greater feeling of connection with your environment, including people, animals, plants and even the physical objects around you. Acknowledge this connection.

Axiom

Gratitude is both an acknowledgement to the universe that you recognize and accept its gifts and a validation to yourself that you are indeed worthy of accepting them.

Gratitude at the beginning of a relationship brings joy and new energies

Gratitude during a relationship brings a sense of deeper bonding.

Gratitude at the end of a relationship helps bring closure and a restoration of integrity, so that new beginnings can emerge.

Relationship Cleansing

Relationships as Exchanges of Energy

This section describes a very powerful yet simple exercise you can do with yourself to help unlock stuck energies. You will not believe how powerful this exercise is, until you actually try it.

The purpose of this exercise is to free up trapped energies, portions of your spirit, that are still connected to past relationships. These relationships can be of any kind, from intimate love relationships, to family, friends and co-workers. Every person you have ever known has had an energetic relationship with you, meaning a relationship on an energy level. Every relationship, no matter how long lasting or brief, involves an exchange of energy.

Some relationships deal heavily with the exchange of energy in its aspects of power and control. These relationships in particular can be powerful influences on our personal energy field, and their effects can last for many years, even a lifetime (or longer).

Attaining Closure in Relationships: Achieving Balance

In fact, just when is a relationship "over"? If you are still carrying an energetic connection to some emotional event of a past relationship, consciously or unconsciously, and this energetic connection holds part of your spirit, then to some degree you are still carrying on a active relationship. You don't have to be physically seeing this person on a daily basis to be carrying on an energetic interchange with them. From the field of quantum physics, the principle of "non-locality" describes just how our energies affect others at a distance, instantaneously. We maintain energetic connections long after relationships appear to have ended. If your relationships were of a loving kind, there is no problem with remaining in a loving state with regard to that person.

Sending love energy consciously to ones we have known in the past is a wonderful gift, and is healing for both people involved. However, if you have unresolved emotional issues or traumatic experiences with someone that were never fully resolved, you are carrying forward into present time the energetic connection with that person. This type of energetic connection actually drains some of your personal power *away from* present time. If you consider how many relationships we have over the course of our lives that involve unresolved issues of power and control, you can quickly see how this cumulative effect can be a source of tremendous drain to our energetic bodies, sapping our zest and vitality for life.

Acknowledgement, Gratitude, Forgiveness, Love, Releasing
As you do this exercise, you will be actively collecting past residual energies from relationships you had thought were over, as well as from relationships which may be ongoing currently. The power of recall, acknowledgement and forgiveness from the heart will help you balance these energies now, in present time.

Practice this Activity: Relationship Cleansing

What you will be doing in this exercise is a simple process involving 5 non-verbal intentions.

1. Acknowledgement
First, you will be recalling a person whom you have or had a relationship with and first acknowledging them as a being. This is where you become aware of the energetic connection you still have with that person. As you "reconnect" with these old energy flows, you open the door to resolving unbalanced energies. As you visualize this person, you give the intention of acknowledgement. This validates the energetic connection you both have with each other.

2. Gratitude
The second step is to give the intent of gratitude for all that person has brought into your life. Gratitude helps open the heart and balances the energy of giving with the energy of receiving.

3. Forgiveness
The third step is to give the intent of forgiveness. Forgive the person for all actions or inaction on their part that you feel has harmed you or held you back in any way. This includes small things for which you feel a "tinge" of resentment toward them, to larger things such as betrayal or actual physical or emotional

harm. Forgiveness releases negative energy from YOUR energy field. By giving the intent to forgive, you are actually healing your own wounds first. Forgiveness of others is a gift to self.

4. Love

The fourth step is to give the intent of love for that person. The intent to love is an affirmation that we are all woven from the same fabric and are children of the universe. The intent to give love consciously opens your heart and affirms your desire to increase your vibration to a higher level. The intent for conscious love is a blessing for you and the other person, and is a real energy that will flow to their heart and lift their vibration higher.

5. Releasing

The fifth step is to give the intent to release the other person from any remaining attachments you have to them, and release them from any thought forms that you may have been imposing on them. This is a powerful step where you bring back your own energy and spirit from where you had sent it previously. Recalling your own energies ultimately brings you greater ability to be focused in present time, and gives you the ability to more fully act with conscious choice-making in determining your own empowered future. Releasing is powerful and is simply done by giving the intent to release. You may give the intent more than once if you wish. You will know when the release has been done.

Releasing a person in this way does not necessarily mean you will never see them again, it does mean that your energetic connection to this person will be at a higher vibrational level. Your connection will not be one of forced, karmic interaction. You will be able to function from a position of empowerment. In many cases, your relationship with this person will take a rapid shift after completing this process.

Practice this Activity:

A 10-Minute Chakra Meditation

This is a very simple yet very powerful meditation on the chakras that you can perform easily in about 10 minutes or less. It has an energizing effect on the chakras as well as a cleansing effect on one's energy field.

This exercise works with the Kundalini energy which is very powerful. Do not do this exercise for more than 10 minutes unless you are experienced with Kundalini energies.

During the preparation phase at the beginning, you may also have incense, a candle and your favorite uplifting music in the background. None of these things should be so intense as to distract you from focusing on the visualizations of the Chakras, however.

The overall purpose of this exercise is energizing and cleansing.

Steps:

Preparation: Sit in a quiet place where you will not be disturbed.

Breathe quietly and calmly. Do not force your breathing, but become conscious of its pattern. Loosen any tight clothing so you can breath comfortably.

1. Focus your attention on the First or Root chakra at the base of your spine. Inhale slowly for a count of five, then exhale slowly for a count of five. Don't focus on the counting, focus on the image of the Root chakra spinning and the breath you are inhaling circling the chakra as you breath in. Relax as you breath out, but

do not spin the chakra in reverse on the exhale. Let it continue to spin normally on both the inhale and the exhale.

Visualize the chakra in your mind's eye as clearly as possible. Sense its location in your body and sense its "feeling" as you do the breathing. If you cannot get a visual image or feeling, just imagine that you are seeing and feeling it. The effect will ultimately be the same.

2. Next, focus your attention on the Second or Naval Chakra at the Sexual energy center. Inhale slowly for a count of five, then exhale slowly for a count of five. As you do this, imagine or visualize the energy flowing up through the root chakra, to the sexual center and wrapping itself around the sexual center chakra. Don't focus on the counting, focus instead on the image of the chakra spinning and the breath you are inhaling circling the chakra as you breath in.

3. Next, focus your attention on the Third or Solar Plexus Chakra. Inhale slowly for a count of five, then exhale slowly for a count of five. As you do this, imagine or visualize the energy flowing up through the root chakra, to the sexual center and up to the Solar Plexus chakra and wrapping itself around the Solar Plexus chakra. Don't focus on the counting, focus instead on the image of the chakra spinning and the breath you are inhaling circling the chakra as you breath in.

4. Next, focus your attention on the Fourth or Heart Chakra at the center of the chest. Inhale slowly for a count of five, then exhale slowly for a count of five. As you do this, imagine or visualize the energy flowing up through the root chakra, to the Sexual center, up to the Solar Plexus Chakra, to the Heart Chakra and wrapping itself around the Heart Chakra. Don't focus on the counting, focus instead on the image of the chakra spinning and

the breath you are inhaling circling the chakra as you breath in. The feeling associated here is Love.

5. Next, focus your attention on the Fifth or Throat Chakra. Inhale slowly for a count of five, then exhale slowly for a count of five. As you do this, imagine or visualize the energy flowing up through the root chakra, to the Sexual center, up to the Solar Plexus Chakra, through the Heart Chakra, to the Throat Chakra and wrapping itself around the this Chakra. Don't focus on the counting, focus instead on the image of the chakra spinning and the breath you are inhaling circling the chakra as you breath in. The feeling associated here is that of truth.

6. Next, focus your attention on the Sixth Chakra, the location of the Third Eye or Ajna Center. Inhale slowly for a count of five, then exhale slowly for a count of five. As you do this, imagine or visualize the energy flowing up through the root chakra, to the Sexual center, up to the Solar Plexus Chakra, through the Heart Chakra, to the Throat Chakra, to the Sixth Chakra and wrapping itself around the this Chakra. Don't focus on the counting, focus instead on the image of the chakra spinning and the breath you are inhaling circling the chakra as you breath in. The feeling associated here is that of insight and inner vision.

7. Next, focus your attention on the Seventh or Crown Chakra located at the top of the head. Inhale slowly for a count of five, then exhale slowly for a count of five. As you do this, imagine or visualize the energy flowing up through the root chakra, to the Sexual center, up to the Solar Plexus Chakra, through the Heart Chakra, to the Throat Chakra, through the Sixth Chakra and to the Seventh Chakra and wrapping itself around the this Chakra. Don't focus on the counting, focus instead on the image of the chakra spinning and the breath you are inhaling circling

the chakra as you breath in. The feeling associated here is that of wisdom.

As you work your way through this exercise, you will feel the energy flowing up your spine, getting stronger as it moves towards the Crown Chakra. If you encounter distracting thoughts during this process, just let them pass. Do not focus on them. When you have finished, you may feel lightness and a tingling sensation. This is the energy working within you. Relax and use this opportunity to expand your thoughts to higher levels of consciousness.

Chapter Four

Personal Experiences
with Healing, Spiritual Growth
and the Energy of the Heart

The following pages contains several very powerful and personal accounts of subtle energy at work, shared by those who have worked directly with these energies. These are stories from the heart, reflecting courage, compassion and a willingness to share.

Healing from the Heart

Heart energy is the most powerful energy in the universe. I have found through my own experience of working with heart energy as a Reiki Master that when the heart is open, and the vibration of love energy can enter the body, it is here where that healing occurs. This is not an easy process. The human body has stored years of accumulated acknowledged and unacknowledged hurts and sorrows. Blockages on a physical level manifest and occur to protect the body from incurring more pain and sorrow. Ironically, the more blockages we create, the more isolation we feel from our essence and the essence of others. Heart energy is present energy in its purest form. When a person "comes from the heart" they come from love.

My intent in a Reiki session is to "enlighten" or to actually bring light into the body. This is done with unconditional love as well as technique. In doing so I must create an energy field that feels safe to the person. When a person feels safe, they can trust, and it is there where their body, mind and spirit relax and the heart can begin to open. I am completely in the moment of now and the outcome of our session becomes non-existent. I am not the healer per se. I am the conduit for healing to occur. If I feel resistance, or an area that needs particular attention, I use color as a channel to bring light and love into the body. When the color turns from a murky to clear I know that the person has made the adjustment necessary to correct the imbalance.

I have no judgment when exchanging energy with a person in a Reiki session, but I have made certain observations. People that feel a sense of responsibility for where they are in their lives and feel the power to be able to change their lives seem to feel at more peace with themselves by the end of our session than people who feel they are victims. I have also found this to be true with people who realize that our energy exchange is not a passive experience, but rather an active one. They may be sound asleep, but on other levels of consciousness they are actively engaged.

My honest intent as a therapist of alternative healing modalities is to help raise the vibration of heart love energy throughout the universe. When I am exchanging heart energy with one person and sending them love, I am exchanging heart energy and love with the collective consciousness of the world. Separateness is a mind thought, Oneness is heart energy.

—Marilyn Schaal
Reiki Master
Senior Cardiac Technician

Reiki and the Heart

Over the last five years of doing Reiki treatments, I have worked with many people who have had heart issues, either physical or emotional. Some have been due to childhood issues, some have resulted from negative love relationships, and others have stored different negative emotions in their hearts over the years.

Reiki helps to release these negative emotions in the heart and replaces them with the high vibration Reiki energy. As these negative emotions and energies release, people become happier, more peaceful, loving, and more open to give, as well as receive love. This also applies to people with physical heart problems, such as rapid heart beat, heart attacks and any sort of heart pain. The only requirement for good health, mentally, emotionally, physically and spiritually is the intent of the person to heal. I have seen many "miracles" occur through Reiki.

Recently, I worked with a couple who were having extreme marital difficulties. The wife was ready to file for divorce but decided to try Reiki as a last resort. She started coming to me for Reiki and within days of her first session, things had already started to shift. She was able to release much of her anger that originated in her childhood. She was doing so well that her husband also started coming in for Reiki sessions.

The husband had an energetic protective shell around him, which kept people at a distance. He had a lot of fear of getting close to people and was addicted to alcohol. Through Reiki, he released his fear of intimacy and his craving for alcohol. His heart started to open.

They are both still receiving Reiki from me and they tell me their marriage is better than ever. They have connected at a deeper level, and their relationship is more loving than either of them ever imagined it could be.

This is the miracle of Reiki. Have the intent to open your heart, and your life will become filled with love, peace and joy.

—Sharon Wegrzyn
Reiki Master/Teacher
Karuna Reiki Master/Teacher

A Healing of the Heart

My personal experience with healing of the heart energy is that it is a lot like peeling away the layers of an onion. You think you are completely healed and another layer is exposed. This can be disheartening except that with every layer that is peeled away you gain new tools to use in the future so the process seems to get easier and quicker!

This healing of the heart is greatly enhanced through Wholistic healing techniques such as Yoga, Reiki, and EMF Balancing Technique®.

One of the most dramatic heart openings I ever experienced was like an ice pick cracking the "armor" of my own heart. I received this healing through two very dear Reiki Master friends of mine in a very brief but thorough healing session in 1984. This cracking of the armor paved the way to incredible heart healing.

"Armor" happens as our hearts are hardened through the tragedies of living. My father was an angry alcoholic who took it out mostly on my mother, who was an enabler. There is a lot of my childhood I do not remember because it was too horrible. At the age of two I was sexually abused by my grandfather. I started to remember as I sought healing for the dysfunctional areas of my life. By that time, my grandfather had already died.

These dysfunctional areas included paralytic migraine headaches from the age of fifteen that Western Medicine had no reason or cure for. By the time I was twenty-one my co-workers had to take me by the hand and lead me out of the office and drive me home because I could not see or talk, and could barely walk. I also had sexual dysfunction that did not allow me to live a fulfilled sexual life.

I have been practicing Yoga since 1979 and teaching since 1986 as a relief from my migraine headaches through deep breathing and relaxation techniques. I have also been receiving Reiki healing since 1984, practicing since 1988, and began teaching in 1993. December 2000 I became a teacher of EMF® Balancing Technique to further enhance my development and teaching skills.

In my twenty-two years experience with the Wholistic healing arts, I've noticed that they work from the inside out. The healing energy brings up from the subconscious mind those things that are creating problems in our life to the conscious mind so they can be processed, healed and brought into wholeness. All we need is a sincere desire and heart felt willingness to be free and whole.

With the migraine headaches I realized that I was holding in my emotions and not expressing my true needs because as a child I thought it was safer to be seen and not heard. Always be a good girl, don't cause waves, and you'll be left alone. As an adult this caused a tremendous amount of internal pressure on my mind and body. I allowed my co-workers to use me as a doormat and internalized all the resentment and anger. Through a series of events, a lot of my anger and frustration was vented one day on an unfortunate co-worker back in the late 80's. Because I spoke out for myself, I won the respect of all my co-workers and I have been speaking from my heart ever since. As long as I continue to speak my truth from my heart I am free of migraines.

As far as the sexual dysfunction, I started consciously working on this in 1994-1996. Through a series of Reiki sessions I was guided to the inner knowing about the root of the problem and was given a higher understanding of all the events and people involved and was able to find peace in my own mind and body. Today, I am completely free of this dysfunction. Thank you God!!!

I have witnessed this over and over in my clients who come for healing from some dysfunction in their life whether it be mental (child or sexual abuse), emotional (depression) or physical (over weight, diabetes, cancer, MS, alcohol and drug abuse). Most often these clients become Wholistic practitioners also.

I am thrilled to say that both my parents are Reiki Masters and are living happily together, celebrating their 48th year of marriage! What a healing of their hearts.

—Melinda M. DeBoer
International Wholistic Health Consultant
Sr. Licensed Reiki Master/Teacher
International Center for Reiki Training
Southfield, Michigan,USA
www.reikifire.com

Heart's Energy— Spirit's Wisdom

Several years ago, my guides gave me a wonderful process for working to restore heart back into the lives of my clients. I am a spiritual coach working with people who want to bring balance into their lives and live from a place of spirit's wisdom— the name of my business. The first time I used this as directed by my guides, the results were phenomenal for my client. Never have I seen such a dramatic shift in such a short period of time. I since have used it as a very important tool in connecting clients with their spiritual essence and it has always brought heart to their lives. Let me share one of many stories with you.

Carolyn was in her early 40's, overweight, working in a technical industry, was in a 6-year relationship and was depressed. In her words, all of this was "way past stale." Her life seemed to be heavy, no fun and she said she was depressed with it all and didn't see things getting any better. She felt stuck. I thought that this was a perfect moment to use the process my spirit guides had given me. I named it the "Essence Recovery Pattern." I knew "talking" about it wouldn't get us much movement since it was so analytical and fit too easily into her technical programming track.

What I love about the process they gave me is that it bypasses intellect and takes the client into an altered state to just feel. I went through the first steps of the process and asked her to find words to describe what she was feeling even though the words would be inadequate. She described peace, a rightness, energy movement, openness. There was no blame, wrong or right, and no shoulds in this place. Her heart truly opened to who she is. I could feel her spirit expanding and breathing life into her body. Within 30 minutes, her face was flushed with excitement. Tears were running down her face as she finally re-connected with her essence. This process acts much like a soul retrieval I was taught from my shaman teacher, yet it is almost playful.

Her spirit infused her body with its essence and she said her heart was open, fresh like a cool wind had just blown out all the cobwebs. In a neutral yet truthful tone she said, "There's no heart in anything I have going on right now." Just a neutral knowing of truth. I asked her "How can you live more fully from this place you are experiencing now?". In the next half an hour, we mapped out what steps she could take that would support her having heart in her life for real. She was renewed and said she hadn't felt this much energy for many years. It felt good.

Over the next several months, Carolyn was to ask herself this question with everything she did; "Does this have heart for me?" This question and the feeling I anchored in for her using NLP (Neuro-Linguistic Programming) helped her to make many needed and timely changes in her life. She lost significant weight, completed and exited her relationship, and quit her job. She is now working in a field that holds heart for her every day. She is in relationship with herself for the time being and exploring her lost dreams and what has heart for her.

Without the heart experience generated from this process, it would be daunting to make the magnitude of changes Carolyn made in just a few short months. When we are connected to our essence and it reveals truth to us, our heart opens. Once the connection is made, it becomes easier to go for what we want. When we step outside the heart place, we tend to give up on our dreams, live for other people, live from the small ego place. Heart is the only security we have. It will not lie to us. It will reveal ourselves to ourselves. From our hearts, life is God in joy.

—Linda Nichole Carrington, Ph.D.,
Intuitive Certified Life Coach and energy worker.
President of Spirit's Wisdom, specializing in intuitive coaching
for professional, personal and spiritual goals
Coachcarrington @aol.com

Heart Center Clearing

I would like to share the following two memorable experiences my husband Michael and I had when clearing the heart center of two of my clients.

While clearing the front heart center in Phase I of the EMF Balancing Technique, our client, a sensitive opened her eyes and stared right through me with a rapt expression on her face. She then exclaimed, "I am surrounded by a choir of golden Angels." She later remarked, I have never seen so much gold energy in one place before. While I was doing the session, I felt like I no longer had arms. They were simply a part of the energy. This woman is a metaphysician for many years and is the owner of the Metaphysical Store/Center where I do much of my work.

In a second experience with another client during an EMF Balancing Technique session, my client saw a golden being appear by her head as I worked on the high heart center in the back. She also is a sensitive and works at the center.

—Patricia Lawn and Michael Lawn
Reiki Masters
EMF Balancing Technique Advanced Practitioners/Teachers

The Power of Subtle Energy Healing

I'd like to briefly share three of my many experiences with the power of subtle energy healing.

The first story is of a young man who unfortunately reached a place in his life and thought he had run out of options. In a desperate state of mind he sought solace from his pain in the self-destructive manner of attempting suicide. I was asked to come in and help as a healer to do whatever I could to help. When I first encountered him he was in the intensive care unit ("ICU") on life support, unable to utter a sound and unaware of anyone in the room. He had many friends who stayed at the hospital day and night and prayed for his recovery. His mother had requested that the members of his faith pray for him and if anyone knew of someone that might assist with trying to save his life. I worked with a member of his church and through that connection I offered to do whatever I could. As I would scan his body in between my use of Therapeutic Touch (a subtle energy healing modality) I encouraged his family to persevere in their efforts by touching and speaking to him continually as well.

Fortunately this young man had a very open-minded nurse attending to him during this critical period who supported whatever efforts were used to help him. I came back to work with him several times. On several of those occasions I was joined by a colleague of mine, Teresa, who uses color and sound therapy. We noticed after a short time that he pressed his brother's hand and smiled up at him. Up until that time, the doctors had little hope for his recovery. Today, he continues to improve slowly. It is our hopes that he will soon be able to live a normal and healthy life.

My second story is that of a cardiac surgery patient. This particular patient was experiencing an abnormal amount of bleeding after his surgery. The operation had gone smoothly yet after his surgery he starting bleeding. Although every patient certainly has their own unique experience, in this case this particular patient required an excessive amount of combined efforts to stop his bleeding. We exhausted our energies and blood products to try and stop his bleeding. Then finally the physician looked at me and told me to go and do my thing. So I went to assess the patient and do my "thing" (subtle energy work) and came back with a positive report for the doctor. The surgeon still does not understand what I did nor did he really care. He felt if it could help, why not? It continually amazes me how until we reach desperation and exhaustion, we often fail to open up to other possibilities. In this case it helped keep a patient from coming back to surgery again and possibly opened the physician's eyes to other possibilities in the area of healing.

My third story surrounds a patient who came for an open-heart procedure who was quite ill. He was a young man in his 50's who had to have a valve replacement and coronary artery bypass grafts. He had some complications and needed a balloon pump insertion into his femoral artery to help the pumping of his heart. This unfortunately caused some problems for blood supply to his foot. After a few days the doctors were talking about the possibility that he might loose his foot. I had been talking and working with him and he confided in me his concern that after all he had gone through what would he do if he was to loose his foot. I suggested we partner and work together to heal his leg and increase the circulation. I would encourage him to visualize that he had circulation in his foot. We worked everyday together and he did indeed walk out of the hospital. To my knowledge he has done well and continues to do so.

—Patty Rosser, Cardiac Nurse
Therapeutic Touch Practitioner
Host of "Adventures in Health", *Access Sacramento* (TV)

The Heart in Transition

In 1999, my father died of cancer. Although after his initial examination the doctor said he had about 6 months left to live, he only survived another 8 weeks. He was the second oldest of 15 children, and had 3 children of his own. His loss was felt by many. With the help of my brother and sister and myself, my mother moved out of her home, which she could no longer maintain, and into a small but comfortable apartment. After 46 years of marriage, she was suddenly on her own. My mother is someone who had given much support and encouragement to other people throughout her life. After my dad's death, friends and family tried to be very supportive to her during this difficult time. She said that the hardest part of the adjustment was that she did not like living alone. In less than 10 months, she too was also diagnosed with cancer. Since my mother and I were 3,000 miles apart, distance energy work was possible, but not regular in person treatments. When sensing her energy, I felt her heart was very heavy, and the treatment with drugs being given by the hospital was taking its toll on her physical strength. She carried pain in her heart from a difficult childhood, and the recent loss of my father seemed to add a weight to that. I felt her accept the Reiki energy channeled toward her, but I also felt a reluctance on her part to accept more.

I sensed that her spirit knew that recovery for her would have meant continuing to live alone, without my father and the life they had become used to. There was no mechanism for introducing alternative treatments at this stage and this was not something that was part of her belief systems. Still, the presence of loving energy, in person or over a distance, from her three children was of great comfort to her during this time. This I could feel very strongly. I felt that the distance energy treatments gave us a connection that was otherwise not possible due to physical separation. Very soon after her hospital treatment for the cancer began, she died suddenly of heart failure. Longer term suffering, at least, was spared her. Things do not always work out the way we would like to have them work out. But I believe that spirit is part of our lives at every minute and that all things happen in support of a higher purpose. Perhaps this is a reminder that we do not control the outcome of our journey, but only the manner in which we choose to view our experiences. I believe that the distance energy sessions may have eased her transition somewhat, and I am grateful that during her life, she was able share so much with others and with me.

—Mark Greenia
Massage Therapist, Reiki Master
EMF Balancing Technique Practitioner

Reiki and the Heart Energy

Reiki is the essence of unconditional love. Its presence in my life has served as a catalyst for personal and spiritual growth. As a Reiki Master teacher and practitioner, many people have looked to me for guidance and support as they have journeyed toward greater health and well-being. However, one client comes to mind, who through her profound love and generosity, guided me to a greater understanding of healing. Her example taught me to appreciate the miraculous power of our heart connection with others.

Barbara was the first client who walked through the door when I opened my Reiki center in Kentucky several years ago. She was deeply spiritual and believed in the power of hands-on healing. Barbara was so eager to experience Reiki that she took advantage of my special offer – 3 treatments for the price of 2. During the initial two sessions, I noticed a considerable amount of congested energy around her heart. I asked if she was aware of any problems in that area and she conceded that she had been experiencing chest pains. As I worked with the Reiki energy at each of her chakras, Barbara spontaneously began to offer forgiveness to every person who came to mind, including herself. She understood the connection between physical symptoms and mental/emotional issues. She consciously took responsibility for holding onto past hurts and chose to release them. On my recommendation, she also scheduled a check-up with her physician. We both felt serious concern for her health.

Barbara was anxious to return for her third Reiki treatment while she awaited the results of her medical tests. She was eager to avoid any possibility of surgery. She had one more session left and that was all she could afford. When she called to set up a time there was hesitation in her voice and then surprisingly she announced that she wanted to offer her session to a friend as a gift certificate. Joan was a professional woman in a high stress position. Barbara felt Joan needed the treatment more than she did. I knew how much Barbara enjoyed being immersed in the Reiki energies during a treatment. In light of her recent health problems, she especially needed time to relax and to heal herself. I questioned her decision at first, but with great faith, she reaffirmed that it was the right thing for her to do. I offered to send Barbara distant Reiki as an alternative to an actual hands-on session. I intuitively knew not to interfere with her generous act of kindness.

When Joan arrived for a Reiki treatment, she was nervous and self-conscious not knowing what to expect. I assured her that Reiki would help her relax and would allow her own healing abilities to bring her body back into balance. At the time I assumed that she was there for stress reduction only. I knew nothing of her medical history. During the session, however, I was drawn to work at her heart center. Four days after the treatment I received a phone call from Barbara informing me that Joan had been diagnosed with a coronary artery blockage prior to seeing me. She had postponed hospitalization because of a family obligation and was able to fit the Reiki treatment in before returning for more medical tests. When she went for further testing the blockage was gone. Barbara also excitedly explained that her own medical tests had come back normal!

The nature of Reiki energy is to heal all those who come in contact with it – those who give, as well as, those who receive. Barbara's belief that what you do for another, you do for yourself, allowed Reiki to benefit her and Joan. By clearing her energy centers of old wounds, she was able to open her heart to feel more deeply the connection of love and compassion that naturally exists between friends and then to act on it. Her kindness was a gift not just to Joan and herself, but it provided a beautiful life lesson for me. Thank you, Barbara!

—Michelle R. Brennan MS, MS
Counselor of Psychology and Communication Disorders
Usui and Karuna Reiki® Master Teacher

www.ReikiExchange.com

Chapter Five

The Physical Heart

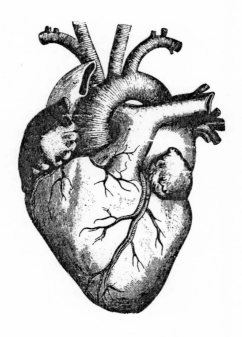

Figure 5

The Physical Nature of the Heart

Hopefully, other sections of this book left you feeling good and helped increase your understanding of the subtle yet powerful energy forces at work all around us and in us. Reading this chapter may not make you feel good as good. There is no easy way to present information on widespread heart related diseases and early deaths involving so many people. I felt it would be irresponsible to not mention this at all, so that is why it is included in this chapter. Almost everyone knows someone who has been affected by cardiovascular problems, or has even lost a loved one because of it.

It is very important to understand the magnitude of the physical problems concerning the heart and circulatory system that affect millions of people. Such problems are directly related to the physical heart organ and its life-circulating system of arteries and vessels.

Obtaining a general understanding of some of the physical maladies related to the heart is appropriate to our overall understanding of heart energies. There is a vast amount of information available in other sources that deal with the biological nature of the heart, the different types of heart related diseases, and the various approaches to dealing with heart disease. This chapter does not attempt to summarize all this data nor does it attempt to give medical advice of any kind. This chapter provides some selected topics of information that help put the nature of heart related physical problems into perspective. In addition, rather than disburse medical and statistical information throughout this entire book, it seemed more appropriate to put all such physical related information together in one location. This chapter looks at the physical, biological nature of the heart from a broad, high level perspective.

For those who work directly in the healing arts, as well as those who are not practitioners but nevertheless seek to improve their knowledge and understanding of the human condition, it is vital to realize the scope of heart related physical problems that face our fellow human beings. According to statistics published by the American Heart Association, more people on this planet die from cardiovascular disease than from *any other* cause. This knowledge helps give us a focal point as to where some of higher healing energies are needed.

The focus on energy work in relation to heart disease is not meant to imply that clogged arteries or damaged heart tissue can be immediately repaired by energy work alone. I believe that energy work can definitely assist healing and recovery processes and should be looked at as a highly beneficial tool that can assist those who have any form of cardiovascular or heart problems.

A major question that should be focused on is how did we get into this situation of such a widespread problem? Can we take effective measures to address heart-related problems before they require radical surgery, or before they do permanent damage to tissues? This is where a holistic approach to health and the use of subtle energy balancing can be of great benefit in preventing physical damage to the body's organs. *All changes in the physical world that we observe are preceded by subatomic changes— changes in the energy quanta that underlie all forms of matter.* These energy quanta respond to subtle energy processes. I believe that Reiki and other forms of energy work can and do provide the catalyst for beneficial subatomic changes in our bodies that then manifest in a return to health and vitality. I believe the loving touch of energy work, coupled with reasonable care of the body through exercise, responsible eating habits and nutrition can ease the potential suffering and prevent the early deaths of vast numbers of people.

Western medical science has labeled and categorized numerous diseases of the cardiovascular system, and has applied its own unique naming terminology to describe a wide range of conditions. Therefore, in order to understand the nature of the problem as it is defined in western medical terms, some medical terminology must be introduced and defined. **Appendix B** defines a list of key terms in the cardiovascular field. It is recommended that you familiarize yourself with that list before reading further in this section. The remainder of this chapter has been made as clear as possible, without becoming too technical or glossing over any important concepts, however, Appendix B will give you a helpful background in terminology.

"Heart 101"— The Anatomy of the Heart

The heart is a muscular organ consisting of four chambers. The two upper chambers are called atriums, the two lower chambers are called ventricles. These four chambers pump blood through the body in a rhythmic pattern with the help of the four valves in the heart. The movement of blood through the body can be felt as a "pulse" at various points such as the wrist and the neck.

Blood moves through the four chambers in the heart before circulating through the body. During each heartbeat, blood returns from the body through the veins and enters the right atrium and moves through the valve into the right ventricle below it.

Simultaneously, blood from the lungs that is rich in oxygen enters the left atrium on the other side of the heart. The blood passes from the left atrium through a valve into the left ventricle. Next, the right ventricle contracts after getting blood from the right atrium, sending blood out to the lungs to get fresh oxygen. At the same time, the left ventricle then contracts after getting blood

from the left atrium. As the left ventricle contracts, it pumps blood through the aorta out to the arteries throughout the body.
The heart has two valves that prevent blood from flowing back between the atriums and ventricles. It also has another two valves that prevent blood from flowing backward from the arteries and into the ventricles. A heart failure occurs when the ventricles cannot pump sufficient volume of blood to meet the body's needs.

Although the heart itself is full of blood, it does not have the ability to extract oxygen and nutrients directly from the blood inside its chambers. The heart needs to rely on the arteries on the surface of the heart to nourish it and keep it functioning properly. The arteries on the surface of the heart are known as the coronary arteries. There are three main coronary arteries: the right coronary artery, the left anterior descending coronary artery and the circumflex coronary artery. These three arteries branch into thousands of tiny arteries, carrying oxygen and nutrients to the heart muscle

Facts about the Physical Heart Organ

Each day the average heart beats 100,000 times and pumps about 2,000 gallons of blood. In a 70-year lifetime, an average human heart beats more than 2.5 billion times. That is over 50 million gallons of blood pumped in a single lifetime.

The heart is part of a massively complex circulatory system running throughout the entire body. If all the vessels of the human circulatory system were laid end-to-end, they would extend for about 60,000 miles. That is enough to circle the earth more than two times.

On December 3, 1967 in Cape Town, South Africa, Dr. Christian Barnard performed the first successful human heart transplant. He took the a heart from a 23 year old woman who had died in an automobile accident and successfully transplanted it into a 55 year old patient. Although the recipient died of pneumonia 18 days later, the operation received world-wide publicity as a breakthrough in the field of medicine.

Today, there is an average of about 2,000 heart transplants performed each year.

In July 2001, surgeons from the University of Louisville performed the first completely implanted artificial heart. It was a battery-operated, titanium device, costing about $70,000.

Programmed Cellular Destruction. According to the October 17 issue of the New England Journal of Medicine, two Northeastern University researchers have discovered that when end-stage heart failure sets in, heart cells get so distressed that they program themselves to die. The DNA in the cells fragments, the cells shrink and then self-destruct. According to Jagat Narula, the Associate Director of the Center for Cardiovascular Targeting, end-stage heart failure may result from a number of causes, including coronary disease, hypertension, diabetes or alcohol abuse. In the end-stage of heart failure, the heart enlarges. It fails to pump sufficient amounts of blood throughout the body. Without adequate blood circulation, the body's vital organs rapidly die. The precise cause of the progressive decline in the heart is unknown. With no available treatment for end-stage heart failure available, doctors have relied on heart transplant surgery as the only option left open to their patients.

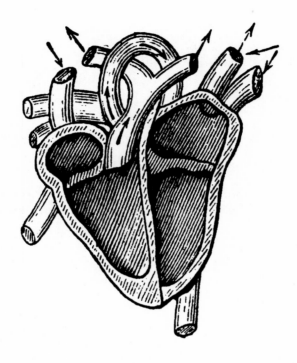

Figure 6 The Human Heart (inside view)

What is "Heart Disease"?

The field of medicine as it relates to the human heart and circulatory system is very broad. The circulatory system is a complex network comprising many parts and thousands of miles of blood vessels. The medical community has various ways of defining what is meant by heart disease, depending on which part of the medical community you listen to. To get a feeling of how large the scope of heart disease is, it may be useful to look at the term "total cardiovascular disease" as used by the American Heart Association. Here are some general guidelines on what comes under the umbrella of Heart Disease and Cardiovascular Disease from the American Heart Association.

- Rheumatic Fever/Rheumatic Heart Disease
- Hypertensive Heart Disease
- Ischemic Heart Disease
- Diseases of Pulmonary (Lung) Circulation (acute or chronic)
- Hypertension with or without Renal Disease
- Stroke
- Athereoclerosis
- Other Diseases of Arteries, Arterioles and capillaries
- Diseases of the Veins and Lymphatic system
- Other Heart Diseases

Data Related to Heart Attacks and Cardiovascular Disease
(From American Heart Association, American Health Association and other sources.)

Cardiovascular disease ("CVD") itself is the leading cause of death in the United States.

On a worldwide basis, cardiovascular disease is the leading cause of death in 31 of the 35 countries reporting death statistics to the World Health Organization.

A person dies of cardiovascular disease-related causes every 33 seconds. While the overall rate of heart disease in the United States has shown a promising decline in recent years, one type of heart disease, heart failure, is on the increase.

While there is a tendency for heart disease to occur most frequently in middle aged and older males, it affects both sexes and many age groups.

Nearly twice as many women in the United States die of heart disease and stroke as from all forms of cancer, including breast cancer.

According to medical statistics, 50 percent of the men who die suddenly of coronary heart disease, have no previous *medical* symptoms. About 50 million Americans age 6 and older have high blood pressure, also called "hypertension." In the United States alone, the number of people leaving hospitals with cardiovascular disease as the first diagnosed illness is around 6 million per year. Deaths from cardiovascular diseases have decreased in some countries but increased in others. In both developed and developing countries, deaths from cardiovascular disease still account for almost 50 percent of all deaths.

10 Leading Causes of Death in the U.S.

- Heart Disease: 724,859
- Cancer: 541,532
- Stroke: 158,448
- Chronic Lung Diseases: 112,584
- Accidents: 97,835
- Pneumonia/Influenza: 91,871
- Diabetes: 64,751
- Suicide: 30,575
- Nephritis: 26,182
- Chronic Liver Diseases: 25,192

Cardiovascular disease is not just a problem in the United States. In China, for example, there are between 1 and 1.5 million stroke deaths each year, and about 600,000 more deaths from all forms of heart disease. Cardiovascular disease in all forms claims about 2.5 million lives— or almost 30 percent of all deaths in China— each year. Coronary heart disease is the leading cause of death in Chinese urban areas. Pulmonary heart disease is the leading cause of death in Chinese rural areas (2001 data from the American Heart Association).

The highest death rates from cardiovascular disease were in the Soviet Union, Romania, Poland, Bulgaria, Hungary, and Czechoslovakia. The lowest were in Japan, France, Spain, Switzerland, and Canada (1991 data).

Heart Attacks

Coronary attacks, known more commonly as heart attacks, result from coronary heart disease. Coronary heart disease, also called coronary artery disease, is a blood vessel disease in the heart. A heart attack occurs when the blood supply to part of the heart muscle itself— the myocardium— is severely reduced or stopped. This occurs when one of the coronary arteries that supply blood to the heart muscle is blocked. The blockage is usually from the buildup of plaque (deposits of fat-like substances) due to arteriosclerosis. The plaque can eventually tear or rupture, triggering a blood clot to form that blocks the artery and leads to a heart attack. Such an event is sometimes called a coronary thrombosis or coronary occlusion.

Causes?

No one can claim to know the exact cause for this widespread proliferation of cardiovascular problems. There are probably multiple causal factors at work, and much research has been done into possible causes, including diet, environment, genetics and perhaps other factors.

If we look back over the past 150 years, we can see several significant changes in the civilization and habits of man in many areas of the earth. Here are four factors which may be highly significant.

Significant Global Changes

1. A global increase in the rapid rate of consumption of earth's resources and an increase in atmospheric toxins, land and water pollution.

2. A global increase in the availability, use and abuse of tobacco and pharmaceutical drugs.

3. A nearly global increase in food additives especially sugars in a wide variety of different forms, and food stabilizers such as hydrogenated oils.

4. A tendency towards increased levels of stress in daily life, due to changes in political, economic and technical forces.

Table 18

Diet, Nutrition and the Healthy Heart

When we are in good communication with our bodies and with our feelings, we are in a better position to determine our state of physical health before something major goes wrong. If we are not in touch with our bodies and our feelings, we will not hear or feel the signals that our bodies give us when our physiology goes out of balance. What does this mean? This means that if we are aware of the body's subtle energy flows, its rhythms, its general state of health, then we will be more easily become aware of signals of imbalance in the body in its early stages. The body has an excellent early warning system, if we are only wise enough to listen to it. Most people do not listen to their body's subtle signals. It seems as though we lead busy lives that have no room for listening to the deep but powerful communication signals that the body in its wisdom is sending forth on a day by day, minute by minute basis.

According to medical statistics, 50 percent of the men who die suddenly of coronary heart disease, have no previous *medical* symptoms. This means there were no perceptible warning signs, *except* perhaps for those subtle warning signs that the body was sending when no one was listening. If we are to consider the powerful energy forces that exist in the Heart Chakra as we discussed earlier in this book, then there must be signals of potential imbalance in the heart energies long before the ultimate signals— heart attack, stroke, and death. It is my belief that we can learn to detect these signals, and more importantly, act to correct any imbalances before they become life threatening.

The Importance of Taking Care of Yourself

Axiom

"Self love" is a state of being where one's consciousawareness is in tune with the love energy of one's own energy field. One resonates with one's own love energy before this energy can expand outward to encompass others.

The Meaning of Self Love

The concept of "self love" does not mean selfishness based on an inflated ego. Self love means being in touch with your heart center and being attuned to the wavelength of love vibrations that provide you with the communication channels to your physiology. *The heart center is a communication switchboard from your physiology to your psyche.* Listen to your heart. It has a wealth of wisdom spanning eons of time, far beyond the intellectual data you have collected over a relatively brief span of years. Self love includes feeling good about yourself and wanting to take care of your body and promote a healthy lifestyle.

Listening to the Body's Signals

When you are in touch with your physiology and the subtle signals it sends you all the time, you will be better able to judge what foods and nutrients your body needs and which are potentially harmful to it.

Because most of us are not in touch with the subtle signals of our physiology, we eat based on many factors that have *nothing to do* with actual hunger for nourishment. We tend to eat as a form of recreation when we are bored. We also tend to eat as a form of social interaction. We eat to experience the sensations of taste, including the "high" from sugars, the "buzz" from alcohol, and other sensory delights. These sensations distract us from feeling our emotional states. We eat for the purpose of distraction, or just to keep busy doing something (snacking, munching). We eat out of habit and in response to the mass media advertising to eat three meals a day, plus snacks, plus desert fads, party foods and other "fun" foods. Eating has become detached from the process of nourishment and nutrition.

Making Responsible Choices in Nutrition

There has been increasing scientific evidence over the past few decades that there are very valuable health benefits to be gained from diets, which are high in fruit, vegetables, whole grains, and legumes, and diets that include fish, nuts and low-fat dairy products. During the same time period, the availability of fast foods and other pre-packaged, pre-processed foods has grown tremendously. Sugar has been added to the western diet in ever increasing quantities over the past 75 years. Now, we have so much sugar (under many different names) and so many products with partially hydrogenated oils that it has become a challenge to find products in the mainstream marketplace without these additives. It is important to read labels, and to know what you are reading.

If we are uninformed or irresponsible in the selection of our store-bought foods and restaurant foods, we could be putting our bodies at risk for high levels of certain additives that are contributing factors to throwing our bodies off balance nutritionally. These items include sugar (in its various forms) and hydrogenated oils (or partially hydrogenated oils).

Some may argue that diet, life style, and even heredity, are the root causes of physical heart problems and cardiovascular disease. However, if one eats poorly on a regular basis, fails to engage in any activity that expresses the body's vitality and zest for life, and engages in other unhealthy practices, indulges in unhealthy emotional states of mind, one might ask where is the self-love in this behavior? Is the person acting in a way that promotes his or her own higher energies. What emotional influences are behind the conscious choices the person is making? We either choose to act lovingly and responsibly to others, and ourselves or we choose to act irresponsibly. There are no in-between states. Holding mental, emotional and spiritual attitudes that promote love, health and vitality is a conscious choice. Acting in way that supports those attitudes is a conscious choice.

Beware of Sugar in Stealth Mode

High quantities of sugar can be devastating to the body's physical energy production systems. Too much sugar throws the body out of balance. Diabetes and hypoglycemia are two energy imbalances related to the body's inability to balance sugar levels. Poor nutritional balance and weight problems that can come from eating too much sugar also contribute to the physical level problems associated with cardiovascular disease. The craving for constant sweetness can almost be considered an emotional or sensory addiction, or at best, a habit. The quantity of sugar content in food is not always obvious. Sugar content can be hidden under a variety of names. Some food labels will include high fructose corn syrup as one of the top three ingredients. Some fast food and other prepared foods contain high fructose corn syrup, dextrose, honey *and* sucrose! (Read the labels!) These are powerful sugars. A food is likely to be high in sugars if one of these names appears first or second in the ingredient list, or if several different types of sugars are listed.

Sugar in Stealth Mode

- Brown sugar
- Corn sweetener
- Corn syrup
- Dextrose
- Fructose
- Fruit juice concentrate
- Glucose
- High-fructose corn syrup
- Honey
- Invert sugar
- Lactose
- Malt syrup
- Maltose
- Molasses
- Raw sugar
- Sucrose
- Syrup
- Table sugar
- beet sugar
- brown sugar
- cane sugar
- confectioner's sugar
- powdered sugar
- turbinado

Table 19

If you check labels carefully, you will also find added sugars in things like toothpaste, vitamins, low fat health bars, "100% fruit juices," organic breads, and in other places you might not expect to find it.

Diabetes II

Type II diabetes is not a disease of the heart. Diabetes is an imbalance in the body's physical energy production system, specifically the ability to process sugar molecules effectively. Type II diabetes, also called non-insulin-dependent diabetes mellitus, accounts for 85-90 % of the cases of diabetes. It is mentioned here for three reasons:

(1) diabetes II has been on an increase and now affects over 16 million people in the U.S. alone;

(2) individuals with diabetes have two to three times the risk of cardiovascular disease; diabetes is a major cause of stroke; and

(3) Some of the same health related issues related to cardiovascular disease exist for diabetes, such as high fat intake, high calorie intake, lack of adequate physical activity, the presence of obesity, and general diet and nutrition imbalances.

Two key areas that diabetes has in common with cardiovascular disease are:

(a) A connection with our diet and nutrition choices; and

(b) An inability to sense the internal signals of imbalance the body is sending us until the effects become life threatening.

The Concerns about Free Radicals

What are free radicals? A free radical is an atom or molecule with an unpaired electron. Electrons are normally paired. An atom or molecule with an unpaired electron is very unstable and highly reactive. An unpaired electron in a free radical causes it to seek out other molecules so it can steal an electron from them in order to "feel" balanced. This electron theft changes the structure of the other molecules causing them to also become free radicals. This can result in a chain reaction in which the structure of millions of molecules are altered creating changes in our DNA and many other molecules. On a macro scale, it is this transfer of electrons that causes butter to go rancid, causes apples exposed to the air to turn brown, and causes iron to rust. In the human body, this free radical damage is linked to many diseases including circulatory system problems, stroke, memory loss, Lou Gehrig's disease, Parkinson's disease and Huntington's disease, hypertension and accelerated aging.

Free radical damage has been linked to cancer and other afflictions. Hydrogenated oils and partially hydrogenated oils have been linked to the proliferation of free radicals

Our day to day environment contributes immensely to the spread of free radicals. Increased production of free radicals is attributed to the presence of drugs in our bodies, the increased use of radiation, pesticides, air pollutants, solvents, fried foods, alcohol, tobacco smoke, and other toxins.

There have been a number of scientific studies into the beneficial effects of antioxidants in reversing the cellular damage associated with aging, as well as benefits for reducing or preventing some forms of cancer and heart related problems. According to "Environmental Health Perspectives," Volume 109, Number 10, October 2001, dietary antioxidants have long been promoted as a defense against many diseases, such as cancer, cardiovascular disease, and diseases of the immune system. The "big" groups like the American Heart Association are often careful about what they endorse and in some cases they are recommending that further research be done. In any event, the research and available information in this area continues to grow. It is clear at least that free radical damage to cells is something to be avoided, and reversed when possible.

One thing that helps combat free radicals is a category of substances called anti-oxidants. The anti-oxidants contain an electron that can supply the free radical's need without causing damage to cells and other molecules. Anti-oxidants should be an important part of our nutritional plan.

What are Antioxidants? Antioxidants are known as "anti-aging" agents. Antioxidant is a nutrient or chemical that intercepts and neutralizes destructive free radicals in the body. Antioxidants are sometimes called "free radical scavengers." Some examples of antioxidants include vitamin A, vitamin C, vitamin E, some of the B vitamins, and beta-carotene. Other antioxidants include the mineral selenium, as well as the enzyme Glutamine and other amino acids. Some antioxidants prevent the cellular damage from beginning, some antioxidants act to block the cellular damage while it is occurring, and others help repair the damage after it has occurred. Reactive oxygen species (ROS) such as the superoxide (O_2 -) and the hydroxyl radical (OH) are aggressive chemical compounds that can induce tissue destruction and aging.

What Are Hydrogenated Oils?

Partially hydrogenated oil is formed when vegetable oils are processed and made more solid or into a more stable liquid. Small particles of nickel or copper are added and the mix is heated to very high temperatures under pressure for up to eight hours while hydrogen gas is injected.

This processing is called hydrogenation and is done to cause vegetable oil to emulate the consistency of saturated fats and to improve shelf life of foods. The natural molecular structure of the oil is altered from a polyunsaturate to a saturate, which causes the fat molecule to change from a fluid, flexible state to a more static, inactive state. This gives food a "longer life" and saves money on shipping and storage costs for food companies.

Reportedly, single molecules of hydrogenated and partially hydrogenated oils resemble molecules of plastic when viewed under a microscope.

These types of saturated fats have been viewed for years by many health professionals as being a major source of health problems. These modified oils are not assimilatable by the body and will build up a toxic residue in the system over a period of time, raising cholesterol levels that trigger many harmful conditions, including heart disease.

A diet of foods containing hydrogenated oils has also been linked to breast cancer

Where Do You Find Hydrogenated Oils?

In today's western diet, hydrogenated oils are added to a great many products. Almost all cereals, bagels, crackers, margarine, cookies, breads, pizza, donuts, cakes, ice creams, candy, deserts, and other items. Hydrogenated oils appear in many foods that say "low fat" or "organic" or other foods that you might not suspect. It is actually difficult to find packaged foods, especially bread and cereal products without hydrogenated oils, unless you specifically look for them. Sometimes a health food section will have products without hydrogenated oils clearly labeled. Mono-diglycerides are a form of hydrogenated oils.

Fast foods are usually very high in fats and in hydrogenated oils. Fast food french fries are usually cooked in partially hydrogenated oils, and also contain sugar, sodium acid pyrophosphate (a color preservative), TBHQ (Tert-Butylhydroquinone) (a preservative), Dimethylpolysiloxane (an anti-foaming agent). (See Appendix B)

If you wash down your fries with a soft drink, you are adding sugar and caffeine as well. The combination of sugars, caffeine and items your body cannot easily digest, such as hydrogenated oils, you are putting a high degree of stress on the body and throwing its chemical/digestive energy processing systems way out of balance. Your body immediately reacts to the high intake of sugar, salt, fats and caffeine all at once. Some people become "fast food junkies" as their body's become accustomed to feeling this chemical "buzz" in their systems. This buzz should be a signal to us that our body's natural rhythms are being pushed out of balance.

(See Appendix D for information on companies that produce foods that do not contain hydrogenated oils.)

Emotional and Energetic Factors

that Influence the Heart

Emotional, psychological and other environmental stress factors seem to greatly influence the nature of heart related diseases.

In addition to physical conditions, and nutritional factors, other factors influencing an increased risk of heart disease include

---

Emotional/Psychological Risk Factors

and the Heart

- inadequate social support or lack of social networks
- lack of close family and friendship support, feelings of isolation
- work environment stress
- job loss
- depression
- continual anxiety
- aggressive and hostile personality traits
- operating with a continual sense of time urgency

Table 20

Depression: an Energetic Crisis of the Heart

Axiom

Depression is a feeling of powerlessness. When an individual cannot locate the source of his or her own power, a state of lethargy ensues, where what little remaining energy the person has is turned inward on themselves, thus draining their power further.

The remedy for depression is to return the individual to a state of energetic empowerment.

Empowerment is achieved through an increase in one's own responsibility over one's personal intent and regaining control over one's energy production centers.

One of the areas of difficulty facing a growing number of people in our society is depression. Many people in different age groups experience depression. It occurs among the young teen-age population, among the middle aged and among older people. A large number of people enter into depression after a heart attack. Those afflicted with depression often spend more time recovering and may be prone to other difficulties.

Although there has been much written about the subject of depression, it is still not sufficiently understood. All too often it is looked upon by western medicine as a condition to be treated by chemical remedies. Treating symptoms of depression before understanding the underlying causes is foolhardy at best and potentially dangerous at worst. It is also extremely unfair to those who are suffering the agonies of depression, whether in its mild or extreme forms.

Depression in extreme cases is thought to be a chemical imbalance in the brain. It is important to remember that the brain and the heart are linked together in our total energetic system. The electromagnetic impulses generated by the heart are much stronger than those generated by the brain. The brain and the heart send signals back and forth to each other. When the brain's electromagnetic wave generation is in sync with the heart it is called "entrainment." When the brain and the heart are at "odds" with each other, the body begins to go out of balance. Over a longer period, this imbalance can result in physical problems.

Feelings of depression can predispose one to not taking care of themselves, either physically, mentally, emotionally or spiritually. Long term depression can affect the strength of the heart energies. People who feel depressed sometimes turn to drugs, alcohol and other distractions in an attempt to suppress or cover up their feelings. Depression can worsen when someone is then diagnosed with a life threatening physical ailment. Sometimes after a major surgery patients will experience a depression.

When dealing with depression and/or serious physical illnesses, the whole person must be considered. By the "whole person" we mean all aspects of how the person sees himself or herself in the world. Do they feel they live in a loving world? Or, do they feel they live in a harsh and dangerous world? Do they feel they are contributing meaningfully to others on a daily basis? Or, do they feel their lives are aimless, repetitive? Do they feel they make a positive impact to their fellow human beings? These are not esoteric philosophical questions. They are vital questions, the answers to which will tell you whether someone is predisposed to eventual depression and physical deterioration.

Depression and Energy Flows

It may sound odd to talk about depression and energy flows in the same sentence. However, they are very closely related. It is vitally important to understand and deal with the manifestations of what many people refer to as depression in a whole new light. Depression needs to be examined in terms of *energy*. You are a unique and wonderful energy being. Each of us is an energy being of immense potential and creativity. We, as energy beings, have created for ourselves, bodies of light. These light bodies vibrate at various frequencies. We interact with each other through the energy vibrations. Some of our vibrational frequencies are low enough to appear as solid. This is the physical body. However, the vast majority of our energy exists at a vibratory state far above the physical. Those healers who work with subtle energies directly know the power that our energetic bodies have to influence our mental, emotional, spiritual and physical well being. Depression is an energy loss from the body. Stopping this energy loss and balancing the body's energy centers is a major element of alleviating the energetic causes beneath a depression.

The Three Types of Depression

As described in more detail in the book *Energy Dynamics: Conscious Human Evolution*, there are three basic types of depression. Psychological, which includes the mental and emotional, Spiritual, and Physiological (of the body). They are not completely independent from each other. However, talking about them as three different types makes it easier to explain and understand what the various aspects of each one are.

Psychological depression is caused by an inability to reconcile the impulses and signals one receives from the personality, and from the cultural dynamic with those that come from the Higher Self. A psychological depression is alleviated by addressing the imbalances in the emotional and mental energies of the being.

This aspect of depression is one where the emotional energies and mental energies are at odds with each other. A conflict ensues internally which taps into the person's basic energies and leaves them feeling powerless and confused. Severe depression is an indication of a severe imbalance in these energies.

Spiritual depression, is caused by a misalignment of one's basic intentions with the directions that one should be taking for one's own personal growth, greater awareness and greater love. A spiritual depression can be either subtle or profound. There is usually some degree of spiritual depression at the root of any other type of depression. A spiritual depression is corrected by examining our basic intentions and seeking to bring those intentions into alignment with the divine aspects of our nature.

Physiological depression, is caused in part by an abuse of the body. Using harmful drugs, abusing prescription drugs, overeating, undereating, overwork, stress, junk food bingeing, ignoring personal hygiene, ignoring the body's need to rest or to exercise, all contribute to a deterioration of the physical body.

When the body's energy production systems are abused, the energy levels become erratic. Abuse of drugs, including prescription drugs, can cause the body to go numb and become shut off from basic physical and emotional feelings. Abuse of alcohol and stimulants mask and confuse one's feelings and depress the body's endocrine system, nervous system and its overall metabolism. Prolonged use of antidepressants can suppress or depress the ability to "feel" one's own feelings. Such abuse can knock the body even further out of balance.

A physiological depression can be subtle, in which the person seems to be able to function normally, or it can be so strong that a person cannot even cope with the challenges of daily life. A drug-induced physiological depression can lead to other problems and is related to spiritual and psychological depression. One cannot successfully meet the challenge of a spiritual or psychological depression while the body is in a state of abuse or severe energy imbalance. However, one cannot remedy a spiritual depression through prescriptions drugs aimed at masking the body's physical symptoms. The **whole being** must be treated in order to achieve a state of balance, wholeness and health.

Environmental Influences

The influence of one's immediate environment has a lot to do with how prone one is to depression and how effectively one is able to deal with a depression should it occur. In a loving, supportive environment a person has a better chance of recovering to a state of balance than in an environment where external energies are highly agitated or where other people are depressed, whether physiologically, psychologically or spiritually. In environments where the external energies are not supportive and where there exists fear, anger, power struggles, or physical or verbal abuse, the ability of a person to overcome the added weight of depression is severely hampered. It may be possible, indeed highly therapeutic, for the person to leave the environment first, and then work on their personal challenges with the depression. Finding another more supportive environment may be difficult, but it is a major factor in recovery and should be given a high level of priority. One may sometimes find that just leaving a certain environment will do much to alleviate a depression all by itself. Engaging in activities that provide a creative outlet for one's energies and performing activities that allow one to contribute in a meaningful way to the benefit of others will greatly help alleviate depression. Support groups (those not focused on drugs or blame) can help create a supportive environment and one in which a person can examine his or her own goals and intentions and acquire new focus in life. Energy balancing, in this scenario, would be an excellent complement to such a program of recovery and would greatly assist a person's return to balance and wholeness.

Guidelines for Physical Health

- Do not overeat. Eat smaller meals that are easier to digest and process.
- Eat when hungry. Do not eat when not hungry.
- Keep fat intake low.
- Avoid saturated fats.
- Avoid partially hydrogenated oils.
- Avoid processed foods and drinks with added sugars.
- Avoid most fast foods.
- Choose lowfat milk products or nonfat milk products.
- Increase your intake of fresh vegetables and fresh fruits.
- Avoid over salting foods.
- Avoid consuming too much alcohol.
- Take appropriate nutritional supplements.
- Give yourself adequate time daily to reflect on spiritual goals.
- Cultivate a thought habit of gratitude for the good things you have.
- Forgive others, do not hold anger in your heart or anywhere in your body.
- Release negative thoughts and energies, focus on higher vibrational thoughts.
- Practice an activity (yoga, tai chi, meditation) that helps integrate body energies.
- Seek out an activity that allows you to express your creativity and embrace it.
- Choose to perform some activity that involves service to others.
- Actively create a loving environment around you.

Table 21

Body Weight and Cardiovascular Risks

Carrying too much physical body weight can increase the risk of high blood pressure, heart disease, stroke, diabetes, certain types of cancer and other illness. Since many people eat for reasons other than being genuinely hungry and needing nourishment, there are many people eating when their body does not require food. The body is not in a position to properly digest and assimilate food when it does not need nourishment. Continuing to put food in the body when it does not need it can cause an imbalance in the body. The science of Ayurveda teaches that one should not eat when one is not hungry. Sounds obvious, however in our society many people have lost touch with the body's true hunger signals and instead react to "false" hunger signals caused by an imbalance in sugar levels in the body, not from an actual need for food. This is one of the real problems with eating too much sugar. It can throw off the metabolism to the point where hunger signals are masked and/or confused.

In her excellent tape series *"Advanced Energy Anatomy,"* Caroline Myss says that an overweight condition can be related to a suppression of the person's creative energies. The person may be holding back from engaging in activities that would otherwise help contribute to a balanced energetic system.

The Importance of Proper Digestion

Eating food when the body is not really in need of nourishment can throw the digestive system off balance. Eating food for reasons other than nourishment is related to an imbalance in the third chakra energies. The digestive fire related to the energies of the second and third chakras, needs to be active in order to burn ("digest") food and assimilate it into the body. When digestion is not happening, the body can build up toxins that slow down the metabolism and further reduce the ability to assimilate nutrients. Therefore it is important to maintain a healthy digestion and to eat foods when the body needs refueling, and not saturate the body with excess food when it is not hungry.

To *reduce* body weight, engage in activities that promote digestion and burning of calories (including stored energies).

- Increase activity levels, more walking, running, swimming, running, biking
- Decrease intake of fatty foods, decrease intake of sugars, decrease heavy meats
- Decrease overall food volume (carefully/gradually)
- Take digestive enzymes/herbs to promote the digestive fire and increase efficiency

To *maintain* body weight, engage in activities that promote balance.

- Balance food intake with the body's actual need for nourishment
- Balance nutritional intake— include fruits, vegetables, grains, and proteins
- Balance activity with non-activity, balance motion with non-motion

Nutritional Supplements

Nutritional supplements can be an excellent way to provide the body with nutrients to assist it in maintaining health and balance, and even reverse some of the effects of free radicals and other influences. New discoveries in the area of enhancing nutritional supplements with the power of light have given rise to new potentials.

Dr.Todd Ovakaitys M.D., founder of Gematria, has done significant research in the area of laser enhanced nutritional supplements and the advantages of free form amino acids over intact or partially digested proteins. His research and the process he has developed is a revolutionary approach to integrating a understanding of the human electromagnetic systems and quantum physics with the nutritional needs of the body.

> "I realized that the huge body of DNA information is coded and that understanding the code was the key to being able to work with DNA in a specific way as opposed to the way currently being used by medicine. The most critical piece of information revealed was that DNA communicates through electromagnetics, and it's the coils within coils that generate the electromagnetic signals used for communication throughout the body. It then became apparent to me that the system is so intimately attuned to electromagnetic signals that if you, through mathematics, sacred geometry, and the correct electronics created the right fields; you could literally instruct and reprogram the cell to do almost anything."

See Appendix K for a description of the laser enhanced nutritional supplements produced by Gematria, which incorporate a revolutionary process of laser energy enhancement developed by Dr.Todd Ovakaitys M.D.

Resources for Chapter Five

Statistical Information Courtesy of:
- *The American Heart Association*
- *The American Health Association*
- *The World Health Organization*
- *Centers for Disease Control*
- *U.S. Department of Agriculture*
- *United Network for Organ Sharing*
- *Access Excellence, Genentech*
- *and other sources*

Chapter Six

Axioms of Higher Consciousness

What Is an Axiom?

> "An Axiom is a fundamental principle or agreed-upon condition of reality upon which other aspects of reality seem to rely, or through which other aspects of reality can be better understood."

Intelligent, co-creative evolution of the spirit requires that we be conscious of our own belief systems. It is important to examine and understand the Axioms that underlie our belief structures. A greater understanding of the fundamental factors and components of our belief systems will provide us with a more holistic viewpoint as we take a more active part in our own evolution. In the previous book, *Energy Dynamics: Conscious Human Evolution*, over 100 Axioms were presented that dealt with our energetic nature as beings of light, and fundamental principals of our interaction with others, and the nature of our existence.

The Axioms presented here build on those concepts and introduce new ones. The prior book's Axioms are not repeated here, and one should read the prior Axioms separately to experience their benefit. The Axioms that follow here are focused on a wide variety of topics that each has a place in our evolutionary process at this time.

One of the benefits of reading the Axioms is that if they ring true for you, they begin a process of energizing neural pathways in the brain to help you assimilate and understand other similar knowledge. They have an organizing influence on your thought processes because they deal with fundamental concepts of awareness and the quantum nature of our universe. Reading the Axioms, in whatever sequence you choose to read them, is a consciousness raising activity.

Space-Time

Axiom

The reality of the environment that we experience around us is the result of our focused attention on a specific range of energy frequencies.

There are frequencies of energy that exist above and below that which we normally focus on. They exist right here with us, right now. They co-exist with us, but we are not attuned to their vibrational levels. These other ranges of vibration can be thought of as levels or "dimensions."

Higher or lower levels do not necessarily imply better or worse, simply different, although the higher levels are associated with finer energies and beings of higher frequencies of light.

When we change our vibrational perception to different rates or frequencies, we bring into our perceptual range those things, beings, or events that are in alignment with those frequencies. Like energy attracts like energy.

The quality that separates one dimension from another is the vibrational rate of the energy involved.

Space-Time-Motion

Axiom

Space-time is a continuum. The rate of time's "passing" is related to motion.

Where there is no motion, there is no time.

Motion is a function of our perception. Our perception influences how we perceive motion and how we perceive the passage of time.

The act of perceiving objects and motion creates space, since there can be no movement without a space in which to move, and there can be no space without something in it which moves and thus defines the space.

Absolute non-motion does not exist. Therefore, all matter and energy in any given space-time is in motion. The "time" in space-time is not necessarily "linear" time.

Linear time is a human construct.

Phase-Shifting

Axiom

What we call spirits* are beings at vibrations of light above our normal, customary range of perception. They exist in dimensions where everything vibrates at that frequency range. They can slow their vibrational rate slightly, which is often sufficient to bring them into resonance with us long enough to communicate with us (through thought, feeling or energy).

A being or object in one dimension can phase into another dimension through a change in vibrational rate. If you perceive a being or object as it begins this phase shift it will appear as if it is vanishing. It is in fact vibrating outside of your normal perceptual range.

This is much like watching a bumblebee as it vibrates its wings. At a certain speed, the wings become invisible. They still exist in space-time, but human vibrational range of perception is not attuned to perceiving the higher vibrational rate. When the wings stop vibrating, they become visible again.

(*"spirits" as used here may refer to a wider range of entities, other than human.)

Linear Time and The Power of Forgiveness

Axiom

Linear, sequential time is a human construct designed to fixate events into a framework and thus explain, define and attempt to control these events.

Linear, sequential time is not the same for everyone. Most arguments between people can be traced back to the fact that they are not placing events in the same time-space sequence. An individual's perceptions of linear, sequential time are often unique to that person, and thus two or more individuals may not completely agree on "what happened when and to whom."

Individuals may recall the same event completely differently. Both interpretations may be correct. Since we can change our personal perception of an event, we can change our reality about it. Past and future events are also perceptions, subject to change.

At the root of most arguments is a disagreement concerning the nature of a past, present or future event. "Forgiveness" is powerful tool since it recognizes our ultimate state as co-creators of our reality. There is no ultimate, objective reality to which we must subscribe. There are only variations in how we interpret our individual experiences. Forgiveness acknowledges the higher level of goodness in a person and allows both parties in an argument to maintain their "rightness."

Raising Vibrations

Axiom

Raising one's vibration helps put one in contact with higher intelligences, higher beings of light and beautiful spiritual energies.

We can assist each other by consciously raising our own vibration and the vibrations of those we meet. We actually assist others in their spiritual growth when we do this.

When we exchange energies, when we love another, we participate in the raising of vibrations that leads us closer to our Higher Self and to All That Is.

Oversoul— The Higher Self

Axiom

The Oversoul or Higher Self is a collective consciousness that sees beyond the veil of space-time and beyond the illusion of the life-death separation. The Higher Self sees all our incarnations as occurring simultaneously.

Our various subtle energy bodies are each aware of the others. They operate as an integrated whole that functions according to energetic pathways that we ourselves have created. The fact that we are not "aware" of each separate subtle energy body independently is a function of our consciousness, not a lack of consciousness.

Higher Self's Perspective

Axiom

The Higher Self sees all our various incarnations as aspects of itself that are each engaged in a unique and very special learning experience. We are aware of and in constant touch with our Higher Self, even though we are not consciously aware of it. This may sound like a contradiction. It seems contradictory unless we understand the difference between our localized, day-to-day "awareness" and the greater aspect of our consciousness that permeates all aspects of our being.

From the Higher Self's perspective, all past and future lives are happening right now, at the same "time." From the individual Soul's perspective, there is a veil of energy separating past, present and future lives. This allows the Soul to focus on certain aspects of its lessons and gain the highest possible experiential value from those lessons.

If the energy veil is too dense, however, the individual Soul can sometimes be denied the ability to learn from the experiences of its other "selves" and this can bring about the conditions of effort, confusion, despair, hopelessness and a stuck feeling. During such periods, it is helpful to communicate directly with our Higher Self. We need to ask for guidance, (insight, grace, love, energy) to help bring clarity to life's challenges. All prayers and all requests are always heard. The Higher Self will respond.

Other Aspects of Ourselves

Axiom

Other aspects of ourselves can and do exist in the same space-time stream as we do. Sometimes we meet and interact with these selves as part of our learning experience. These are highly unique opportunities for growth, since the energetic connections between us and our other "selves" can be immensely powerful. They can be a catalyst for change and growth at emotional and spiritual levels. We often feel a special kinship with such other selves, even though we may not know exactly why. Being other aspects of our self, they are still, however, very much individual entities with their own personalities, karmic energies, and life contracts. They are not "shadow selves" or "non-entities" or lesser beings of any kind.

"Soul Mate"

Axiom

Our Higher Self sees each individual aspect of its greater whole as being fully formed, fully alive, conscious and capable of selective choice-making. Our Higher Self loves all aspects of itself, all aspects of "us" equally. No aspect is considered bad or of lesser value. The love energies of the Higher Self are the binding forces that hold all aspects of our selves together along a common, higher evolutionary path.

The term "soul mate" best describes the relationship between ourselves and these other aspects of ourselves. However, the term soul mate has been used by others in ways that imply a single, special connection that comes about only between two people. Soul mate in the sense we are using it here, refers to different aspects of the same Higher Self, that come together for a brief or a long period, to interact energetically with each other for the purposes of their mutual growth and spiritual evolution.

The Doors of Perception

Axiom

Perception is the act of selectively filtering input from reflected images of our creation. The "human" perceptual range is an agreed upon framework of frequencies which we agree upon for the purpose of sharing experience with each other.

We can periodically re-energize our creative energies by choosing to widen our perceptual filters, to bring into our personal experience, reflections of those aspects of creation that we are not normally consciously aware of.

The Energy Matrix

Your Vibrational Signature

Axiom

There exists an Energy Matrix which aligns the subtle molecular forces of all atoms and subatomic particles of the body into a specific pattern, and which holds that pattern as long as the energy matrix remains unchanged. This energy matrix is unique to each individual and holds the specific organizing instructions that make each one of us unique. This energy matrix is our energy personality to some extent and is comprised of the collective consciousness of all our cells and their subatomic parts.

The matrix holds the subatomic particles together in a cohesive but somewhat loose arrangement. It is cohesive in that our physical form appears to remain the same. It is loosely arranged in that all particles are allowed freedom of vibration and motion within certain parameters. The "form" is maintained by the imposition of the energy matrix upon the vibratory mass of particles that is our physical body.

This matrix extends outward from the body as well, and includes levels of the energy bodies surrounding our physical body. This unique energy matrix is our personalized vibrational energy signature, our personal symbolic representation of ourselves.

Past Lives and Karma

Axiom

"Past lives" to not control your current life situations. Your current beliefs have far more influence on your daily life and your current experiences than do any past (or future) events.

If you have present time energy focused on past events or on past trauma, the lack of this energy in present time is what drains your power. The past incidents themselves have no power. It is only your own consciousness when focused on external events, that seems to give those events power.

Karma is based on the fact that you do not completely forget your past actions. Therefore, actions in the past seem to effect you now.

Through present time responsible choice making, you can eliminate (or transcend) any aspect of karma that you might interpret as negative or unwanted.

If you continually find yourself replaying a karmic drama in your life, over and over, it is your beliefs about the dreams that need to be examined by your conscious aware mind.

Your personal beliefs are empowered by your conscious awareness and it is this power that in turn seems to have an effect on you. Your present time beliefs about any aspect of existence will magnetize others with similar beliefs and they will appear in your life.

Sensuality, Sexuality and Intimacy

Axiom

Sensuality is the quality of taking and giving of information through the senses. Sensuality is an energetic connection through all the senses, not just the five most commonly known senses. Sensual intimacy is the sharing of this energy interchange with another person.

*To be **sensual** is to be in touch with the subtle fibers that connect you to things in your environment in a way that allows you to perceive their unique frequencies, beauty and aliveness. To be sensual is to live **with** the universe, enjoying it at each step along your path.*

Through the senses, we learn to identify aspects of our environment that tell us about ourselves. Sensuality extends our reach. Sensuality is a connection to the wider world of things, events and ideas.

Infinity

Axiom

Infinity is the absence of the consideration that there are ultimate boundaries beyond which nothing can be sensed.

Infinity is the playground of potentiality and creativity.

Dreams

Axiom

Dreams are a powerful aspect of our existence. Dreams provide us the opportunity to tap into, process, explore and create solutions to problems and experiment with new realities without the hindrance of the rational mind and outside of the constraints of physical universe space-time.

Dreams act as a communication medium between various aspects of ourselves. Dreams provide a communication medium with other beings.

All forms of life dream.

We do not remember all of our various dreams because it is not necessary for us to do so.

Certain dreams convey messages that we should endeavor to bring forth into our conscious awareness.

Daydreams and Imagination

Axiom

Daydreams allow you to actively create new realities while simultaneously exploring what those realities look like in comparison with your so-called normal reality.

You engage your inner creativity through active daydreaming.

It is through daydreaming and creative imaginations that you re-energize your psyche. In daydreaming you stand in the doorway between the waking world of your normal awareness and the world of your unfettered imagination.

As you pass through the door, your "conscious" mind and its rational constructs are left behind and you are open to the experiences of your larger senses. This can be a healthy and therapeutic process.

Daydreaming is an immensely powerful activity. One more powerful than you allow yourself to acknowledge. In daydreaming, your conscious rational mind is not as shut down as it is in normal sleep.

In daydreaming you have the ability to maintain a stronger link with your day-to-day reality. This enables the creativity and the content to flow more easily between worlds. Nightly dreams are a much deeper form of creative expression than daydreams and serve a different purpose.

Daydreaming is good practice for the art of creative visualization.

Daydreaming is also good practice for the more complex art of lucid dreaming, which involves becoming conscious within one's nightly dreams.

Energy, Movement, Balance

Axiom

The physical body is designed to facilitate the learning process on the physical plane. The body can increase its vibration through physical movement. Flowing movements such as those in a subtle dance allow the body's energy flows to open up. Subtle, flowing movements of the body can raise its vibration and calm the emotions.

Accumulations of dense energy patterns in or around the body tend to pull the body into a state of non-movement. Slowness, dullness, heaviness, tightness and inflexibility are all symptoms of a reduction in subtle energy flows within the body. Using will and intent to get the body moving will raise its energy level and will disburse denser energies.

Proximity to others who are open to subtle energy flows will also tend to unpack and release one's own compacted energy masses.

Other Dimensions

Axiom

Perception is the act of selectively filtering input from reflected images of our creation. The "human" perceptual range is an agreed upon framework of frequencies which we agree upon for the purpose of sharing experience with each other.

We can periodically re-energize our creative energies by choosing to widen our perceptual filters, to bring into our personal experience, reflections of those aspects of creation that we are not normally consciously aware of.

Sleep

Axiom

Sleep is an altered state where the body and mind rejuvenate themselves, and where consciousness lets go of the bonds of logical thought that constrict its ability to make quantum leaps in creativity.

Sleep is an opportunity to enter another world. It is a doorway to other aspects of ourselves.

Physical, mental and spiritual vitality is enhanced by sleep since it is through sleep that we unleash powerful levels of creativity that we do not allow ourselves the pleasure of experiencing during our "waking" state.

Emotional Suffering

Axiom

Emotional suffering usually comes about from an experience of loss, or from a perceived loss. Something or someone has been taken from us without our consent.

Emotional suffering is felt most strongly in the heart center, however, all parts of the physical body respond immediately to the feeling loss, grief or anguish.

Oftentimes it is necessary to feel the feelings of suffering in order to grow beyond it. Let yourself feel sorrow, sadness or suffering, rather than negate its existence. Feel what the message is there to tell you. Sometimes it is just a feeling. Experience it.

Crying tears shows that the heart is open to feeling its own feelings. Value the ability to cry and the ability to feel the emotion in the moment. Crying can release stuck energies and painful emotions, and make one feel cleansed and refreshed. It can also leave one exhausted, calm, peaceful, purified or whole.

When you cry, all the cells of your body cry. They all share in the feeling and in the release. It is a total body experience.

Spiritual Suffering

Axiom

Sometimes, a spiritual suffering is a call to action, the beginnings of new growth and change. A new birth. First painful, then giving way finally to a new joy.

The experience of suffering comes about as a signal from ourselves that we need to change our spiritual, mental, emotional or physical behavior pattern. The pain of spiritual suffering is a gentle nudge from our higher self to move onward.

If we remain in a state of pain or suffering for too long period of time, it is an indication that we are not allowing the flow of change to proceed. Attachment (as relayed in the teachings of the Gautama Buddha) can result in suffering when the attachment is used to resist change. The flow of change is necessary to the progress of growth.

Suffering turns to joy when we allow the path of change to open to our higher energies. The stone cold heaviness of suffering and pain blossoms into a warm, expanding fountain of light when the suffering is viewed as a signpost for our next path instead of a punishment for unknown deeds.

Temporary suffering is an urging to allow love energy to flow into and through you, thus opening the doors to change and spiritual growth.

Joy is a natural state of being that indicates you are on your path of growth and have touched, even if briefly, the connection to your God-self.

Astrology

Axiom

The study of astrology is the application of intuitive insight to the positions of planetary bodies at any given instant to interpret the reflections of the vast array of universal forces at work. Planetary positions depict focus and alignment. From moment to moment that alignment changes, pulsates, flows into its next state. Relative and apparent positions of planetary bodies, and of particles themselves, have a direct relationship to what we consider to be Space-Time.

At the physical level, vibration is a Space-Time event. The planetary relationships reflect vibrational states associated with Space-Time events. The universe's vibrational song at the time of your physical birth is forever imprinted on your biofield.

Planetary positions reflect universal patterns and potentialities.

They do not dictate the outcome of events, nor do they dictate our choices.

Anxiety

Axiom

Anxiety is a manifestation of an energy disorder.

Anxiety is caused by an energy imbalance in the chakra energy system.

Anxiety is closely tied to a feeling of "motion out of control". The motion is that of energy leaving one or more of the body's energy centers without the individual's conscious intent for it to do so. This leaves the individual feeling like part of themselves is out of control.

Closely tied to anxiety are the feelings of fear and impending disaster. The individual feels that something is happening outside of their control, and this something has the power to affect them.

The most direct approach to treating anxiety is not to mask the feelings associated with it, but to address the root cause of the energetic imbalance.

Physical Touch

Axiom

Physical touch between bodies sets up an energy interchange at many levels. First the energy fields interact, then the biological nerve senses interact, then the body cells at a subatomic level interact. At each level, an energy exchange takes place. Only a few seconds of actual contact is needed to exchange a vast array of data between two people.

The key bit of information exchanged is that of vibrational frequency. One body senses the vibrational frequency of the other to determine if the vibrations are threatening or supportive. A determination is made as to whether the energies are harmonious and balanced, or whether there is discord and agitation.

A determination is also made as to whether the other's body is radiating energy, co-creating the space around it, or whether the other's body is attempting to absorb energy from the things around it.

Contact with a body that is radiating energy in a co-creative manner is usually a pleasant experience.

Contact with a body that is draining energy away from things around it is usually an unpleasant experience.

Only a few milliseconds of time are required for all this information to be exchanged and the determinations recorded.

In most cases, after this initial interchange takes place, the energy bodies of both of the individuals involved attempt to attain a comfortable level of balance with each other so that they may interact on a harmonious frequency. In cases where one or both of the individuals seeks to gain control over the other, this attainment of balance will not occur. This is the energetic root of conflict.

Storms and Weather Patterns

Axiom

Storms and weather patterns are a reflection of psychic energy at work. The planet is a living "breathing" entity with an electromagnetic field surrounding it. It responds to the forces of its own cycles and interactions with the sun and moon. It also responds to the emotional energies of beings living on it. Storms and weather patterns are not random phenomena. The emotional and psychic energy of groups of people resonates into the earth's magnetic field and can cause shifts in weather and the manifestation of all sorts of weather phenomena.

Electrical storms, for example, are a release of vast amounts of emotional and psychic energy into the atmosphere. Storms are periods of cleansing and shifting of energies. Groups can project their energies into the environment and bring about massive global shifts, usually in their immediate area. However, the energy of groups can also cause shifts remotely in other parts of the globe. Every storm and weather condition has a certain "feel" to it. Generating that feeling again, on a mass scale, can bring about similar weather effects.

Talent

Axiom

A talent is a selected focus of ability taken up by choice, by an individual, to explore an area of existence in detail and share with other aspects of the personality the knowledge gained by the application of that talent to the physical surroundings. Talents can be improved and refined over a lifetime, or over several lifetimes. An individual integrates its experience with the application of the talent to the environment and thus creates a unique and new aspect of the personality.

A talent can become a trait of the larger personality and can contain, over time, experiences of how that talent can be used. The personality shares this knowledge through the Oversoul and through its interaction with other beings. This is also how civilizations learn as a group and how knowledge can be passed from one body of people to another.

Death

Axiom

Death is a transcendence from one mode of learning to another mode of learning.

Consciousness continues beyond death.

Emotions and emotional connections we have to other beings can continue after death. Emotional connections and thoughts (beliefs) help propel us from one level or dimension of realty to another.

Our emotional energies and our thoughts will determine how we perceive our reality after death, as they do in life. The difference is one of speed. After death, our reality is affected by our thoughts and feelings almost instantaneously. This is the biggest transition a being must make— Absorbing the realization that we are self-empowered, co-creators of our reality. Every observation contains within it the seeds of some deep-seated belief. As we observe, we also create based on our beliefs.

The learning school of the physical world is providing us with a slow-motion playing field upon which to experiment, test and observe how our co-creative powers affect what we perceive. We co-create the physical through cooperation with those around us.

Through the process of death we transcend the physical— and the learning continues. In fact, we use the process of death to advance our ability to assimilate what we have experienced in this "life" so that we may rely on that experience to advance to higher levels of consciousness.

As self-aware fragments of the Divine, we use the death experience to provide us with a shift from one level of consciousness to another. To make the energetic shift from daily physical awareness to a non-physical reality level without going through the process of death is possible. In our present level of development, death is part of our co-created reality structures and is a convenient method for transcendence. It is not the only method.

One of the purposes of "fatal" illness is to focus our attention on the death experience itself as there is much to be learned in this process.

Death as a Growth Process

Axiom

We are not alone in the death process. Guides and higher beings are always available to provide assistance and comfort during the transition process. Some provide assistance as a matter of course, others provide assistance when called upon.

Fear of death is a fear of growing to the next level of our spiritual development. There is an unknown aspect of this growth experience.

Focusing on and experiencing the Divine Love that is available to us always will melt the fear from our hearts and ease our transition.

One of our roles on the Earth plane is to assist others in their transition through the death process by providing them with loving support and high energy thoughts.

During the death process, the Oversoul gently folds us back into itself, into our Higher Self where we integrate experiences of the lifetime just past . Through the Oversoul, we share with other aspects of our self, what we have learned and we begin to build a feeling matrix of where our next learning lessons will take us.

The level and depth of love that exists in the Oversoul is extremely powerful and contains a beauty and joyousness we seldom experience on the Earth plane.

Reincarnation

Axiom

Reincarnation is the application of the vital energy of being to the playing field of physical existence. As a being manifests and integrates itself into the physical world for the purpose of learning how to deal with energies of its own creation, it acquires experience. It may pull back from its interaction with denser physical energies for periods of time in order to correlate that experience into itself. It then may reenter the physical arena to fill in gaps in experience or to expand on experiences it wishes to know more about, or to acquire whole new realms of experience, thus entering once again the time-stream of the physical for the purposes of integration.

Prior periods of integration give the being a greater depth of understanding with which to formulate new realities in which to learn and test its new knowledge. Periods of integration with the physical universe provide knowledge and experience to a being which it can then rely on at other periods and other of its incarnations. Multiple incarnations are possible and learning occurs in multiple dimensions at once. Reincarnation is not a linear function. It is a multidimensional phenomenon in which we play a much more active, conscious role than we realize.

Layers of Mind

Axiom

The Heart is part of the Mind. Overemphasis on the value of analytical thought has created a collection of mind chatter that interferes with the ability to feel the thoughts of the Heart. The Heart Center energies are part of the overall Mind of an individual, which is not the brain, but a collection of multidimensional energies stored in an energy field around the individual and in both physical and non-physical space.

Humankind's evolution and integration into the physical world required at some point in the past an emphasis on the development of analytical thought, somewhat independent of the body's intuitive feeling and instinctual drives. That analytical development has been largely achieved and a re-integration of that function into the larger overall mind is now required for the human to advance into the next stage of evolution as a new being. That is happening now across the planet.

Right now, we live as a planetary species with two distinctly different evolutionary states. Two "kinds" of human. One consists of a fragmented mind where the layers are not integrated one with the other. The new emerging being is one where the layers of mind are integrated with each other and with spirit. This is an evolutionary leap. Right now, both the new form and the old form are co-existing on the planet. We are entering a period of major adjustment and change on the planet as more people transition to this new level of being and the old paradigms of existence fall away. We are weaving for ourselves a new and expanded consciousness at each moment. Those of like-mind seek each other out in order to co-create this new level of reality and to assist others who are ready to make this transition. This is accomplished through raising the frequencies of light and vibrational states. This is the role of the new artisans of the future. This is your role now.

Appendices

Appendix A

Courage of the Heart

Chris's story of one of strength and commitment. After an accident in 1995 left her in a coma for twenty-one days, she awoke to find she had to learn to walk and talk all over again. Her world as a gymnast and gymnastics coach was forever changed. Since that time, she has worked ceaselessly to bring herself into a new life. She has worked with and helped others along the way, and continues to coach children's gymnastics part time whenever possible. Here is her inspiring poem on goals.

Goals

A goal is obtained
after a long, hard **drive.**
The ambitiousness we hold
in our hearts we cannot **hide.**

Our destiny to live prosperously,
strong and healthy **lives,**
are in the governings we choose,
which our minds and souls **derive.**

They say, "be all you can be,"
and "to thine own self be **true,"**
but it really comes down to…
your inner spirit drives **you.**

Let your energies flow free,
keep your heart and mind so **clear,**
that you'll find goals attainable
and your drive very easy to **steer.**

—Christine Greenia Mencarelli

Appendix B

Medical Terminology

As with any complex or technical subject, an understanding of the basic terminology is vital to comprehending the material. There are a great many technical terms associated with the heart and circulatory system. Here is a list of key words that are worth defining and becoming familiar with.

- Angina Pectoris— a pain in the chest caused by an insufficient blood flow to the heart area, making it difficult for the heart to do its job.
- Angioplasty— the surgical process of inserting a catheter (tube) from an artery in the leg up to the obstructed coronary artery. A balloon attached to the tip of the catheter is then inflated and deflated several times to compress the plaque buildup inside the artery. This is a process of opening the artery manually, and effects are sometimes temporary. (Some 926,000 angioplasties were done in the United States in 1998.)
- Aorta— the main artery that carries blood away from the heart.
- Artery— a tubular vessel that carries blood away from the heart.
- Arteriosclerosis— a hardening of the arteries.
- Atrium— one of the hollow cavities of the heart.
- Capillary— tiny, thin-walled tubes that carry blood between arteries and veins.
- Cardiac arrhythmia— an irregular heart beat, sometimes caused by heart disease.

- Cardiac failure— an inability of the heart to pump blood in sufficient quantity to meet the body's needs.
- Cardiac— pertaining to the heart, from the Greek word Kardiakos.
- Cardiac arrhythmia— abnormal heart rhythms.
- Cardiac defibrillation— a common emergency procedure that is performed by delivering an electric shock to the heart with a machine called a defibrillator. Defibrillation stops the rapid, uncoordinated heart contractions (called fibrillation).
- Cardiomyopathy— a disease in which the heart muscle becomes inflamed and doesn't work as well as it should.
- Cardiovascular— pertaining to the heart and the blood vessels.
- Cardiovascular disease— diseases of the heart and blood vessels.
- Cholesterol— Cholesterol is a soft, waxy substance found among the lipids (fats) in the blood and in all body cells. It's an important part of a healthy system because it's used to form cell membranes, some hormones and other needed tissues. Too high a level of cholesterol in the blood is a major risk factor for coronary heart disease, which leads to heart attack. Cholesterol and other fats can't dissolve in the blood. They have to be transported to and from the cells by special carriers called lipoproteins. There are several kinds, but the ones to be most aware of are low-density lipoprotein (LDL) and high-density lipoprotein (HDL). . If too much LDL cholesterol circulates in the blood, it can slowly build up in the walls of the arteries feeding the heart and brain. HDL cholesterol is known as "good" cholesterol because a high level of HDL seems to protect against heart attack. The total cholesterol levels in adults of 240 mg/dL or higher are considered high risk, and levels from 200 to 239 mg/dL are considered borderline-high risk. According to the American Heart Association, an estimated 100.9 million American adults have total blood

cholesterol values of 200 mg/dL and higher, and about 40.6 million American adults have levels of 240 or higher.

- Coronary— pertaining to a circle or crown.
- Coronary arteries— the two arteries that supply blood to the heart muscles.
- Coronary artery disease— a condition where the arteries cannot get enough blood to the heart, usually caused by hardening of the arteries making.
- Coronary bypass— an operation to bypass non-functioning arteries to restore blood flow (About 553,000 coronary artery bypass graft operations were done in the United States in 1998.)
- Coronary occlusion— a blockage or closure of one of the coronary arteries, usually by a blood clot.
- Coronary thrombosis— is the term for the most common variety of heart attack. The technical name for a heart attack. Heart attacks occur when the heart muscle becomes damaged through lack of oxygen. This usually happens when a coronary artery or one of its branches becomes blocked by a blood clot. The result of coronary thrombosis is *cardiac* or *myocardial infarction*, death of part of the heart muscle. (About 25 percent of the people who die from heart attacks have no prior symptoms. Some people experience heart attacks and do not even realize they are having a heart attack.)
- Echocardiography – the use of ultrasound technology to create pictures of the heart. This technology allows doctors to study the movement of the heart muscle to determine how well it is functioning.
- Electrocardiograph— a machine that can measure and record the electrical impulses generated by the heart as it beats. Abbreviated ECG.
- Embolism— a blood clot that travels through the blood stream and causes a blockage.
- Heart Attack— See Coronary thrombosis.

- Hypertension— high blood pressure, usually caused by narrowing of the arteries. Individuals affected with hypertension are often at risk for heart disease, kidney failure, and stroke.
- Hypertrophic Cardiomyopathy— an excessive enlargement and thickening of the heart muscle.
- Ischemia— A localized tissue anemia due to obstruction of the inflow of arterial blood. Ischemia refers to the effects of inadequate blood supply. To function properly, your heart requires a constant supply of oxygen-rich blood. If the coronary arteries, which deliver blood to the heart, become too narrow from arteriosclerosis, not enough blood gets to the heart. If the coronary arteries become completely blocked, heart tissue begins to die from lack of oxygen, and a heart attack occurs.
- Myocardium— The muscular wall of the heart. The outer surface is called the epicardium and the inner lining is called the endocardium.
- Pericardium— The thin sac that surrounds the heart and the roots of the great blood vessels.
- Quadruple bypass— A complex surgical procedure that involves taking a blood vessel from the chest or leg and using it to bypass a blocked artery in the heart. The vessel is removed from the chest or leg and sewn into the heart. If three arteries are repaired, it is called a triple bypass. If four arteries are repaired it is called a quadruple bypass.
- Thymus glands— Glands consisting of two separate lobes which reside just above, and in contact with the heart.
- Vein— tubular branching vessels that carry blood from capillaries toward the heart.
- Ventricle— a chamber of the heart that receives blood from the atrium of the same side and pumps it into the arteries.

Appendix C

Providing Care for People with Immune Deficiency

By Karen Ball, LMT

Only as We Heal Ourselves Can Our Presence Become Healing. The more we are willing to acknowledge, express and work with our beliefs regarding illness, death, pain and lifestyles different from our own, the more we will be able to offer our clients a sense of peace, hope and acceptance.

The person living with AIDS (PLWA) has been traumatized on every level. This person deserves our utmost care and compassion. Slow, gentle, loving work offers the client an opportunity to soften, open and relax.

Be aware of the desire to adhere to a predetermined agenda, at the expense of the client's needs in the moment. When we are concerned with details, technique, performance and/or being "right", we are acting out a sense of responsibility *for* our clients. When we feel responsible *to* our clients, we are concerned with relating person-to-person.

Greatest Risk: By far, the greatest risk is to the person with a compromised immune system. Common everyday pathogens can easily "lay this person out" for weeks and weeks, as well as further tax the already depleted immune system. For this reason, if you feel sick (ex. a cold), or are aware of carrying an easily spread microbe, consider staying home. Being in close proximity to a person with immune deficiency poses a major threat to that person's well being.

HIV and AIDS Conditions:

Guidelines for Massage
HIV, the virus credited with causing AIDS, is not highly contagious.

Unlike flu or tuberculosis, it is not spread by coughs and sneezes.

Unlike malaria or the plague, it is not transmitted by insects.

Unlike cholera, it is not ingested through contaminated food or water.

Unlike smallpox, *HIV cannot be spread by casual skin contact. Massage therapy therefore is a low-risk occupation when it comes to HIV/AIDS.*

The spread of HIV results from certain specific behaviors; behaviors that are generally within our control. That is both the good news and the bad!

Death figures from complications due to AIDS are dwarfed by the number of deaths from other entirely preventable causes. For example, one-quarter million children die every week from undernourishment. *Malnutrition is the leading cause of immune deficiency worldwide. It is a weak immune system that invites the effects of opportunistic parasites and viruses, including HIV.*

Precautions that should have been explained during the first weeks of all massage therapy training programs, if followed scrupulously, will keep the therapist safe from HIV, as well as other infectious microbes. Anxiety dissipates when the therapist is well informed.

There is an increased risk of tuberculosis infection when in contact with individuals with suppressed immune systems. All health care practitioners are encouraged to get regular skin tests for tuberculosis if in contact with PLWAs. A universal telephone screening practice of inquiring as to whether the person is dealing with a persistent cough or fever is certainly prudent. Anyone with a persistent cough and/or fever should see a physician for evaluation of the condition before receiving massage therapy.

Theoretically, in order to transmit HIV during a massage, there would have to be an *open* sore on *both* the practitioner's and client's bodies that *makes contact*. Intact healthy skin is adequate protection from exposure. Use rubbing alcohol, vinegar or lemon juice to detect open cuts on your hands.

Source:

From AIDS Online, an online educational course by Karen Ball, LMT, for massage therapists and bodyworkers. For further information and detailed guidelines please see http://www.aidscourse.com.

Appendix D
Contact Information

Energy Work Modalities and

Subtle Energy Research

Subtle Energy and Energy Medicine
ISSSEEM Central Office
International Society for the Study of
Subtle Energies and Energy Medicine
11005 Ralston Rd., #100D
Arvada, CO 80004
Phone (303) 425-4625 Fax (303) 425-4685
issseem@compuserve.com
www.issseem.org

ISSSEEM is one of the leaders in the effort to synthesize traditional wisdom and shamanic knowledge about subtle energies and energy medicine with scientific theory and study it with scientific method. Designed as a bridge between scientifically-inclined intuitives and intuitively-inclined scientists, ISSSEEM supports experimental exploration of the phenomena long associated with the practice of energy healing. Through conferences, a quarterly magazine, *Bridges*, and a peer-reviewed scientific journal, *Subtle Energies*, the Society serves its members and strives to stimulate theory, research, and discussion in the larger scientific community.

The EMF Balancing Technique
The Energy Extension, Inc.
595 West Main Street, PMB 77
Norwich, CT 06360
860-889-3451
energyinc@aol.com
www.EMFBalancingTechnique.com

The International Center for Reiki Training
21421 Hilltop Street, Unit #28
Southfield, Michigan 48034
(800) 332-8112 Local: (248) 948-8112 Fax: (248) 948-9534
center@reiki.org
www.reiki.org

Energy Works
(Kirlian camera equipment, biofeedback, massage, etc.)
Energy Works
1085 Tantra Park Circle
Boulder, CO 80303
Phone (303) 554-9812
Eworks@milehigh.net
www.kirlian.org

Institute of HeartMath
14700 West Park Ave.
Boulder Creek, CA 95006
Phone (831) 338-8500 Fax (831) 338-8504
info@heartmath.org

The Institute of Heartmath® is a non-profit research and education organization. The goal of the Institute for Heartmath is to conduct research on the human heart and its role in establishing physiological, mental and emotional coherence and to develop effective interventions to improve learning, performance, behaviors, health and quality of life.

Massage Therapy

American Massage Therapy Association
820 Davis Street, Suite 100
Evanston, IL 60201-4444
Phone (847) 864-0123 Fax (847) 864-1178
www.amtamassage.org/home.htm

Baby Massage Video Tape ($25)
Baby Touch, LLC
3043 Central Street SE
Olympia, WA 98501
Phone (877) 782-6476 Fax (775) 855-5215
info@babymassage.net.

Touch Research Institutes (TRI)
University of Miami School of Medicine
P.O. Box 016820
Miami Fl, 33101
Phone (305) 243-6781 Fax (305) 243-6488
tfield@med.miami.edu
www.miami.edu/touch-research/

The first Touch Research Institute was formally established in 1992 by Director Tiffany Field, Ph.D. at the University of Miami School of Medicine via a start-up grant from Johnson & Johnson. The TRI was the first center in the world devoted solely to the study of touch and its application in science and medicine. The TRI's distinguished team of researchers, representing Duke, Harvard, Maryland, and other universities, strive to better define touch as it promotes health and contributes to the treatment of disease. Research efforts that began in 1982 and continue today have shown that touch therapy has numerous beneficial effects on health and well-being. The second TRI is located in the Philippines. A third TRI is located at the University of Paris and studies the role of touch in perception, learning, and psychopathology. A fourth TRI is located at the UCLA Medical School Pediatric Pain Center and is focused on the use of touch therapies with children's pain syndromes.

Massage—Biotone—Professional products for massage therapy
Phone: (800) 445-6457
Info@biotone.com
www.biotone.com

Living Earth Crafts (Massage tables)
Phone (800) 358-8292
www.livingearthcrafts.com

Essential Oils—Young Living
Young Living Essential Oils
250 South Main Street
Payson, UT 84561
www.youngliving.net/corporate
Webinfo@youngliving.com
Phone: (800) 763-9963 (Orders—distributor #262-369)

Nutrition and Nutritional Supplements

Foods without Hydrogenated Oils

David L. Dewey, an author/columnist, provides a web site with information on companies that produce foods that do not contain hydrogenated oils.
www.dldewey.com

Free Radical Research—The Oxygen Society
2950 Buskirk Avenue, Suite 170
Walnut Creek, CA 94596.
Phone (925) 472-5904 Fax (925) 472-5901
info@oxygensociety.org.
www.sfrr.org

Established in 1987, the Oxygen Society is a professional organization comprised of over 1,200 scientists, researchers and clinicians with an interest in the field of free radical biology, chemistry and medicine. The association is the North and South American affiliate chapter of the International Society for Free Radical Research

Gematria Products Inc. (Laser energized nutritional supplements.)
2075 Corte Del Nogal
Suite A
Carlsbad, CA 92009
Phone (760) 931-8563
www.Gematria.com

Medical Information/Health Organizations/

Support Groups

American Diabetes Association
1701 North Beauregard Street
Alexandria, VA 22311
1-800-DIABETES (1-800-342-2383)
www.diabetes.org

American Heart Association
7272 Greenville Avenue
Dallas, TX 75231-4596
(800) AHA-USA1 (242-8721)
www.americanheart.org

Citizens for Public Action on
Blood Pressure and Cholesterol
PO Box 30374
Bethesda, MD 20824
Phone (202) 362-7563 Fax (202) 362-7565

Coronary Club, Inc.
9500 Euclid Avenue, E-37
Cleveland, OH 44195
(216) 444-3690 (800) 829-2506

Mended Hearts, Inc.
7272 Greenville Avenue
Dallas, TX 75231
(214) 706-1442
www.mendedhearts.org

National Center for Nutrition and Dietetics
216 W. Jackson Blvd.
Chicago, IL 60606-6995
Phone (312) 899-0040 Fax: (312) 899-1979
www.eatright.org/ncnd.html

National Heart, Lung, and Blood Institute
Information Center Public Health Service
P.O. Box 30105
Bethesda, MD 20824
(301) 251-1222
www.nhlbi.nih.gov

U.S. Department of Health and Human Services
Centers for Disease Control and Prevention
National Center for Health Statistics
Division of Data Services
Hyattsville, MD 20782-2003
(301) 458-4636
www.hhs.gov

Will Rogers Institute
1640 Marengo Street, Suite 406
Los Angeles, CA 90033
Phone (888) 994-3863 Fax (323) 223-0035
www.wrinstitute.org

Ayurveda

The Ayurvedic Institute (Treatments, Studies, Training)
11311 Menaul Boulevard NE
Albuquerque, NM 87112
Phone (505) 291-9698
Info@ayurveda.com
www.ayurveda.com

American Institute of Vedic Studies
P.O. Box 8357
Santa Fe, NM 87504-8357
Phone (505) 983-9385
Vedicinst@aol.com
www.vedanet.com

Bazaar of India Imports
1810 University Ave.
Berkeley, CA 94703
Phone (800) 261-7662
info@ayur-veda.com
www.Ayur-veda.com

Appendix E
You Can Sponsor a Child

Here is an activity, a commitment, which will benefit others as well as help you open your heart through the process of giving.

There are many organizations that provide a process through which you can sponsor a child for $15 or $20 per month, which provides that child and their family with medical care, emergency food and vitamins, educational materials, clothes, improved living conditions and other basic needs.

You can also write to the child you sponsor and receive information back on their progress and growth.

This is a beautiful experience and one that lets you step outside of yourself and your problems, and contributes love and encouragement to another.

There are many such organizations. Here is one that I have personal knowledge of and one that has been around for a long time. They sponsor over 250,000 children in 9 countries around the world. The provide medical care, emergency treatment, relief to families who are victims of disaster, and much needed educational and basic living supplies.

The organization staff are very friendly and helpful. Their web site explains the entire program and has photographs of those children in need of sponsors. Sponsorship is $15 per month for a child, which is probably the lowest of any sponsorship program.

Please visit their web site— www.Children.org

Children International
P.O. Box 219055
Kansas City, MO 64121
(800) 888-3089

Appendix F
Recommended Music

"The Journey Home"
Hemi-Sync Metamusic
Developed by the Monroe Institute
Monroe Products/P.O. Box 505
Lovingston, VA 22949
(804) 263-8692
www.Hemi-Sync.com

Metamusic incorporates evocative sounds and specially blended Hemi-Sync frequencies to guide you into focused, whole-brain states of consciousness. The Hemi-Sync sound patterns on this recording help you achieve and sustain synchronized brain-wave activity in both hemispheres of your brain, an optimal condition of improving human performance. Stereo headphones are required to get the full benefit from the hemi-sync technology, but this music can also be used without headphones as background music during energy sessions or body work.

"Reiki: The Light Touch"
Merlin's Magic
Inner Worlds Music
154 Betasso Road, Boulder, Co 80302
(800) 444-9678

This CD contains sixty minutes of beautiful, serenely blissful instrumental music for healing and happiness. This recording was specifically composed and arranged by Andreas Mock of Merlin's Magic to be played during Reiki treatments, but its soothing sounds are also wonderful for many other forms of body work, energy balancing, meditation or relaxation. This music includes the lovely sounds of acoustic guitar, piano, keyboards, violin, viola and deeply resonant Tibetan bells. Fantastic!

"Sequencia"
Susan Alexjander
Logos Series
Box 8162
Berkeley, CA 94707

Beautiful, peaceful music derived from the molecular vibrations of DNA. This CD is very unique. Good to play while reading, relaxing or during massage. Raise your energy vibrations, gently!

"Sounds of Eternity"
Harmony Wind Harps
P.O. Box 3039
Pagosa Springs, CO 81147
(970) 264-2962
www.stationlink.com/windharp

Harmony Wind Harps(TM) are interactive outdoor acoustic sculptures which generate harmonic sounds by translating the subtle energies of the wind and earth vibrations into a full spectrum symphony of sound. These sleep contemporary designs are built using the principles of Sacred Geometry. (available on cassette only)

"Treasure Falls"
Maureen Kelly and Sundhara Barrable
P.O. Box 4820
Pagosa Springs, CO 81147
(970) 264-2962
www.stationlink.com/treasure

Beautiful music on folk harp and flute, composed and recorded in a single session in Pagosa Springs, Colorado. (available on cassette only)

"The Silent Path"
Robert Coxon
(800) 352-6657
kryonbooks@kryon.com
www.kryon.com/k_coxon.html

Robert Coxon provides his most angelic music to date. Exquisite melodic orchestrations, blending acoustic instruments with rich synthesizer textures and the ethereal sound of a giant sacred bowl, create an optimum setting for total relaxation and total well-being on all levels. Coxon uses a combination of synthesizer and real instruments to create magnificent melodies with a lush symphonic background

"Essence" & *"Love is Space"*
by Deva Premal
Deva, Miten; Prabhu Productions
www.mitendevapremal.com
(fax) (979) 249-3653

A variety of beautiful songs, chants and music encompassing the feelings of joy and compassion. Taken from various ancient sources in Tibet, India and elsewhere, Deva and Miten's music is profoundly uplifting and healing.

Appendix G
Recommended Online References
and Resources

Energy Work— Body Work— Spiritual Growth

Luminarch Resources: Spirit/Mind/Body
Articles, References and Links on Reiki, Energy Balancing, Massage, Ayurveda, Meditation, & more.
www.Luminarch.com

EnergyDynamics: Conscious Human Evolution
Axioms and Resources for Personal Growth, Balance and the Evolution of Your Body's Energy Systems
www.EnergyDynamics.org

The EMF Balancing Technique(r) by Peggy Phoenix Dubro.
Energy Extension Inc., Peggy and Steve Dubro
www.EMFBalancingTechnique.com

Kryon (Books, Tapes, Seminars, Information & More; Lee Carroll)
www.Kryon.com

International Center for Reiki Training
www.Reiki.org

InnerWords Magazine
Words from the Heart, Touching Other Hearts— A beautiful magazine focusing on personal and spiritual growth, greater health, and increased awareness. Articles, advertisements, book reviews, services and more.
www.InnerWords.com

American Massage Therapy Association
www.amtamassage.org/home.htm

The Monthly Aspectarian— magazine and online resource page, spirit/mind/body
www.lightworks.com/MonthlyAspectarian/

The Ayurvedic Institute (Treatments, Studies, Training)
www.Ayurveda.com

The Monroe Institute (Catalog, Workshops, Hemisync Technology, & more)
www.MonroeInstitute.org

Bodywork Central (Massage, etc.)
www.BodyWorkCentral.com

Yoga Research and Education Center (YREC)
www.yrec.org/feuerstein.html

Touch Research Institutes (TRI)
University of Miami School of Medicine
www.miami.edu/touch-research/

My Healer's Creed (online) (Kay Cook)
http://pages.prodigy.net/kaycook

Aids Online Course (Karen Ball, LMT)
www.aidscourse.com/

ISSSEEM
International Society for the Study of Subtle Energies and Energy Medicine
www.issseem.org

Doven Starr Reiki Site
www.usui-reiki.org

EnergySchool.com (Yin-Yang material and more)
www.EnergySchool.com

Other Online References

Artwork of Cheryl Yambrach Rose
www.CherylRose.com

Gematria Products— Laser Energized Nutritional Supplements
www.Gematria.com

The Oxygen Society (Free Radical Research)
www.sfrr.org

Children International (Sponsor a Child in Need)
www.Children.org

The Mineral and Gemstone Kingdom
www.minerals.net

Appendix H
Restful Sleep Formula

- 1 Cup of warm milk
- 500 mg of Kava Kava
- 2 mg of Melatonin
- 500 mg of Magnesium
- 1000 mg of Calcium

Taken about 15 minutes before bedtime, this combination gently relaxes the body and mind and helps promote sleep. You can start with ½ of the above dosage to see it that works for you. Do *not* take this with alcohol, sleeping pills or any prescription medication or over-the-counter medication.

Taken in the middle of the night, it may also help you get back to sleep.

Calcium and Magnesium can usually be found together as a supplement in most health flood sections.

You may want to reduce or omit some of the ingredients above from time to time, so the body does not get used to the formula. For example, skip the Kava Kava portion for a week and return to it if needed.

Other tips for restful sleep include:

- limit or omit caffeine intake after 4:00 p.m., and none after 6:00 p.m.
- limit or omit late meals, i.e., after 8:00 p.m.

- take an early evening walk followed by stretching exercises 2 or 3 hours before bed
- have a "wind down" period before bed; no violent movies or other excitement.
- listen to soothing music or sleep inducing music (e.g., "Super Sleep" by Monroe Inst.)
- meditation or light reading may suite your wind down time also

(If you have severe medical problems or severe sleep disorders, consult your medical practitioner.)

Appendix I
Glossary

Anahata (1) (the Fourth Chakra) This chakra is represented as having twelve petals. It is located at the heart, in the center of the chest. It is also associated with the cardiac plexus and the thymus gland. (2) This is the first chakra above the diaphragm. This chakra center is associated with the lungs as well as the heart. Prana and the element of air are focused here. It is a center of nurturing both of self (lungs/heart) and others (breasts) and the seat of the higher emotions, feelings, (e.g. love, empathy, compassion). This is the first center that deals with issues that truly transcend the individual self. It is often seen as the center that integrates the lower and higher chakras. This is often represented by the six-pointed star, the combination of downward and upward pointing triangles. A cross, centered at the heart chakra symbolizes the integration of male and female, yin and yang, as well as the upper and lower. The energy that comes through the heart, that is relatively free of the attachment associated with the lower chakras, is more properly termed feeling, as opposed to emotion. As the attachment drops away true compassion can appear. (Source: *Yoga and Psychotherapy: the Evolution of Consciousness*, Swami Rama, Rudolph Ballentine, and Alan Weinstock). (3) The Fourth Chakra is called Anahata, it is located above the heart and it affects ones issues in the areas of acceptance, generosity and sense of security. When this center is in a state of imbalance, one may show signs of jealousy. Some of the crystals used to help balance the Fourth Chakra energies include Green Jade, Aventurine and Rosequartz.

Antioxidant Antioxidants are known as "anti-aging" agents. An Antioxidant is a nutrient or chemical that intercepts and neutralizes destructive free radicals in the body. (A free radical is an atom with an unpaired electron.) Antioxidants are sometimes called "free radical scavengers." Some examples of antioxidants include vitamin A, vitamin C, vitamin E, some of the B vitamins, and beta-carotene. Other antioxidants include the mineral selenium, as well as the enzyme Glutamine and other amino acids. Some antioxidants prevent the cellular damage from beginning, some antioxidants stop the damage while it is occurring, and others help repair the damage after it has occurred. Reactive oxygen species (ROS) such as the superoxide (O_2 -) and the hydroxyl radical (OH) are aggressive chemical compounds that can induce tissue destruction and aging. (See also **Free Radical**)

Ascension (1) The process of raising one's vibration through the power of intent. The intent to start the ascension status of enlightenment is an intent to break out of the mold of being in the "flock." The Human in the new energy, casting off his karma and contract, and moving into the next incarnation without Human death. Then, without an existing contract, creating one as he goes. (Source: Kryon book VII, "*Letters from Home*" Kryon/Lee Carroll, The Kryon Writings, 1999). (2) The act of rising, ascending; going up.

Aura The Aura is a collection of energy vibrations that surround an object or life form. The human aura is partly composed of electromagnetic radiation at various vibrations and wavelengths. The exact nature (vibrational level) of the aura varies depending on the energy level of the person, and the type of emotional energy the person is emanating. Some people can see the aura as a display of colors. The colors correspond to the various wavelengths of the energy being emitted. The meaning of the various colors of the aura has been researched and is sometimes used as an indicator of the emotional, physical or spiritual health of the person being observed. Some colors of the aura can be detected using Kirilian photography.

Ayurveda The word Ayurveda means "the Science of Life." It is a science of health and healing which originated in India over 6,000 years ago. Ayurveda is part of the ancient Vedic Sciences, which include herbal medicine, dietetics, body work, surgery, psychology and spirituality, documented in the sacred writings or Vedas.

Balance (1) Noun. The condition of balance, in terms of energy, means that your energy fields and energy centers are open to the natural flow of energy in and out of your system, as you interact with other people and with your environment. Being out of balance is a condition where the energies of the body are out of phase to a point where their natural and graceful of flow is impeded. Dis-ease is the result of an out-of-balance condition. Dis-ease may manifest as a physical ailment if the imbalance is allowed to continue for any length of time. (2) Verb. To work with the body's energy fields and fibers to bring about a state of optimal health, equilibrium and energy flow.

Balancing Energy (See **Energy**)

Binaural Beat Binaural beats are auditory responses, which originate in the superior olivary nucleus of each hemisphere of the human brain. Binaural beats result from the interaction of two different auditory impulses. Using headphones, a different signal is sent to each ear. When there is a difference in frequency of between 1 and 30 Hz between the left and right head speakers, a tone is experienced in the brain as a sound. For example, a 380 Hz tone is played in one ear and a 370 Hz tone is played in the other ear. The brain will "hear a 10 Hz tone, that is a binaural beat. Binaural music has been studies and used as an aid to raising human consciousness. (Reference: Inteligen, Inc.).

Brainwave Frequencies The human brain emits various electromagnetic waves at certain frequencies. These frequencies have been associated with certain mental states of awareness.

Chi A Chinese name for life force energy. (See also **Chi Kung** and **Tai Chi.**)

Chi Kung (pronounced "Chee Gung") Chi Kung is a Chinese term having various spellings in English, such as Chi Gung and Qigong. The term "Chi" refers to universal energy, universal life force. The Japanese call this "Ki." You will recognize the root word in such practices as "Tai Chi," "Aikido," etc. The term "Kung" means to "practice, cultivate, or refine. Chi Kung is based on Chinese healing traditions that go back thousands of years. The practice of Chi Kung helps bring about a calmness of the mind and emotions, and health and vitality to the body. There are many, many forms of Chi Kung. The Chinese consider Tai Chi to be a form of Chi Kung.

Classical Physics (see **Newtonian Physics**)

Cosmic Lattice The Cosmic Lattice is the energy of Spirit. It is the energy of the universe. The Cosmic Lattice communicates with human biology through a series of magnetic resonant frequencies. (See Kryon Book VII: *Letters from Home*, p. 342, The Cosmic Lattice, 1999, Kryon/Lee Carroll).

Cultural Dynamics Cultural Dynamics are those group energy forces and thought forms that tend to guide or influence the interactions of our personality with other personalities on this plane. Cultural Dynamics are a type of Group Personality, which governs the way we interact with others by establishing acceptable and non-acceptable behaviors. For example, if our particular culture has a thought form agreement that expressing love and affection in public is poor taste, that dynamic will influence how we relate to one another at the personality level within our day-to-day experience. Each society and time period has its own Cultural Dynamics.

Crystal A crystal is a solid material with ordered internal molecular structure of regularly repeating three-dimensional patterns. Natural crystals are formed in the earth. Man grows synthetic crystals in specially controlled environments. (See also **Quartz Crystal**).

Crystal Healing The use of crystals in energy manipulation to facilitate and improve the flow of energy within the body's energetic pathways. Different crystals have specific vibratory rates that correspond to certain areas of the body (certain energy centers or energy conditions). The vibratory rates of specific crystals correspond to certain positive attributes that make that particular crystal a suitable aid for facilitating healing of a specific area or condition.

deBroglie, Louis (1892-1987) In 1923, French aristocrat and Nobel Prize winner Louis deBroglie's Ph.D. thesis submitted to the University of Sorbonne, in Paris postulated that matter had a wave-like attribute. Albert Einstein agreed with deBroglie's theory and it was consistent with Einstein's famous $E=mc(2)$ equation.

DHEA DHEA stands for Dehydroepiandrosterone. DHEA is the most abundant hormone produced by the adrenal glands. In the body, DHEA is converted to testosterone and estrogen. The brain normally contains the highest concentration of DHEA over other body tissues. Research indicates DHEA therapeutic effects in many chronic conditions including cardiovascular disease, diabetes, obesity, multiple sclerosis, Parkinson's disease, Alzheimer's disease, disorders of the immune system, depression, and osteoporosis. It is reported to have anti-aging properties.

DNA DNA is the molecule Deoxyribonucleic acid. It has been called the building block of life. Biochemically, DNA is a complex molecule composed of genetic instructions for the development of the body. DNA is found in almost all the cells of the body, including white blood cells, skin, hair roots and body tissue. Traces of DNA can be detected in body fluids such as saliva, semen and perspiration

DNA music DNA music is algorithmic music created by the base sequences and properties of the DNA molecule. One such example is a musical collection called "*Sequencia*," by Susan Alexjander.

Earth Frequency The frequency of the Earth has been measured at about 8.6 Hz or 8.6 cycles per second.

Electromagnetic Radiation The term "Electromagnetic" refers to the composite theories of electricity and magnetism. Electromagnetic radiation is a self-propagating composite of an electric field plus a magnetic field. A change in the magnetic field produces a change in the electric field and a change in the electric field produces a change in the magnetic field. The Scottish physicist James Clerk Maxwell developed the unified theories of electric and magnetic phenomena in a complete mathematical theory.

Electromagnetic Spectrum The Electromagnetic Spectrum is a representation of the various frequencies of energy in our universe, which includes the entire radio, light and radiation wavelengths from the very large to the extremely small.

EMF— Electromagnetic Field. An electromagnetic field is a manifestation of energy generated by the movement (vibration)

of energy in a specific pattern. All objects have an electromagnetic field. In the human, the electromagnetic field surrounding the body is a subtle but powerful vibrational energy field that interacts with and is part of the energy of the mind, emotions and the physiology. Disharmonious vibratory patterns are areas of the field which are out of balance. These disharmonious vibratory patterns are representations of, and can influence, the physical, mental, and emotional state of the individual. The origin of the field is the spirit. The field exists because spirit intends that it exist.

Endocrine System A system of glands in the body that secrete substances directly into the circulatory system to help integrate and control the body's metabolism. The endocrine glands include the pituitary, thyroid, parathyroids, adrenals, islets of Langerhans, ovaries, and testes

Endocrinology Endocrinology is the study of the chemical communication systems in the body that control a vast array of physiological processes. The Endocrine system is a communication system that contains transmitters (the hormone producing cells), signals (the hormones themselves) and receivers (also called receptors).

Energizing the Chakras The focusing of energy on or through the key energy vortices of the body, such as the seven primary Chakras. While standing, energizing can be accomplished by drawing energy up from the earth, through your feet, legs, thighs, and up along the spine. It can be accomplished while sitting, drawing energy up through the root Chakra and up the spine.

Energy (1) Energy is a vibrational potentiality capable of being directed, transformed, transmuted and transferred. At a gross level, energy can be thought of as vibrating particles in constant motion. However, the particles themselves are not solid and do not have defined locations in space. Therefore, they are not truly particles, as we understand the term. Matter is a solidified form of energy, based on our perception of what it means to be solid. Matter and energy are relative states, which rely on our perception and interpretation for their existence. Light and all forms of electromagnetics are energy. An energy field is simply a collection of energy patterns that are in a higher in vibrational state than the type of energy we normally refer to as "matter." All matter has energy fields; all matter is energy. There is no sharp dividing line between an object of matter and an energy field. One blurs into the other. Energy can be focused and directed through the conscious intent of an aware being. All forms of life have an energy pattern. When the pattern is disrupted by disharmonious energy wavelengths, physical, emotional or mental problems can result. Balancing energy is the act of removing obstacles to the free flow of energy within its basic pattern that allows the life form to more closely approximate its native state of wholeness, health and vitality. Evolution is an increase in the vibrational rate of an energy field over time, towards a higher state of being. (2) Energy is the "stuff" which spirit uses to manifest form, such as light, objects, or beings.

Energy Medicine The application of the knowledge of subtle energy flows and the basic nature of the human energy fields to the condition of mind/body interactions to promote health, healing and vitality. Energy medicine takes into account the nature of man/woman as a spiritual being and addresses the journey to wholeness as a return to higher vibrational states of energy, by removing obstacles which burden or block normal healthy energies. Energy medicine, in practice, includes a variety of modalities and techniques which when carefully used in combination can improve the overall health and functioning of the human system.

Entrainment (1) The phenomena of entrainment is observable in both physical and biological systems. If a tuning fork, for example, is struck and produces a vibration at 410 Hz (410 cycles per second) and brought into the vicinity of a similar tuning fork, the second tuning fork will also start to vibrate at the 410 frequency. This is the act of entrainment. In biological systems entrainment can occur when the frequency of the heart matches the frequency of the brain, for example, or when the heart frequencies of two different people come into synchronization. Entrainment is the tendency for two oscillating bodies to lock into phase so that they vibrate in harmony. It can also be defined as a synchronization of two or more rhythmic cycles. (2) A phenomenon seen throughout nature, whereby systems or organisms exhibiting periodic behavior will fall into sync and oscillate at the same frequency and phase. Specifically: **heart-brain entrainment** is a state in which very low frequency brain waves and heart rhythms are frequency-locked (entrained). This phenomenon has been associated with significant shifts in perception and heightened intuitive awareness. (Adapted from HeartMath Glossary.)

Feng Shui Feng Shui is an ancient eastern system that works with the circulation and flow of the life force (ch'i) in the living and working environment to create balance and harmony. Feng Shui is based on the scientific principle that everything is energy and that all things in the universe are connected by a common bond. (*Feng Shui: Your Personal Feng Shui Journey*, Carole J. Hyder, Crossings Press, 1998).

Free Radicals Free radicals are atoms with unpaired electrons. Free radicals are believed to cause aging, cancer, cardiovascular disease, and other body degeneration. Many free radicals are produced as a normal part of cellular metabolism, which takes place in the cell's mitochondria. Free radicals are also produced in the body through stress, exposure to ultraviolet rays of the sun, tobacco smoking, environmental pollution, exposure to radiation, and other causes. Free radicals are also formed when food is cooked in hydrogenated oils.

Frequency In physics, frequency is the number of periodic oscillations, vibrations or waves per unit of time; usually expressed in cycles per second ("cps" now more commonly represented by Hertz, or "Hz.")

Genome All the DNA contained in an organism or a cell, which includes both the chromosomes within the nucleus and the DNA in mitochondria. The genome is the genetic blueprint that gives instructions of how to create life. It is assumed that the total human genome consists of 80,000 genes containing 3.8 billion base pairs.

Grounding The earth is a massive, powerful, yet gentle receptor for bioelectric energies as well as celestial and cosmic energies. When one or more of your energy bodies becomes energized, or you have experienced an energy surge due to a release of blocked energy centers, it is a good practice to spend a minute or so grounding your self. Grounding can be accomplished by standing (barefoot is best) on the earth and envisioning energy gently flowing down to the earth and your energy fields becoming stable. Even more powerful results can be obtained by sitting naked on the earth, where your Root Chakra comes in direct contact with the earth. If you are not able to stop and get in direct contact with the earth, holding several hematite stones in your hands for several minutes can also help. Hematite is a metallic like stone with very good grounding properties. For some people, eating earthy foods such as organic peanut butter or bananas can be grounding as well.

Hatha-Yoga: The unitive discipline of the force (meaning the serpent power or *kundalinî-shakti*); or forceful unitive discipline. (Yoga Research and Education Center).

Heisenberg, Werner (1901-1976) Werner Heisenberg was one of the greatest physicists of the twentieth century. He is best known as a founder of quantum mechanics, and especially for the *uncertainty principle* in quantum theory. Heisenberg is also known for his controversial role as a leader of Germany's nuclear fission research during the 1940's. After World War II, Heisenberg was active in elementary particle physics and West German science policy. (Source: American Institute of Physics).

Hertz (Hz) The unit of measurement for frequency. 1 Hz is equal to 1 cycle per second.

High Blood Pressure (see **Hypertension**)

Holistic Healing— Holistic healing refers to a type of healing that treats the whole person and acknowledges the inter-relatedness of the body, mind and spirit in addressing the total health of a person.

Hormones Hormones are chemical messengers in the body that are secreted into the bloodstream or other circulatory system fluids by one type of cell that affects the functioning of other types of cells. Hormones are produced by the body to affect certain types of cells and certain processes. Cells that are affected by such hormones have specific receptors for those hormones. For example, adrenaline is a hormone produced by the adrenal glands.

Hypertension— Hypertension is high blood pressure. Blood pressure is the pressure inside the blood vessels. It is measured in two stages, one when the heart is relaxed (called diastolic pressure) and one when the heart is contracting (called systolic pressure). High-normal blood pressure is defined as a diastolic pressure between 85 and 89 or a systolic pressure between 130 and

139. Hypertension is indicated when a person's systolic pressure is 140 or higher, or when the diastolic pressure is 90 or higher. In reporting blood pressure it is usually reported systolic over diastolic such as "110 over 80" for example, meaning 100 systolic and 80 diastolic.

Category	Systolic Pressure	Diastolic Pressure
• Normal	less than 130	less than 85
• High Normal	130-139	85-89
• Hypertension	140 or greater	90 or greater

Intent Intent is focus of mind and will. It is the absolute focus of consciousness in the present moment, the NOW. All creativity comes from the application of our awareness to our environment. All prior conditions can be changed through application of intent. In energy work, intent is the aspect of the healing process that allows change. The intent is not to end a condition or event, the intent is always for the unimpeded flow of universal energy towards the highest good for those involved.

Karma Karma is a Sanskrit word that means "action." Karma can be understood as the law of causality. According to the Buddha's teaching, all actions, whether of thought, word or deed, are like seeds that will eventually bear fruit in experience, whether in this or future lives. (Source: *A Flash of Lightning in the Dark of Night: A Guide to the Bodhisattva's Way of Life*. The Dalai Lama, Shambala, 1994.)

Kirlian Photography Kirlian photography is a means of taking pictures of the nonphysical world without a camera. It provides a technology of viewing the patterns of energy and force fields that permeate all things. The technique can serve as a medical diagnostic instrument, too. The Kirlian effect is useful for recording energy balances and harmonies in all forms of life. The effect was discovered and documented in 1939 by a Russian technician Semyon D. Kirlian and his wife Valentina.

Kriyas Kriyas are physical and psychological manifestations that often appear during the process of Kundalini Rising. They may be gradual and subtle, or they may be very extreme and profound. Kriyas can consist of such things as shaking, trembling, heat sensations up the spine or other Chakra areas, tingling of the spine and extremities and other areas. As the Kundalini energy rises it can cause profound changes in the physical body, mind and energy bodies. As the energy moves upward, the Kriyas can become intense and noticeable in the head, neck, brow and around the ears. Sensations of cracking, popping, buzzing and musical notes or songs can be experienced.

Kundalinî-Yoga: The unitive discipline of the serpent power (*kundalinî-shakti*), which is fundamental to the Tantric tradition, including Hatha-Yoga. (Yoga Research and Education Center). Kundalini Yoga is specifically directed towards awakening the Kundalini life force through a complex series of exercises. Focus is also on the breath and the use of mantras. Kundalini Yoga requires a greater degree of commitment than basic Hatha Yoga, since it goes deeper into the nature of the Chakra energies and how these affect our entire being.

Light A form of energy. Light is a high vibrational state of energy that mirrors aspects of our own human energy field. The difference between visible light and non-visible light is *our* ability to perceive within a given rage of vibration, not an inherent difference in the light itself. Some people see a broader range of light frequencies than others. Since light is a form of energy, it is possible to sense or "see" light with other senses than just the eyes. Although traditional physics states that light has a uniform unchanging speed of 186,000 miles per second, there are forms of "light" that travel faster that that. In the world of energies, the concepts of "speed," "distance," "time," and "space" are so closely related to our act of perceiving them that we cannot talk of independent characteristics of light or energy without making it clear that we are creators of what we are perceiving. Conscious aware beings can manipulate light in a variety of ways. Vibrational medicine and energy balancing are manipulations of non-visible light through the application of conscious intent. Discoveries in quantum physics in the past 80 years have significantly changed our understanding of light and its relationship to matter, as well as its relationship to our perception of the universe we seek to understand. We actually create our universe through creating light. Our act of perceiving light is part of this creation process. The universe does not exist unless we choose to perceive it. It is by perceiving light, that we create light. (See also **energy.**)

Lymphatic Massage A type of massage therapy that focuses on the lymphatic system. It promotes a healthy exchange of lymphatic fluids and helps the body's self-protection mechanisms of the immune system.

Lymphatic System The lymphatic system in humans consists of the bone marrow, spleen, thymus gland, lymph nodes, appendix, tonsils, and a other organs. The lymphatic system stores the white blood cells that are a vital part of the body's physical immune system. The lymphatic system collects, filters and transports a clear fluid called "lymph" which exists outside the cells of the body. The lymph fluid bathes the body's tissues and plays a key role in fighting infection.

Lymph Nodes Lymph nodes are specialized dilations of lymphatic tissue which are supported within by a thin mesh of connective tissue or fibers. These fibers contain high numbers of lymphocytes and macrophages. Lymph nodes occur along the entire length of the lymphatic system. The lymph nodes drain the lymph from the system out through ducts and into the bloodstream. Lymph nodes pump infection-fighting cells called leukocytes into the bloodstream when needed.

Meditation Meditation is the process of getting in touch with oneself, through quieting the thoughts and tuning in to the experience of being. Chanting and specific physical postures are not meditation, they are activities added to the practice of meditation. They are not necessary for meditation. To meditate, simply sit quietly and "feel" your surroundings and your own beingness. Meditation is the act of becoming receptive and aware of the state of being. Meditation is a highly personal and subjective process. Done on a regular basis, it brings tremendous benefit to balancing the energies of the mind, body and spirit. Since the body's natural state is one of balance and self-reparation, the closer one is able to get to this natural state, the greater the benefits that are realized. One of the main benefits of mediation in the field of energy work is to quiet the internal, mental chatter that takes up much of our thinking processes during our waking hours.

Melatonin Melatonin is secreted by the pineal gland, which is a pea-size structure at the center of the brain. At night, melatonin is produced to help our bodies regulate sleep-wake cycles. The amount of melatonin produced by our body seems to lessen as we get older. Melatonin may reduce free radical damage; as well as stimulate the immune system; and bring about other beneficial effects. Recommended dosages vary and are still the subject of scientific research. Typical over the counter tablet dosage range from 3 mg (3 milligrams, or 3,000th of a gram) and 3 mcg (3 micrograms, or 3,000,000th of a gram).

Newtonian Physics (also called **Classical Physics**) Newtonian Physics is based on the works of Sir Isaac Newton (1643-1727) who drew upon the works of Galileo Galilei (1564-1642) and others. Newtonian Physics describes the actions of large bodies in the physical universe according to basic laws of motion and gravity. Newtonian Physics was found to not hold true when one observed motion and interaction of energy particles at the subatomic level. Subatomic physics is a field of study known as Quantum Physics, which deals with a view of the universe based on probabilities, energy quanta and the fundamental principles of Max Planck, Werner Heisenberg and others.

Perineum The Perineum is the area between the anus and the lower part of the external genitals. It is associated with the location of the root chakra.

Quantum (plural = **Quanta**) A Quantum is a small indivisible quantity. The word comes from the Latin term meaning basically "how much."

Quantum Physics Quantum physics is a branch of science that deals with discrete, indivisible units of energy called *"quanta."* It is a collection of theories about the nature of the universe that have their basis in the principles of Max Planck (1858-1947) and Werner Heisenberg.(1901-1976). Max Planck's Quantum Principle was that energy was absorbed or released only in discrete quanta or packets. Heisenberg's Uncertainty Principle states that one can never be exactly sure both the positions of a particle and its velocity at the same time. The more we are certain about one, the less certain we can be about the other. Quantum Physics is a very different way of looking at the universe than that used by classical physics or Newtonian Physics.

Quartz Crystal Quartz is a common mineral found in many rocks. Quartz is the hardest of all common minerals and its structure is very stable. The chemical composition of a quartz crystal is silicon and oxygen, and its symbol is SiO_2. Pure quartz crystal contains only silicon and oxygen and no other elements. This is sometimes called rock crystal and is usually very clear and often looks like glass. Quartz crystal has an unusual property called the "piezoelectric effect." The crystal vibrates with a specific frequency. The frequency of the vibration of a crystal depends on how thick it is. Quartz crystals have been used in many electrical and electronic devices where a constant frequency needs to be maintained. Quartz is sometimes used in making lenses. Quartz will allow the transmission of many ultraviolet rays that will not pass through glass.

Resonance (1) Magnetic Resonance is the absorption or emission of electromagnetic radiation by electrons or atomic nuclei in response to the application of certain magnetic fields. Principles of magnetic resonance can be applied in the laboratory to analyze the atomic and nuclear properties of matter. (2) In physics, resonance is the relatively large selective response of an object or a system that vibrates in phase with an externally applied vibration. Early research in to resonance was done using acoustical systems such as musical instruments and the human voice. An example of acoustical resonance is the vibration produced in a violin string of a given pitch when a musical note of the same pitch is sung or played nearby. The two are said to "resonate" together. In very simple terms, resonance is the act of two or more objects or waves vibrating together at the same frequency.

Synchronicity Synchronicity is the awareness of the connectedness of events and how the universe works to provide support for those on a growth path to realize their higher selves. Synchronicity is act of appropriate things, people or events coming together to fulfill a purpose or impart a knowledge of some kind. Running into an old friend who hands you a book that just happens to have answers to some of the questions or issues you were have been working on, may be considered an example of synchronicity. What some people call "coincidences" or "chance encounters" are often synchronistic events, and have an intelligence behind them.

Tai Chi Tai Chi is an ancient Chinese physical and mental discipline, similar to Chi Kung, the practice of which helps develop an increased awareness of the subtle life force energies ("Chi") of the earth and the body. There are various styles of Tai Chi. The "soft" style looks much like an elegant dance form, and helps one achieve greater balance of body, mind and spirit. Tai Chi is also considered a martial art form. The soft form can be taught from the point of view of energy balancing and calming, without any reference to Tai Chi as a martial art. Harder forms may incorporate a sword and have a much greater martial art look to them. The Chinese consider Tai Chi to be a form of Chi Kung (see **Chi Kung**). Practicing Tai Chi is an excellent way to help increase the health of the body and bring piece of mind. Tai Chi is based on the concepts of the Yin-Yang.

Therapeutic Touch A form of subtle energy work that promotes healing and wellness of the body, mind and spirit. The term was derived by Delores Krieger.

Uncertainty Principle (Also known as Heisenberg Uncertainty Principle) The more precisely the position is determined, the less precisely the momentum is known in this instant, and vice versa.—Heisenberg, uncertainty paper, 1927. (Source: American Institute of Physics)

Universal Calibration Lattice (UCL) Fibers of light and energy radiate horizontally from the Chakras. These fibers form figure eight shaped loops that feed into long vertical fibers of energy that surround and permeate our energy anatomy. This is the framework that forms the UCL. The UCL begins in your heart at the very core of your soul/self. It strengthens your biology in a state of grace as a fully Self-enabled human being. This is where your personal connection to the collective All begins. The UCL is the doorway to the Cosmic Lattice. (The EMF Balancing Technique®, Energy Extension, Inc.)

Vedas Ancient scriptures containing a vast storehouse of knowledge stretching back thousands of years. The Vedas form the basis of the Hindu religion and were compiled from knowledge brought through ancient seers and rishis. Ancient teachings on the nature of man and the universe, the mind, spirit and techniques of healing the body can be traced back to these ancient Vedic texts.

Veil An energy field or energy barrier that clouds normal human perception from the greater truths of existence and the nature of the universe. The veil provides a shield which allows us to focus on our earthly lessons without distraction, however, if the veil becomes too heavy, we loose sight of our connection to the divine powers and our true state of unity. As we incorporate new energies into our lives we engage in the activity of lifting this veil to allow greater connection to the energies of the universe and achieve a greater awareness of our role as co-creators of the worlds through which we travel.

Vibrational Medicine The study or practice of the healing arts which acknowledges the existence of spirit and of unseen energy forces that are the basis behind all life. Vibrational medicine sees the manipulation of subtle energies to higher states of vibration as a way to promote a state of balance, facilitate healing, and allow for greater spiritual growth. (See also **Energy Medicine** and **Energy.**)

Wave-Particle Duality This is a concept in Quantum Physics that light (electromagnetic radiation) has a dual nature, that is in some cases it behaves as a wave, and in other cases it behaves like a particle (photon).

Wavelength Wavelength is the distance between identical points in the adjacent cycles of a waveform signal propagated in space or along a wire.

Appendix J
Bibliography and References:
Books, Audio Tapes and Videos

Many of these titles are readily available through online bookstores such as Amazon.com and other publishers listed in this Appendix. Some titles are also available in a variety of formats, including hardcover, paperback, audio tape and video tape.

Andrews, Ted. *The Healer's Manual: A Beginner's Guide to Energy Therapies*. Llewellyn Publications, 1999.

Appell, D. "Fire in the Sky." *New Scientist*. Feb. 27, 1999.

Baginski, Bodo, and Sharamon, Shalila. *Reiki: Universal Life Energy*. Life Rhythm Publications, 1988.

Bagnall, Oscar. *The Origins and Properties of the Human Aura*.

Bailey, A.A. *Esoteric Healing*. Lucis Publishing Company, 1984.

Ballhorn, Rod. "Structural Biology Looks at the Ties That Bind." *Science & Technology Review*. April 1999.

Beattie, Melody. *Journey to the Heart: Daily Meditations on the Path to Freeing Your Soul*. HarperCollins, 1996.

Becker, Robert O. *Cross Currents: The Promise of Electromedicine, the Perils of Electropollution*. J.P. Tarcher, 1991.

Becker, Robert O., and Seldon, Gary. *The Body Electric: Electromagnetism and the Foundation of Life*. William Morrow & Co., 1985.

Bohm, Werner. *Chakras: Roots of Power*. Samuel Weiser, 1991.

Braden, Gregg. *Awakening to Zero Point: The Collective Initiation* (Book, Audio & Video). Radio Bookstore Press. 1993.

Braden, Gregg. *The Collective Initiation* (Audio).

Braden, Gregg. *The Isaiah Effect: Decoding Our Future Through the Lost Science of Prophecy.* Harmony Books, 2000.

Braden, Gregg. *The Physics of Emotion* (Audio).

Braden, Gregg. *Tools for Inner Energy* (Audio).

Braden, Gregg. *Walking Between Worlds: The Science of Compassion* (Audio & Video). 1997.

Bradford, Michael. *The Healing Energy of Your Hands.* Crossing Press, 1995.

Brennan, Barbara Ann. *Hands of Light: A Guide to Healing Through the Human Energy Field.* Bantam Books, 1988.

Brennan, Barbara Ann. *Light Emerging: The Journey Of Personal Healing.* Bantam Books, 1993.

Bruyere, Rosalyn L. *Wheels of Light, Chakras, Auras, and the Healing Energy of the Body.* Fireside, 1994.

Bstan-Dzin-Rgya-Mtsho, Dalai Lama, Nicholas Vreeland (Editor) (2001) *An Open Heart: Practicing Compassion in Everyday Life*

Burks, A.J. *The Aura.*

Burr, H.S. *The Fields of Life: Our Links with the Universe.* Ballantine Books, 1972.

Burroughs, Stanley. *Healing for the Age of Enlightenment.* Burroughs Books, 1993.

Burt, K. *Archetypes of the Zodiac.* Llewellyn Publications, 1988.

Cameron, Pam, and Cameron, Fred. *Bridge Into Light: Your Connection to Spiritual Guidance.* Oughten House Publications, 1993.

Carlson, Richard, and Shield, Benjamin, eds. *Handbook for the Heart: Original Writings on Love.* Little Brown & Co., 1998.

Carroll, Lee, and Tober, Jan. *The Indigo Children: The New Kids Have Arrived.* Hay House, 1999.

Castaneda, Carlos. *A Separate Reality: Further Conversations with Don Juan.* 1991.

Castaneda, Carlos. *The Power of Silence: Further Lessons of Don Juan.* Pocket Books, 1991.

Castaneda, Carlos. *The Teachings of Don Juan: A Yaqui Way of Knowledge.* Pocket Books, 1985.

Chaquette, Sonia, Ph.D *True Balance : A Common Sense Guide for Renewing Your Spirit (2000)*

Chopra, Deepak. *Quantum Healing: Exploring the Frontiers of Mind/Body Medicine.* Bantam Books, 1989.

Chopra, Deepak. *The New Physics of Healing* (Audio). Sounds True, 1992.

Chopra, Deepak. *The Seven Spiritual Laws of Success: A Practical Guide to the Fulfillment of Your Dreams.* Amber-Allen, 1994.

Choquette, Sonia, *True Balance : A Common Sense Guide for Renewing Your Spirit*

Choquette, Sonia, Ph.D *True Balance : A Common Sense Guide for Renewing Your Spirit*

Clow, Barbara Hand. *Chrion: Rainbow Bridge Between the Inner and Outer Planets.* Llewellyn Publications, 1987.

Clow, Barbara Hand. *Heart of the Christos: Starseeding From The Pleiades.* Bear & Company Publishing.

Clow, Barbara Hand. *Liquid Light of Sex: Kundalini Rising at Midlife Crisis.* Bear & Company Publishing, 1991.

Collinge, William, Ph.D., *Subtle Energy: Awakening to the Unseen Forces in Our Lives*

Condron, Barbara, *Kundalini Rising: Mastering Creative Energies*

Dale, Cyndi. *New Chakra Healing, The Revolutionary 32-Center Energy System.* Llewellyn Publications, 1996.

Davie, Dr. Brenda, *The 7 Healing Chakras : Unlocking Your Body's Energy Centers*

Davies, Brenda *The 7 Healing Chakras : Unlocking Your Body's Energy Centers*

Davies, Dr. Brenda, *Unlocking the Heart Chakra : Heal Your Relationships With Love, (2001)*

Davis, Dr. Brenda *Unlocking the Heart Chakra : Heal Your Relationships With Love (2001)*

Eden, Donna, and Feinstein, David. *Energy Medicine: Balance Your Body's Energies for Optimum Health, Joy and Vitality.* Tarcher/Putnam, 1998.

Eichenbaum, Diane. *Soul Signs.* Fireside Books, 1998.

Enlivening the Chakra of the Heart; The Fundamental Spiritual Exercises of Rudolf Steiner (2000)

Frawley, Dr. David. *Ayurvedic Healing: A Comprehensive Guide.* Passage Press, 1989.

Fromm, Mallory. *The Book of Ki: A Practical Guide to the Healing Principles of Life Energy.* Healing Arts Press, 1998.

Gardner-Gordon, Joy *Color and Crystals : A Journey Through the Chakras*

Gardner-Gordon, Joy, *Color and Crystals : A Journey Through the Chakras*

Gerber, Richard. *Vibrational Medicine: New Choices for Healing Ourselves.* Bear & Company Publishing, 1996.

Goldman, J. *Healing Sounds: The Power of Harmonics.* Element Books, 1996.

Gordon, Richard. *Your Healing Hands.* Wingbow Press, 1984.

Goswami, Shyam, *Layayoga: The Definitive Guide to the Chakras and Kundalini,* (1980)

Goswami, Shyan, and Sundar Goswami *Layayoga: The Definitive Guide to the Chakras and Kundalini (1980)*

Gray, Alex. *Sacred Mirrors: The Visionary Art of Alex Grey.* Inner Traditions International, 1990.

Gunther, B. *Energy, Ecstasy, and Your Seven Vital Chakras.* Guild of Tutors Press, 1978.

Hawking, Stephen W. *A Brief History of Time: From the Big Bang to Black Holes.* Bantam Books, 1988.

HeartMath, "The DNA Phantom Effect: Direct Measurement of a New Field in the Vacuum Substructure." *Institute for Heart Math*, 1995.

Hendricks, Gay, and Hendricks, Kathlyn. *Conscious Loving: The Journey to Co-Commitment.* Bantam Books, 1990.

Higley, Connie, and Higley, Alan. *Reference Guide for Essential Oils.* Abundant Health, 1998.

Honervogt, Tanmaya. *The Power of Reiki: An Ancient Hands-on Healing Technique.* Owl Books, 1998.

Horan, Paula. *Abundance Through Reiki.* Lotus Light Publications, 1995.

Huffines, LaUna. *Bridge of Light: Tools of Light for Spiritual Transformation.* H.J. Kramer, 1993.

Huffines, LaUna. *Healing Yourself With Light: How to Connect With the Angelic Healers.* H.J. Kramer, 1995.

Hutton, Bernard J. *Healing Hands.* 1978.

Hyder, Carole J. *Wind and Water: Your Personal Feng Shui Journey.* Crossings Press, 1998.

Irving, Daniel, *Serpent of Fire: A Modern View of Kundalini*

Judith, Anodea *Eastern Body, Western Mind : Psychology and the Chakra System As a Path to the Self*

Judith, Anodea *Wheels of Life : A User's Guide to the Chakra System (Llewellyn's New Age Series)*

Judith, Anodea, *Eastern Body, Western Mind : Psychology and the Chakra System As a Path to the Self*

Judith, Anodea, *Wheels of Life : A User's Guide to the Chakra System (Llewellyn's New Age Series)*

Judith, Anodea, and Vega, Selene. *The Sevenfold Journey, Reclaiming Mind, Body and Spirit Through the Chakras.* Crossing Press, 1993.

Judith, Anodea. *Wheels of Life, A User's Guide To The Chakra System.* Llewellyn Publications, 1999.

Karagulla, Shafica (et al) *The Chakras and the Human Energy Fields*

Karagulla, Shafica, *The Chakras and the Human Energy Fields* Krieger, Dolores. *The Therapeutic Touch: How to Use Your Hands to Help to Heal.* Simon & Schuster, 1992.

Krishna, Gopi, *Kundalini*

Kryon/Carroll, Lee. *Kryon— Don't Think Like a Human* (Kryon Book II). The Kryon Writings, 1994.

Kryon/Carroll, Lee. *Kryon— Letters from Home: Loving Messages from the Family* (Kryon Book VII). The Kryon Writings, 1999.

Kryon/Carroll, Lee. *Kryon— The End Times: New Information for Personal Peace* (Kryon Book I). The Kryon Writings, 1993.

Kryon/Carroll, Lee. *Kryon 2000— Passing the Marker: Understanding the New Millennium Energy* (Kryon Book VIII). The Kryon Writings, 2000.

Krystal, Phyllis Reconnecting the Love Energy: Don't Bypass Your Heart (1995)

Lama, His Holiness the Dalai. *A Flash of Lighting in the Dark of Night: A Guide to the Bodhisattva's Way of Life.*

Lama, His Holiness the Dalai. *The Bodhgaya Interviews.* Snow Lion Publications, 1988.

Leadbeater, C.W. *The Chakras.* Theosophical Publishing House, 1994.

Leary, Lani. *Healing Hands: Meditations for Healing Through the Human Energy Field* (Audio). Sounds True, 1998.

Lee, Patricia. "Therapeutic Quality of Essential Oils— Revival of an Ancient Healing Tool?" *Earthpulse Flashpoints.* Series 1, No. 6.

Lockwood, M., Stamper, R., and Wild, M.N. (World Data Centre) "A Doubling of the Sun's Coronal Magnetic Field during the Last 100 Years." *Nature.* Vol. 399. Jun. 3, 1999. Pp. 437-439.

Lowen, A. *Bioenergetics.* Penguin Books, 1975.

Lowndes, Florin and M. Barton (Translator)

Lubeck, Walter. *Rainbow Reiki: Expanding the Reiki System with Powerful Spiritual Abilities.* Lotus Light Publications, 1997.

MacIvor, V., and La Forest, S. *Vibrations: Healing Through Color, Homeopathy, and Radionics.* Samuel Weiser, 1979.

McLaren, Karla *Your Aura & Your Chakras : The Owner's Manual*

Mitchell, Karyn. *Reiki Mystery School: Transformational Reiki.* Mind Rivers Publishing, 1998.

Mitchell, Karyn. *Reiki: A Torch in Daylight*. Mind Rivers Publishing, 1994.

Mitchell, Karyn. *Reiki: Beyond the Usui System*. Mind Rivers Publishing, 1996.

Monroe, Robert A. *Journeys Out of the Body*. Main Street Books, 1973.

Mookerjee, Ajit, *Kundalini: The Arousal of the Inner Energy*

Motoyama, Hiroshi. *Theories of the Chakras*. 1981.

Motz, Julie. *Hands of Life: An Energy Healer Reveals the Secrets of Using Your Body's Own Energy Medicine for Healing, Recovery, and Transformation*. Bantam Books, 1998.

Muir, Charles, and Muir, Caroline. *Tantra: The Art of Conscious Loving*. Mercury House, 1989.

Mumford, Dr. John *A Chakra & Kundalini Workbook : Psycho-Spiritual Techniques for Health, Rejuvenation, Psychic Powers and Spiritual Realization*

Mumford, Dr. John, *A Chakra & Kundalini Workbook : Psycho-Spiritual Techniques for Health, Rejuvenation, Psychic Powers and Spiritual Realization*

Mumford, *Dr. John, A Chakra & Kundalini Worklbook*

Myss, Caroline. *Advanced Energy Anatomy*, (Audio). Sounds True, 2001

Myss, Caroline. *Energetics of Healing* (Video). 1997.

Myss, Caroline. *Spiritual Power, Spiritual Practice* (Audio). Sounds True, 1998.

Myss, Caroline. *Three Levels of Power and How to Use Them* (Audio). Sounds True, 1998.

Myss, Caroline. *Why People Don't Heal, and How they Can* (Audio/Video). Three Rivers Press, 1998.

Paulson, Genevieve Lewis. *Kundalini and the Chakras: A Practical Manual for Evolution in this Lifetime*. Llewellyn Publications, 1991.

Petter, Frank Arjava. *Reiki Fire: New Information About the Origins of the Reiki Power*. Lotus Light Publications, 1997.

Pressman, Maurie Dr., *Enter the Supermind*, CeShore, (1999)

Rajneesh, Osho, *In Search of the Miraculous : Chakras, Kundalini & the Seven Bodies*

Ramsdale, David, and Ellen Ramsdale, Alan Parker (Illustrator) *Sexual Energy Ecstasy : A Practical Guide to Lovemaking Secrets of the East and West (1993)*

Rand, William Lee. *Reiki for a New Millennium*. Vision Publications, 1998.

Rand, William Lee. *Reiki: The Healing Touch*. Vision Publications, 1991.

Ritberger, Carol *Your Personality, Your Health : Connecting Personality With the Human Energy System, Chakras and Wellness (1998)*

Ritberger, Carol, *Your Personality, Your Health : Connecting Personality With the Human Energy System, Chakras and Wellness* , (1998)

Roberts, Jane. *Seth Speaks: The Eternal Validity of the Soul*. Prentice Hall, 1972.

Roberts, Jane. *The "Unknown" Reality*. 2 vols. Amber-Allen Publishing, Inc.

Roberts, Jane. *The Nature of Personal Reality*. Prentice Hall, 1974.

Roman, Sanaya. *Living with Joy: Keys to Personal Power and Spiritual Transformation*. H.J. Kramer, 1986.

Roman, Sanaya. *Personal Power Through Awareness: A Guide for Sensitive People*. H.J. Kramer, 1986.

Roman, Sanaya. *Soul Love: Awakening Your Heart Centers*. H.J. Kramer, 1997.

Rsjneesh, Osho *In Search of the Miraculous : Chakras, Kundalini & the Seven Bodies*

Schwartz, Jack. *The Human Energy Systems*. E.F. Dutton, 1980.

Seidman, Maruti. *Guide to Polarity Therapy*. North Atlantic Books, 1999.

Selby, John, *Kundalini Awakening: A Gentle Guide to Chakra Activation and Spiritual Growth*

Sherwood, Keith *Chakra Therapy : For Personal Growth & Healing (1998)*

Sherwood, Keith, *Chakra Therapy : For Personal Growth & Healing,* (1998)

Simon, David. *Vital Energy: The 7 Keys to Invigorate Body, Mind & Soul.* John Wiley & Sons, 2000.

Simpson, Liz. *The Book of Chakra Healing.* Sterling Publishing, 1999.

Simpson, Liz. *The Book of Crystal Healing.* Sterling Publishing, 1997.

Space Environment Center. "Glossary of Solar-Terrestrial Terms." Space Environment Center, 2000. <http://www.sec.noaa.gov/info/glossary.html>.

Sui, Choa Kok. *Pranic Healing.* Samuel Weiser, Inc., 1990.

Thie, John F. *Touch for Health*, Devorss & Co., 1979.

Thompson, R. "Power Failure in Canada During 1989." *IPS Radio & Space Services*, 1995.

Tiwari, Maya. *Secrets of Healing (Ayurveda).* Lotus Light Press, 1995.

Uhl, Marianne. *Chakra Energy Massage.* Lotus Light, 1996.

Wauters, Ambika. *Chakras and their Archetypes: Uniting Energy Awareness and Spiritual Growth.* The Crossing Press, 1997.

Welch, Pamela. *The Energy Body Connection: The Healing Experience of Self-Embodiment.* Llewellyn Publications, 1999.

Welwood, John, *Journey of the Heart : The Path of Conscious Love,* (1996)

White, John. *Kundalini: Evolution and Enlightenment.* Paragon House, 1990.

White, Ruth *Using Your Chakras : A New Approach to Healing Your Life*

White, Ruth. *Working With Your Chakras: A Physical Emotional and Spiritual Approach*, Samuel Weiser, 1994.

Wolf, Fred Alan. *The Body Quantum: The New Physics of Body, Mind, and Heath*. Macmillan Publishing Co., 1986.

Wolf, Fred Alan. *The Spiritual Universe: How Quantum Physics Proves the Existence of the Soul*. Moment Point Press, 1998.

Yao, Joseph. *Acutherapy*. 1984.

Yogananda, Paramahansa. *The Law of Success*. Self Realization Fellowship, 1980.

Zukav, Gary. *Soul Stories* (Book & Audio). Simon & Schuster, 1999.

Zukav, Gary. *The Dancing Wu Li Masters: An Overview of the New Physics* (Book & Audio). 1994.

Zukav, Gary. *The Seat of the Soul* (Book, Audio). Fireside Books, 1990.

Appendix K

Nutrition Takes a Quantum Leap: Gematria Products and Laser Energized Supplements

An evolution is occurring in healthcare as more natural medicines gain acceptance. Interestingly, this acceptance is largely the result of increased scientific investigation and the public's awareness of this research. It appears that medical researchers now have in their possession the technology and understanding necessary to more fully appreciate the value of "natural" therapies. In essence, many natural therapies are being improved or refined through scientific investigation. Science is paving the way for the medicine of the future—a medicine that recognizes the healing power of nature.

—Michael T. Murray, ND,
Encyclopedia of Natural Supplements, (1996)

The Gematria Story

What could be more natural than the foods we eat? Unfortunately, the mass production, and chemical enhancement of foods of the late 20th and early 21st centuries have denatured the best therapeutic tool we have. If all we would eat were organic foods locally grown with loving care, we would wipe out most of the known diseases because the human body is a resilient mechanism capable of high levels of self balance & and self repair. But when the toxins produced by our lifestyles build up in the cells, tissues, and organs of the body, impairment and aging begin. The good news is that with the proper nutrition and supplements, health and a greater youth can return.

Let us begin the story with that of the single carbon. 50,000 peer reviewed scientific studies and 5 decades of research conclude that single carbon transfers are essential to human health. From building the bases of DNA to putting the final touches on complex protein structures with thousands of atoms, single carbons are the brick and mortar of organic chemistry.

The simplest organic molecule contains a single carbon surrounded by 4 atoms of hydrogen. Called methane, it has the shape of a perfect 4-sided pyramid called a tetrahedron. In this structure, the carbon is in the very center of the pyramid shape and a hydrogen atom occupies each of the 4 corners. If a hydrogen atom is removed from one corner of the methane pyramid, the carbon atom in the center can now bond with another atom. The chemical group just formed— with a carbon and three hydrogen atoms— is called a methyl group. This is the most fundamental organic group, without which life as we know it would be impossible.

Birth

When a human ovum is fertilized, an enormously complex task of development and differentiation ensues to give rise to an infant with a multitude of different cells and tissues. The body uses methyl groups, attaching to the DNA base cytosine, as anchors on the DNA itself to organize the function of every type of cell. The specific pattern of DNA methylation is unique for every cell. The DNA methylation pattern tells each cell what part of the DNA can be active and which should be dormant.

When an infant is born, the methylation of cytosine ranges from 2-6%, the fraction dependent on the unique pattern for each cell type. This pattern is like a fingerprint for each cell and gives the cell a blueprint for which proteins and enzymes and activities it will carry into function.

Aging, Disease, & Cellular Decay

Methyl groups are widely used in the body for detoxification and DNA repair. Using an estimated average of 3% methylation of cytosine at birth, the nuclear DNA of each cell would have approximately 90 million methyl groups. As reviewed by a recent article in the journal Medical Hypothesis, the body controls development and aging by the loss of methyl groups from DNA.

Cellular information and control systems become increasingly fuzzy, as DNA methyl groups are lost. Certain cancers tend to occur at a 20% DNA methyl group loss. In autoimmune diseases like lupus and rheumatoid arthritis, a specific immune cell called the lymphocyte has been shown to lose 50% of its DNA methyl groups; loss of information integrity in this powerful type of immune cell causes an attack of self against self, as lymphocytes attack otherwise normal, healthy tissues.

Degeneration and death usually occurs when about 40% of the methyl groups have been lost from DNA demethylation. An average loss of roughly 36 million DNA methyl groups per cell therefore represents a limit to biological survival. An average loss of 1800 DNA methyl groups per cell per day limits a lifespan to about 60-65 years, whereas a loss of only 1200 groups per cell per day is consistent with increased survival to age 90-95.

Our new formula Heart Gems has the full array of nutrients proven to enhance and restore methyl group transfers. In the body, the main driver of supplying methyl groups is called tri-methylglycine or TMG, an amino acid that offers three extra methyl groups per molecule. Also called betaine, TMG is a safe and natural product derived from sugar beets.

Heart Gems has 10 different validated vitamins, minerals, and methyl group suppliers to boost methyl metabolism strongly in each and every cell. Just providing one of these factors has been associated with a 7-17 year life extension compared to those not thus supplemented. The biologic effects of this formula are so profound that if it were widely used, actuarial survival for the entire country could be expected to increase, with significantly greater longevity, fewer and milder chronic diseases, and im-proved quality of life for the population as a whole.

Homocysteine is a metabolic byproduct in the body. The elevation of which is associated with loss of methyl groups from DNA. El-evation of homocysteine is also associated with accelerated short-ening of the ends of chromosomes called telomeres; both of these effects may cause aging. Heart Gems is an activated combination of the most powerful nutrients ever studied for lowering harmful homocysteine in the blood while increasing the production of the highly beneficial SAMe (S-adenosylmethionine).

Homocysteine is also highly toxic to blood vessels and its level may be up to 40 times more predictive of the risk of heart disease than the cholesterol level. 44% of U.S. deaths are due to heart disease. The average homocysteine level in the U.S. population is at an unhealthy 10. Above the level of 7, every 3-point rise in homocysteine increases heart attack risk by 35%.

Elevated homocysteine levels are also strongly associated with the development of Alzheimer's disease, strokes, and increased complications in diabetes, lupus, and other chronic diseases. *A 1998 article in Medical Hypothesis presents evidence that " aging may be almost entirely due to a loss of methyl groups within the cells, with elevated homocysteine a marker for impaired methyl group transfers throughout the body". This study concludes that aging may be reversible if aged cells could be stimulated to restore methyl group transfer functions rather than losing them.*

Homocysteine levels are increased with smoking, alcohol overuse, oral contraceptive use, red meat ingestion, high fat diets, and aging. One study showed that drinking 4 cups of coffee per day elevates homocysteine levels by 10%.

The action of TMG is to convert homocysteine to the essential amino acid methionine, which can then be converted to SAMe. Choline in Heart Gems also provides methyl groups and can boost learning and memory. The ingredient inositol may also help to lower homocysteine levels, while making cell membranes more fluid, increasing regenerative capacity. Folic acid and vitamins B6 and B12 are key cofactors required for homocysteine detoxification and can further reduce homocysteine levels. Zinc and magnesium are other essential metabolic cofactors for lowering homocysteine that are provided as a highly absorbable and biologically active amino acid chelates.

In almost all cases, adjusting the intake level of this formula to the metabolic situation will be likely to lower homocysteine levels into the lowest risk zone below 7. Significant homocysteine lowering typically occurs within 1-3 months, which can be validated individually with a homocysteine blood test. Using this formula, one patient showed a lowering of homocysteine level from 15 to 4 in only 60 days, equating to an over 75% reduction in cardiac risk and warranting long term use.

Extensive research has shown that the Heart Gems ingredients are very effective at increasing SAMe (S-adenosyl-methionine) production in the body. Clinical studies have shown SAMe to be very powerful at elevating mood quickly and safely, healing joints, relieving aches and pains even of fibromyalgia, and preventing and healing liver damage. SAMe is the specific methyl group donor that the body uses to restore methyl groups to DNA, the ultimate anti-aging effect at the DNA level.

In addition to reducing homocysteine levels, the Heart Gems formula can also increase the beneficial internal production of methionine, SAMe, DMG (dimethylglycine), glutathione, and melatonin. Some of the more significant reported benefits of these internally generated Heart Gems byproducts are summarized in the following table:

Methyl Group Donation (TMG, SAMe, and Choline)
- Methyl groups break down harmful chemicals.
- Required for growth of new cells.
- Prevents DNA mutations and strand breaks.
- Prevents expression of disease causing genes.
- May reduce the risk of genetically induced cancers.
- Protects against alcohol induced liver injury.
- May slow and even reverse aging.

SAMe (S-adenosylmethionine)
- Increases serotonin levels and can be a potent mood elevator.
- Helps repair and preserve joint function.
- Potent relief of joint pain.
- Cell membrane stabilizer.
- Intimately involved in DNA protection and repair.
- Enhances ATP, the fundamental cellular energy molecule.
- Well being promoter.
- Repairs liver injury.
- Protects the heart.
- Builds myelin sheaths around nerves.
- Maintains and repairs brain cells.
- Treats schizophrenia and dementia
- Supports nerve repair in demyelinating diseases (like multiple sclerosis).
- May relieve symptoms in arthritis and fibromyalgia.

Melatonin
- Promotes rejuvenative sleep.
- Immune enhancer.
- May reduce risk of cancer.

Glutathione
- One of the most powerful antioxidants ever studied.
- Potent anti-cancer effects.
- Anti-aging actions.

DMG (Dimethylglycine)
- Increases physical energy.
- Enhances athletic performance.
- Improves function of autistic children.

Folic Acid
- Reduces risk of heart attacks and stroke.
- Lowers risk of colon cancer.
- Decreases incidence of birth defects.

Lipotropic or Fat-directed Factors (Methionine, Choline, and Inositol)

- Improves fluidity of cell membranes (required for cell regeneration).
- Supports production and repair of myelin sheaths of nerves.
- Detoxifies heavy metals and environmental toxins.
- Reduces toxic effects of cigarette smoke and smog.
- Protects against injury from ionizing radiation.
- May enhance learning and memory.
- Improves metabolism of fat and cholesterol.

The Heart Gems components are activated with a patented laser technology designed to energize the methyl groups of trimethylglycine and promote their transfer.

The recommended use of Heart Gems is one capsule three times daily with meals. For many persons, this level of intake will reduce homocysteine levels to the lowest risk range. Some persons may require 3-6 times this basic amount for optimum results. This is especially true for persons with marked elevations of homocysteine, or for persons with severe liver disease or genetic enzyme abnormalities. Enhanced mood and increased physical energy are markers that suggest adequate intake. Blood testing for homocysteine levels is the most certain way to be sure the desired results have been achieved.

It is suggested that one capsule three times per day be taken for the first month. After that, the use can be increased to strive for desired levels of energy and mood enhancement, relief of joint symptoms, or support of liver or brain nutrition. This formula is a long-term rebuilder, restorer, and preventative, and usually requires several weeks of use before the effects are perceived.

The components of the formula are very safe. TMG has no side effects except for brief tension headaches if large quantities are taken on an empty stomach. Choline may occasionally deepen the depressive phase of manic-depressive illness. Chronic intake of large amounts of vitamin B6, over 300-500mg per day, may rarely cause nerve inflammation. Even at the highest suggested intake of Heart Gems, this threshold for B6 would not be exceeded. Clinical studies have shown that up to nine capsules three times per day may be taken safely in extreme cases in which this high an intake level may be needed for best results.

Persons who have taken this homocysteine lowering combination of nutrients for 10 or more years report a marked reduction in colds, increased energy and endurance, and reduced blood sugar levels. Fat may melt off the body with ease with a return to more youthful body proportions. Some people describe that this nutrient blend makes them feel like young adults or even teenagers again.

Each 3 capsule serving of HeartGems provides every cell in the body with 50 million methyl groups. This gives each cell a great surplus of methyl groups to slow and reverse the loss of these life-preserving groups from DNA. Methyl groups not used to remethylate DNA can participate in a wide range of highly beneficial functions such as the following:

- Building the bases of DNA itself.
- Making the myelin sheaths of nerves.
- Rejuvenating proteins that have degenerated.
- Detoxifying organic poisons.
- Producing chemical messengers in the brain.
- Reducing risks of heart attacks, strokes, and cancer.
- Repairing joint cartilage and relieving joint pain.
- Inactivating histamine to relieve allergic responses.

- Boosting mood through enhanced serotonin production.
- Increasing energy, endurance, and stamina.
- Improving fluidity and repair of cell membranes.
- Providing essential conditions for cell regeneration.

We have just completed a major randomized, prospective, placebo-controlled double blind study of the Heart Gems formula. Forty subjects participated in a 6-month study, the first 3 months testing the Heart Gems formula versus placebo.

Preliminary results from the over 8000 pages of clinical and lab data generated have revealed:

- *Subjects taking Heart Gems had a highly statistically significant drop in homocysteine levels, a major cardiac risk factor. Based on large population studies, this degree of homocysteine drop is consistent with an over 33% reduction of cardiovascular risk and a 15-20 year reduction in physiologic age chemistry.*
- *Persons in the placebo group had no significant change in homocysteine levels.*
- *Using a highly validated symptom survey, persons taking Heart Gems had a highly significant reduction in body aches and pains.*
- *Persons taking Heart Gems showed a highly statistically significant reduction of symptoms of depression, boosting mood dramatically in some cases.*
- *Overall symptoms of all kinds were highly significantly reduced in persons taking the active formula.*

In addition, perhaps for the first time ever observed with safe natural substances, persons taking the Heart Gems formula showed a highly statistically significant reduction in symptoms

of hostility. *The implications of this observation for a happier and more harmonious global society are vast and very hopeful.*

According to the medical literature, the chemistry of the Heart-Gems formula may help balance the immune system in auto-immune conditions. The following study subject with severe active lupus gives an indication of the kind of benefit that may result— since starting the formula she reports:

"I have had an increase in energy and strength. This is continuing almost daily. I have had lesions on my feet that made it difficult to walk freely without pain. The lesions are now about 95% gone for the first time in several years. I have had the same kind of lesions on my hands, making it difficult to use them for any general task like opening a cupboard door. My hand lesions are now about 90% gone."

Intensive data analysis is now under way, with the intent to share the statistical results with the general medical community. There are several aspects of this study that have never before been reported in the literature. It is possible that this research will foster the greater study and use of these activated nutritional substances to benefit many people.

For more information on Gematria products, see
ww.Gematria.com.
Gematria Products, Inc.
2075 Corte Del Nogal
Suite A
Carlsbad, CA 92009
(760) 931-8563

Appendix L

Integration of Psychology and Biology Love Energy: The Life Force: The Fountain of Youth

by Clancy D. McKenzie, M.D.
Capital University, Washington, D.C.

Proper nutrition, exercise and relaxation are recognized as vital ingredients for a long and healthy life. But there is a fourth ingredient that largely has been overlooked. This fourth factor is love, which can add as much to one's energy level and to one's longevity as any of the other factors. In fact, biblical accounts indicate that love energy potentially can add hundreds of years to one's life— yet this comparatively important factor has not been studied scientifically to the same extent as the other three factors.

Even though most of us do not see this love energy readily, this does not mean it does not exist or does not have great impact. Take for example a person who eats nothing but junk food, smokes, doesn't exercise, drinks beer and sports a pot-belly. Let him fall in love, and suddenly he has as much energy as a person who lives on energy food and exercises daily. Suddenly he can work day and night. What is the mechanism for this enormous flow of energy and where does it come from? How can we harness it and use it at will? These questions are especially important in the health fields, because this energy might also be the healing energy, or the life force itself.

To begin to understand love energy, let me first give a definition that will make more sense as time goes on. I define love as an attention or energy directed outward, and the byproduct of which is happiness. The opposite is need or desire, which is the same attention or energy directed back to the self, and the byproduct of which is unhappiness. Reverse the direction of flow of attention or energy and you get the opposite feeling. Fall in love and you are in a state of bliss— but as soon as you want the other person to love you, you are miserable.

Fall in love and you have so much energy you can work day and night, but as soon as you reverse the direction of flow and focus attention on the self *"Oh woe is me, aches and pains, etc."* you have so little energy you can hardly move.

Subliminally we do see evidence of this love energy, but we have not really analyzed it in modern times. We see this energy, for example, when a person falls in love, because we say *"he's beaming, glowing, radiant, vibrant, turned on."* Thus we see, at some level, the aura— which brightens in intensity proportionate to the increase in flow of love energy. Holy people, or saintly individuals, are those who become extremely loving, and they are depicted as having bright auras or halos, or as being surrounded by light. This *"aura"* that we see might have another name: In a dream state I heard the words: *"The aura is the edge of the soul."* Interesting. I wasn't thinking about this or looking for it. It was as though someone was passing by and just wanted to tell me that. So was this a part of my own mind? Or was it some kind of a visitor?

This love energy is the life force itself, or the healing energy. Need or desire, which is the exact opposite, roughly can be equated with what is sometimes called *"sin,"* and we have read *"the wages of sin are death."* Or, *"Touch the forbidden fruit and you shall surely die."* This is energy flowing in a direction opposite to the direction of flow of the life force, and opposite direction of the flow of love energy. There are scores of biblical accounts of holy people who lived for hundreds of years. These are also people who were known to be very loving and who are depicted as having very bright auras.

In another dream-state I saw the fountain of youth. I wasn't looking for it; it was simply there, revealed to me and for what reason I do not know. It is not in some distant corner of the earth: It is within every person. It is a beautiful fountain of love energy in each person, waiting to spring fourth. What I saw was a beautiful outpouring of love energy, radiating outward about arm's length. I instantly knew it was the fountain of youth— and along with the vision was the clear awareness that as soon as the person wants to live forever, he/she shuts off the flow. (One can forever want to help people, but to want to live forever is the wrong direction of flow of this attention or energy.)

This just might be what is described as the energy of the soul. You might have heard about yogis advising to draw energy from the soul, and we have heard the words *"soul power."* How is this energy used? How do we draw from this enormous, boundless, unlimited source of energy and let it flow through us? One way is to do the task for someone else. This gives much more energy. Examples: a person who dedicates winning a race for a child who is dying of leukemia— versus running the race for the self. One's chances of winning are enhanced if one dedicates the race to someone else. Another example of this was in the Tyson versus Holyfield fights. Holyfield dedicated the victory to God, whereas Tyson was fighting strictly for his own glory.

I'm not saying this is 100%, but it appears to be a factor— and the strength of this factor might depend on the intensity of the desire to do the task for someone else.

A most precious 23-year-old daughter of one of my patients had Hodgkin's lymphoma, and prior to receiving another round of chemotherapy she overheard her doctor telling another physician *"I'm afraid this is the beginning of the end for her."*

I encouraged her to explore alternative methods, but the next chemotherapy was set to begin the following week. So I told her about programmed dreams and recommended she have a dream that would tell her exactly what to do.

In her programmed dream she was helping someone else who had a serious problem, and when we discussed her dream she added *"that's how I recovered so fast from the first round of chemotherapy, by focusing my attention on helping someone else."*

I really wish she had explored alternative medicine approaches, but I recognized that she was right on course with the love energy, the life force, the healing energy. She made a quick recovery from the effects of chemotherapy and I am hoping that the love energy enabled the treatment to be successful.

How to increase love energy:
While traveling across India I met with a highly evolved Kundalini yogi and I asked him how to become total love energy toward all people all the time. When this holy man finally stopped laughing, he wrote on slate with chalk (because he had not spoken for 30 years) and his disciple translated: *"When you want to hit a target with an arrow you aim only at the bulls eye."* This makes sense, because we all reach out with a love-need combination, and to the extent there is need, there can be hurt feelings when

those needs are not met, and the danger of hurt feelings prevents us from reaching out more fully. When reaching toward total love, toward the bull's eye, there can be no rejection— and this allows us to reach out more fully. Furthermore, if we are loving the purest form of love energy, then we are identifying with, and emulating, that very source itself.

Bahkti yoga is the discipline of intensifying love energy. The total effort is to intensify love, and to experience constant love. The day is filled with devotional love. This can be practiced with or without formalized religion.

In our own daily lives we can sort through each thought, word, feeling, action— and put it on the scale to determine love versus need. By *"need"* I mean desire. This is most useful in psycho-therapy. If a person is miserable it is because he wants something. If a husband or wife complains bitterly about the spouse, this has NOTHING to do with loving the other person; it has only to do with caring exclusively about the self and wanting more for the self.

Enhancing the love energy of the patient is an effective way to increase the healing process. This holds true for both psychologi-cal and physical healing:

Patients who are injured or who have serious physical illnesses, often are focused on the self and the illness. This shuts off the flow of the healing energy. Depressed persons are focused on the self, and this is the opposite of being in love or loving someone else. Persons who have physical injuries or terminal illnesses frequently are quite depressed, which is counterproductive when trying to get well. Anxiety accompanies depression and vice versa for obvious reasons. Anxiety causes depression, which is why sometimes it can be treated with tranquilizing agents. When persons are anxious, they are worried, consciously and unconsciously, about *"what's going to happen to me?"* This is the wrong direction of flow of love energy and will produce unhappiness and loss of energy. It is little wonder that criteria for depression include no interest in anyone or anything, and, loss of energy.

Depressed persons and anxious persons can be cured by treating their conditions through the love dimension alone. A person who becomes totally loving can neither be depressed nor anxious. While I use a multidimensional approach to the treatment of depression, and I consider at least 14 different dimensions of treatment in addition to medication, the one factor I never lose sight of is the direction of flow of love energy, and I always point out when the problem is primarily the patient's need or desire. This same enhancement of love energy is very valuable in treating psychoses, because psychosis— as I will describe in a subsequent lecture— relates to a partial return to infancy, with all the needs of the infant. When a person becomes predominantly loving, this is movement away from the needs of infancy, and movement back into adult mind/brain/reality.

The same holds true for the addictions. At an addictions unit I directed, a counselor voiced the opinion that it was very important to show the patients that the counselor really cares about them. I corrected him on this and said it was much more important that he get the patients to care about him, and do something for him. He then recognized that he himself had overcome his addiction was when he began helping others with theirs.

Enhancement of love energy should be a part of every physical remedy, because it is a vital ingredient to healing. If persons are angry or hateful they will not heal as quickly or as well. There are numerous studies that demonstrate the enhancement of the immune system with love energy or prayer, but these studies are just touching the surface or catching a tiny aspect of this energy. A thorough understanding of the laws of physics which govern this energy is important, because it enables us to identify the direction of flow of this energy, and reverse it at will if it is flowing the wrong direction.

On a number of occasions I have read about a small town in Pennsylvania, named Roseto— which was studied extensively by medical researchers in the 1960s, because its residents were among the healthiest in the United States. Surprisingly enough, the people there smoked as much, exercised as little, and faced just as many stressful situations as other Americans.

After extensive testing the researchers learned that this community, more than any other studied, showed a remarkable cohesiveness and sense of unconditional support for one another. The conclusion drawn from this, and similar findings in the literature, is that all this interpersonal support brings with it the life prolonging and life-saving qualities.

I was interested that this study touched upon this fourth factor for health and longevity, yet at the same time did not differentiate between giving and receiving. Hasn't it been said that it is better to give than to receive? The health and the longevity is a result of the outward flow of this energy. Giving the support is the correct direction of flow of this energy. There is nothing wrong with receiving the support, and in fact it can cause us to be grateful, appreciative and loving— but wanting or desiring support would be energy flowing in the wrong direction and would be counterproductive. It would shut off our fountain of youth.

In the Gita this energy is described in terms of the three Gunas: Satvas, Rajas and Tomas. Satvas is the highest level, followed by Rajas and then Tomas. I equate Satvas with love, or energy flowing outward, Rajas with need or desire, or energy flowing back to the self, and Thomas with apathy, or no energy going anywhere. There are biblical references to this as well. Christ made some reference to preferring persons hot or cold, but definitely, not luke-warm. Tomas is the lowest of the three gunas. It equates to apathy or being luke-warm.

In the Gita it states that the route from Tomas to Satvas sometimes is through Rajas, or— stated in English, the route from apathy to love sometimes is through need. Many years ago I developed a means of instantly converting persons from apathy to love, by triggering need but preventing hurt or jealous feelings. It is possible to take the most distant apathetic relationship, trigger need but prevent hurt or jealous feeling, and precipitate intense feelings of love.

For example, the wife of a political figure in Washington gradually became viewed as dull and mundane by her husband— because he was travelling around the world to exciting places and meeting daily with important people. When he would come home, he was exhausted and would open a can of beer and watch a soap opera on television. She became very upset and her needs were intensified by his lack of interest and affection.

Suddenly one day he became very interested in her; we applied the approach of converting tamas to satvas through rajas. This always works if done properly. On my advice, she told him that she really cared about him, that he was number-one in her life, and that she wanted him to do whatever made him happy. She understood he was tired when he came home after a very hard day and just needed to relax and put his feet up and have a can of beer. This was OK with her— but meanwhile she was going stare-crazy just looking at the four walls and having no one to talk with. So would he mind, would he object, would it be OK if she went out to the local nightclub just to socialize, dance, meet people and have a good time. She presented this in such a way that of course he had to say go ahead, enjoy yourself.

Note there was nothing to stir jealousy or anger: She did not say *"You are not paying attention to me so I am going to go out and meet other people who will pay attention to me."* Instead she asked *"do you mind if,,"* and he gave her permission. She of course does not need permission, but she needs to not stir feelings of hurt, anger and jealousy— if she wants his love and interest instead.

This middle-aged housewife was far too anxious about stepping out alone to actually go into the nightclub, so she drove around the block several times and went to a fast food restaurant, lingering and not returning home until about midnight. Her husband was up and waiting for her. He was interested in how her evening went, and she told what a wonderful time she had and the interesting people she met. His level of interest in her skyrocketed, and for the next several months everywhere he traveled around the country he invited her to go with him. This was good for him and for her, because he felt better too when his love energy was intensified.

After a few months his level of interest settled back down and so she tried the approach once more. This time she made the mistake of stirring hurt, anger, need and jealousy. When she returned home at midnight he was already asleep, so she fell asleep on the sofa, and then at 4AM went tip toeing upstairs. He awakened infuriated, calling her names saying he wanted nothing to do with her. But had she said *"I met a great group of people and probably won't get back until 4AM,"* there would have been no jealousy whatsoever, just interest directed outward, toward her, which is love.

When you understand the flow of love energy you can redirect it at will. To help a person recover from a serious illness, get that person to help someone else— or to help others with the same illness. One of my patients with AIDS is experiencing a substantial improvement in his condition since he has started counseling people in the hospital who are dying from the disease. Get the patient's energy flowing outward, have the patient help others, encourage the person's religious practices— and here you might have to redirect the person from the give me, give me, give me prayers to *"I love you, I love you, I love you"* type prayer.

Fear is the antithesis of love and it is counterproductive: It focuses attention and energy on the self. Picturing the self to be well, the body free from disease, knowing and trusting this is so, and helping others recover— perhaps from similar problems— is far more productive. For the healing process it is important to avoid anger, hatred, bitterness, worry— and to focus instead on intensifying love, caring, doing for others with no regard for anything in return, and the expression of devotional love and appreciation. All of this enhances the life force, the healing energy, and the recovery process.

This love energy appears to follow precise laws, that are like other laws of physics, and which appear to be quantitative. Of all things to study in medicine today, it is the analysis of this love energy itself which might be the most rewarding and productive. It is this love energy to which I hope to devote a large portion of the remainder of my life. Likely it is the most important factor for healing and for longevity since Seleye discovered stress, yet it is equally as invisible as was stress at the turn of the previous century.

Epilogue
The Energy Facilitator's Role

Now, more than ever before in our recorded history, we can tune into what is happening anywhere on the earth. We can get "real time" images of disaster or images of compassion brought right into our living rooms. With this increased knowledge and awareness of world events comes a greater responsibility on our part to do something about them. We have a responsibility to co-create a brighter future. A future where love is present— where compassion flows from one to another. A future where fear and hatred are replaced by love and acceptance. This is all possible and no one holds the key but ourselves. Our primary task is to raise ourselves as individuals to a level where we can hold the energies of love and compassion and share these with our family, friends, and all those around us. As we do this, their energies will flow into ours and we will become stronger. Our individual sphere of influence energetically will grow and expand to encompass more individuals. This is part of the role of the energy facilitator. Our task at hand, and our challenge, is holding the light of increased vibrations and higher levels of love energy. Being able to hold such energies and direct them outward to others is at once a beautiful gift and a unique and powerful challenge.

As the levels of energy available to us increase, we have a greater opportunity now to incorporate these into our lives. More and more people are becoming aware of subtle energies and their effect on our lives. This is a reflection of the growing conscious-ness which we are witnessing and which we are a part of. We are both participants in and recipients of this new energy and the new consciousness that goes with it.

As we raise our consciousness and our vibration individually, we assist in the raising of the planetary vibration and in the evolution of our species. At this point in time, this is our assignment.

Printed in the United States
1286400004B/1-18